Silvana Greco
Moses Dobruska and the Invention of Social Philosophy

Silvana Greco

Moses Dobruska and the Invention of Social Philosophy

Utopia, Judaism, and Heresy under the French Revolution

DE GRUYTER
OLDENBOURG

This publication was financed in part by the open access fund for monographs and edited volumes of the Freie Universität Berlin.

The revision of the English text was supported by the Fondazione Palazzo Bondoni Pastorio.

ISBN 978-3-11-067353-1
e-ISBN (PDF) 978-3-11-075882-5
e-ISBN (EPUB) 978-3-11-075886-3
DOI https://doi.org/10.1515/9783110758825

Library of Congress Control Number: 2021947898

Bibliographic information published by the Deutsche Nationalbibliothek
The Deutsche Nationalbibliothek lists this publication in the Deutsche Nationalbibliografie;
detailed bibliographic data are available on the Internet at http://dnb.dnb.de.

Cover image: Christine_Kohler/iStock/Getty Images Plus.
Typesetting: Integra Software Services Pvt. Ltd.
Printing and binding: CPI books GmbH, Leck.

www.degruyter.com

To Giulio, "Doch alles, was uns anrührt, dich und mich, nimmt uns zusammen wie ein Bogenstrich".

Acknowledgements

My gratitude goes, first of all, to my husband Giulio, who supported me with so much love during my research, often cumbersome, on Moses Dobruska and his *Philosophie sociale.*

I am deeply grateful to the scholars who have followed my work with interest and precious indications: Prof. Dr. Karl-Siegbert Rehberg (Technische Universität Dresden), Prof. Dr. Stephan Moebius (Karl-Franzens-Universität Graz), Prof. Dr. Shmuel Feiner (Bar Ilan University, Tel Aviv), Prof. Dr. Maurice Kriegel (École des hautes études en sciences sociales, Paris), Prof. Dr. Giuseppe Veltri (Universität Hamburg), Prof. Dr. Marita Rampazi (University of Pavia) and Prof. Dr. Raphael Ebgi (Università Vita-Salute San Raffaele). I am thankful to Dr. Emma Bolton for her revision of the English.

Finally, my heartfelt thanks go to my students at the Freie Universität Berlin, who have followed my lectures on the sociology of culture and Judaismwith great attention. Their enthusiasm has prompted me to work in depth on the history of the beginnings of sociology. Among them: Patrizia Dell'Acqua, Barbara Ergenzinger, Susanne Gaertner, Elena Medvedev, Anne-Lise Moll-Jenzen, Andrea Raschemann, Henricke Richter.

This publication was enabled by co-funding for open access monographs and anthologies from Freie Universität Berlin.

Contents

1 Introduction

1.1 The Purposes of the Present Study and Its New Perspectives

This study proposes, for the first time, an in-depth analysis of the *Philosophie sociale,* published in Paris at the end of June 1793 by Moses Dobruska[1] (1753–1794). Dobruska was a businessman, scholar, and social philosopher, born into a Jewish family in Moravia, who converted to Catholicism, gained wide recognition at the Habsburg court in Vienna, and then emigrated to France to join the French Revolution. Dobruska, who took on the name Junius Frey during his Parisian sojourn, barely survived his book. Accused of conspiring on behalf of foreign powers, he was guillotined on April 5, 1794, at the height of Terror, on the same day that Georges Jacques Danton was also on the gallows.

When it appeared, the *Philosophie sociale* aroused considerable interest and was read and appreciated by none other than Immanuel Kant. One of the theses of the present research is that the book had some other famous readers, who for various reasons omitted to mention among their sources the work of an author who had died tragically, an outsider of dubious reputation. A blanket of silence, which has lasted until today. It is true that Gershom Scholem, the great kabbalah scholar, dedicated a brilliant bibliographic profile to Moses Dobruska at the end of the 1970s[2] But in accordance with his interests, linked to esoteric and Jewish history, Scholem concentrated on the sectarian environment from which Dobruska came, and on his Masonic activity. Only a few lines in Scholem are dedicated to the *Philosophie sociale,* and the work remained unexplored until now. And it is to the rediscovery of this dense work, sometimes written in a complex way, but full of intuitions and brilliant anticipations of sociological and philosophical-social thought, that I will devote myself in the following pages.[3]

---

[1] Throughout the present study I will use the form 'Dobruska', which appears in contemporary documents, and not 'Dobrushka', which is modern and artificial, although now widely used. See, for example, the title page of the booklet of Arcadian poems published by our author in his early years: Moses Dobruska, *Die zwo Amaryllen, ein Schäferspiel in einem Auszuge* (Prag: Wolfgang Gerle, 1774).

[2] Gershom Scholem, *La vie de Moses Dobruska, alias Franz Thomas von Schönfeld alias Junius Frey* (Paris: Gallimard, 1981). The book is based on a lecture given by Scholem in Paris in May 1979. See below, 7. 4.

[3] Despite the fact that this is a very important field, the history of sociological thought is still open to investigation. Reflecting on the historical course of the discipline, and especially on its eighteenth-century beginnings, as well as having an intrinsic interest, allows us to better understand

The *Philosophie sociale* develops a highly articulated way of thinking about social reality, about the understanding of human beings, who live in society and interact with their fellow human beings, and about their needs and ambitions. The ultimate aspiration of human beings is – according to Dobruska – the achievement of happiness.

The text is a theoretical elaboration through which our author distils seventy "principles", or laws of cause and effect, on which to base the "first part" of a Universal Constitution.[4] These principles represent the social philosophical basis for the body of rules on which the new democratic society, which is to be born from the ashes of the absolute monarchy, will have to stand. The "second part" of the Universal Constitution will be the application of these principles by the people, i.e. by the elected representatives in the assemblies, as well as by the legislative power. Dobruska is convinced that if legislation is based on these principles and applied in accordance with them, the new social structure will finally overcome the sufferings and distortions of the past and move towards coveted happiness.[5]

As I shall demonstrate later on, the constitutional perspective of the *Philosophie sociale* did not fail to exert its own influence on the French political system in the troubled period of Terror. The provisional Constitution decreed by the National Convention on December 4, 1793, proposed by the lawyer Jacques Nicolas Billaud-Varenne (1756–1819), is also based on ideas expressed by Dobruska.

---

the genesis and content of the current sociological work. See, on this subject, the important observations of Christian Dayé, Stephan Moebius, "Einleitung," In *Soziologiegeschichte. Wege und Ziele*, eds. Christian Dayé and Stephan Moebius (Frankfurt: Suhrkamp, 2015), 7–13; Karl-Siegbert Rehberg, "Die Unverzichtbarkeit historischer Selbstreflexion der Soziologie," In *ibidem*, 431–464. Among the most important books on the history of sociology see Raymond Aron, *Les étapes de la pensée sociologique. Montesquieu, Comte, Marx, Tocqueville, Durkheim, Pareto, Weber* (Paris: Gallimard, 1967); Lewis A. Coser, *Masters of Sociological Thought. Ideas in Historical and Social Context*, 2nd ed. (San Diego: Harcourt Publishers, 1977) (I ed. 1971); Franco Ferrarotti, *Lineamenti di storia del pensiero sociologico* (Roma: Donzelli, 2002); Alberto Izzo, *Storia del pensiero sociologico* (Bologna: Il Mulino, 2005). As regards, in particular, the history of the discipline in Germany, see Stephan Moebius, *René König und die "Kölner Schule". Eine soziologiegeschichtliche Annäherung* (Wiesbaden: Springer, 2015); Stephan Moebius, "Die Geschichte der Soziologie im Spiegel der Kölner Zeitschrift für Soziologie und Sozialpsychologie (KZfSS)," *Kölner Zeitschrift für Soziologie und Sozialpsychologie*, Sonderheft 56 (2017): 3–44; *Handbuch Geschichte der deutschsprachigen Soziologie*, eds. Stephan. Moebius, Andrea Ploder, Nicole Holzhauser and Oliver Römer, 3 vols. (Wiesbaden: Springer, 2017–2019).

4 [Moses Dobruska *alias* Junius Frey], *Philosophie sociale, dédiée au peuple françois par un Citoyen de la Section de la République Françoise, ci-devant du Roule* [hencefort *Philosophie sociale*] (Paris: Froullé, 1793), 53.

5 Dobruska, *Philosophie sociale*, 235–236.

Despite these echoes, important and so far neglected, Dobruska's book cannot be reduced to a mere draft for a Universal Constitution, drawn up in the aftermath of the collapse of the *Ancien Régime*, nor to a simplistic political philosophy, as has recently been claimed.

The central nucleus of the work is in fact social reality, seen in its full extent and problematic nature, distinct from both the political and the moral spheres. This knowledge of social reality, which is as scientific as possible, is approached by Moses Dobruska from two different angles and methodologies, which are closely connected and intertwined.

According to the first perspective, which can be seen as anticipating today's contemporary sociology, he intends to describe and analyze social phenomena according to laws of cause and effect, following in the same path as natural sciences such as physics, chemistry, or mathematics. As we will see, Dobruska's ambition for science clashes with the still rudimentary character of his social analysis.

The second angle, which refers instead to "social philosophy", serves a dual purpose. On the one hand, Dobruska conducts a close criticism of the previous social order, through an analysis of the "pathological" phenomena of the *Ancien Régime* – the *mélanges monstreux*, to put it in the words of the book. On the other hand, the philosophical-social perspective is taken to be the tool to build a new order, which allows the achievement of happiness.

In short, we have a descriptive or sociological dimension, as well as an evaluative and normative one, which we could define more properly as philosophical-social. They are two levels, which I distinguish here for clarity, and which nevertheless, in Dobruska's social thought, appear closely interlinked.

It is also evident that the *Philosophie sociale* represents the beginning of a new strain of thought, which still seeks its own interpretative categories, and which formulates concepts and methods in a rough and experimental way.

Moreover, until the mid-nineteenth century, sociology and social philosophy were not separated into two different disciplines, neither in France nor Germany. Both mainly investigate the social sphere, which is clearly distinct from both the political and the moral and legal spheres.

Only in the twentieth century have some authors preferred to emphasize differences and boundaries. According to this approach, the vocation of sociology is to describe and analyze social phenomena as scientifically as possible, through an empirical methodology very similar to that of natural sciences such as physics, chemistry or mathematics.[6] The aim is to understand people's behaviors and their

---

6 For a distinction between social philosophy and sociology and their specificity, see Axel Honneth, ed., *Pathologien des Sozialen. Die Aufgaben der Sozialphilosophie* (Frankfurt: Fischer,

social interactions as they are, rather than as they should be. In short, from such a perspective, sociology has a non-judgmental attitude, in Max Weber's (1864–1920) sense.[7]

Unlike sociology, social philosophy, seen as a branch of practical philosophy,[8] is instead evaluative and normative. It is not content with a mere description of the 'social fact',[9] as Emile Durkheim (1858–1917) would say, but also assesses it ethically. As Axel Honneth points out, this presupposes that the social philosopher has in mind a social ideal, which he compares with existing reality in order to formulate a critical judgment on the social structure that he examines.[10]

It is obvious that there can be a very fruitful dialogue between social philosophy and sociology. If social philosophy, with its critical vocation, points the finger at "social pathologies", sociology can analyze these same dysfunctions with great effectiveness, thanks to the sophisticated empirical tools at its disposal.

In turn, the results of sociological research can represent an important stimulus for philosophical-conceptual reflection. However, this kind of fruitful interaction between the two disciplines has become [too] infrequent in recent years, one might say for an excess of empiricism which increasingly characterizes the social sciences, including sociology.

Although seen by some with suspicion, due to its alleged lack of scientificity, social philosophy does not seem, to many, an anachronistic knowledge that has now been overtaken by the empirical method of the social sciences. Norbert Leser, for example, pointed out that the relationship between philosophy and science, and in particular between social philosophy and sociology, should not be considered as a dichotomy in which the two approaches are mutually exclusive. Instead, it should be conceived as a dialogue of mutual exchange, which enriches both

---

1994); Rahel Jaeggi and Robin Celikates, *Sozialphilosophie. Eine Einführung* (München: Beck, 2017).

7 Max Weber, "Der Sinn der 'Wertfreiheit' der soziologischen und ökonomischen Wissenschaften," *Logos* 7 (1917): 40–88. Others, on the other hand, have rightly pointed out that sociology also has a fundamental vocation of social criticism, which does not conflict with its scientific nature. See, for instance, eds., Stephan Moebius, and Gerhard Schäfer, eds., *Soziologie als Gesellschaftskritik. Wider den Verlust einer aktuellen Tradition* (Hamburg: VSA, 2006).

8 Social philosophy is today generally understood as "that branch of philosophy, which deals with social issues and questions the form of social practices and institutions as well as the forms of life in society" (Jaeggi, Celikates, *Sozialphilosophie*, 1).

9 Emile Durkheim, *Les règles de la méthode sociologique* (Paris: Félix Alcan, 1895), 175: "les faits sociaux sont des choses et doivent être traités comme tells." See also below, 3. 6.

10 Honneth, "Pathologien des Sozialen. Tradition und Aktualität der Sozialphilosophie," in *Die Aufgaben der Sozialphilosophie*, 50.

disciplines. Although they are partly in competition with each other, the two branches of social reflection are also complementary. They need each other to progress.[11]

If we take historical development into account and compare the situation in two major European countries, France and Germany, we see that social philosophy and sociology have had very different processes of institutionalization in the academic field. If, in France, social philosophy plays a marginal role compared to other philosophical disciplines, in Germany it has had, since the nineteenth century, a place of greater importance. In the German intellectual world, social philosophy has gained its own role among other philosophical disciplines, distancing itself from both moral and political philosophy, and has engaged productively in dialogue with the social science closest to it, sociology, for a long time.

If I have dwelt a little at length on the relations between the two disciplines in a diachronic perspective, it is because I believe that the case of the *Philosophie sociale*, so early and, so far, little understood, should be studied with the awareness of subsequent developments, but also without projecting these developments backwards in an anachronistic manner. Dobruska is, so to speak, "upstream": he antedates the origins of a distinction of methods and qualifying contents that would be affirmed only after him and, I believe, thanks to his insights, even if they were not explicitly recognized by the later scholars of the social sphere.

It is in this perspective that I will outline below the two souls of the social *Philosophie sociale*, the sociological and the philosophical-social, with the caveat that what is distinct here in a clear way is united in the dense textual texture of the work.

1.2 Moses Dobruska, or the Sociologist *Ante Litteram*

In Moses Dobruska's book, theoretical reflections and empirical observations on social phenomena emerge, which we can term as sociological.

These sociological reflections on human nature and society allow Moses Dobruska to define the principles or rules of conduct for the Universal Constitution. They are the key concepts of a social science which was gaining ground in France at the time, and which only a few decades later would take its name, in the work of Auguste Comte, first of "social physics" and then of "sociology".

Although the introduction of the term "sociology", understood as the scientific discourse on society, is in this sense attributed to Comte, recent studies have

---

11 Norbert Leser, *Sozialphilosophie. Grundlagen des Studiums* (Wien: Böhlau, 1997), 29–30.

shown that Emmanuel Joseph Sieyès (1748–1836) coined the neologism "sociologie" as early as 1780,[12] in a note which remained, however, unpublished.

Precisely because of his fundamental role in promoting the definition and the very name of the discipline, Auguste Comte is commonly considered the founding father of sociology.[13] The philosopher and sociologist Raymond Aron (1905–1983), according to whom the first theorist of sociology must be considered Charles-Louis Montesquieu (1689–1755), detached himself from this prevailing opinion with good arguments. It is worth mentioning Aron's theoretical passage because, *mutatis mutandis*, it will serve as a starting point for our evaluation of Dobruska:

> It is fashionable nowadays to regard Charles de Secondat, Baron de la Brède et de Montesquieu, as a precursor of sociology, which is justified if the founder is the man (in this case, Auguste Comte) who invented the term. On the other hand, if the sociologist is to be defined by the peculiar aims which I have suggested, then Montesquieu was much more of a sociologist than Auguste Comte. The philosophical interpretation of sociology present in *The Spirit of the Laws* is much more "modern" than the same interpretation in the writings of Auguste Comte. This does not necessarily mean that Montesquieu was superior to Auguste Comte; but it does mean that I do not consider Montesquieu a precursor of sociology, but rather one of its great theorists.[14]

---

12 Until recent years, the authorship of the term sociology "understood as the science of observation of social phenomena" was universally attributed to Auguste Comte: see for instance Giovanni Busino, "Pavane pour l'histoire de la sociologie," *Revue européenne des sciences sociales* 31 (1993): 95. Jacques Guilhaumou, "Sieyès et le non-dit de la sociologie. Du mot à la chose," *Revue d'histoire des sciences humaines* (2006): 117–134, has revealed that the first to use the term was Sieyès, almost fifty years before Auguste Comte. The word *sociologie* emerges in an unpublished manuscript (shelfmark 284 AP 3 d.l. of the Sieyès archives, preserved in the Archives Nationales in Paris). For Sieyès, the object of sociology are social customs.

13 Cf. Lewis A. Coser, *Masters of Sociological Thought. Ideas in Historical and Social Context*, 2nd ed. (San Diego: Harcourt Publishers, 1977)(I ed. 1971), 3: "The new social science that Comte sought to establish he first called 'social physics'; later when he thought that the term had been stolen from him by the Belgian social statistician, Adolphe Quetelet, he coined the word 'sociology', a hybrid term compounded of Latin and Greek parts".

14 Raymond Aron, *Les étapes de la pensée sociologique. Montesquieu, Comte, Marx, Tocqueville, Durkheim, Pareto, Weber*, (Paris: Gallimard,1967), 27: [Il peut paraître surprenant de commencer une histoire de la pensé sociologique par l'étude de Montesquieu. En France, on le considère généralement comme un précurseur de la sociologie et on attribue à Auguste Comte le mérite de l'avoir fondée – à juste titre si le fondateur est celui qui a créé le terme. Mais si le sociologue se définit par une intention spécifique, connaître scientifiquement le social en tant que tel, Montesquieu, est alors, selon moi, tout autant un sociologue qu'Auguste Comte. L'interprétation de la sociologie, implicite dans *L'Esprit des lois*, est, en effet, plus 'moderne' à certains égards que celle d'Auguste Comte. Ce qui ne prouve pas que Montesquieu ait raison contre Auguste Comte, mais seulement que Montesquieu n'est pas à mes yeux un précurseur, mais un des doctrinaires de la sociologie]. Idem, *Main Currents in Sociologcal Thought: Volume*

Aron's argument seems to me to be well founded. It is the intention to understand social reality in a scientific way that makes Montesquieu a founder of sociology.[15] On the basis of the same principle, that is, in accordance with methodological intentionality, we can also see in Moses Dobruska an initiator of sociological thought. As I will demonstrate in the following pages, the *Philosophie sociale* lies between Montesquieu on the one hand and Henri Saint-Simon and Auguste Comte on the other. This intermediate collocation between these authors is not only chronological, but also pertains to the development of conceptual tools.

On the one hand, Dobruska draws inspiration from Montesquieu's writings, especially from *The Spirit of the Laws,*[16] which he knows well.[17]

On the other hand, both Saint-Simon and Comte take a lot of cues from the *Philosophie sociale,* without ever mentioning it. More than one concept which was theorized for the first time by Dobruska can be found in the writings of the two authors, who, as is well known, were united for some time by a relationship of close collaboration. These loans will be discussed in more detail in the last chapter, where I deal with the posthumous fortunes, or perhaps misfortunes, of Dobruska's thought. For now, it is enough to say that both Saint-Simon's and Comte's social theories appear in a different perspective, if read in the light of the *Philosophie sociale.*

The central contribution of Dobruska's sociological thinking concerns five thematic areas: i) the need for a scientific discipline that deals with social issues; ii) social change and the evolution of social organizations; iii) the individual and society; iv) the social, cultural, and political determinants of happiness; v) models of government and the recruitment of public officials.

One. *Montesquieu, Comte, Marx, De Toqueville: The Sociologistis and the Revolution of 1848* (London and New York: Routledge, 2019).

15 It should be remembered that in addition to the well-known founding fathers of sociology on which there is a wealth of literature – including Montesquieu, Comte, Marx, Spencer Durkheim, de Tocqueville, Durkheim, Simmel, Weber, Pareto, Mannheim, and now also Dobruska – there are founding mothers as well. Think, for example, of, Harriet Martineau, Jenny P. d'Héricourt, Beatrice Webb, Jane Adams, Marianne Weber, Mathilde Vaetering, Frieda Wunderlich, Dorothy Swaine Thomas, Marie Jahoda. For further information on the founders of sociology, see Claudia Honegger and Theresa Wobbe, eds., *Frauen in der Soziologie* (München: Beck, 1998).

16 *L'Esprit des lois* was published for the first time, without indication of the author's name in Geneva by the bookseller-publisher Jacques Barillot during the last ten days of October 1748; see Domenico Felice, "Nota al testo," in *Tutte le opere (1721–1754)* by Charles-Louis de Montesquieu facing French text, ed, Idem, (Milano: Bompiani 2014), 885.

17 Several times in his work Dobruska mentions Montesquieu, with whom he dialogues and criticizes. See *Philosophie sociale*, 14, 199, 213–215 (here he refers in particular to *The Spirit of the Laws*).

1.2.1 The Need for a Scientific Discipline Concerning Social Reality

The first reflection, which we find at the beginning of the *Philosophie sociale*, concerns the need for a scientific discipline concerning social reality. Dobruska intends to build a new field of study, using the same methodology of natural sciences such as physics, chemistry, and mathematics, to investigate first social reality or "social art", as he calls it, and only later the political system and its institutions.

Inspired by Montesquieu's *The Spirit of the Laws*, and pervaded by an eighteenth-century optimism, he is convinced that social reality can be "known" through an empirical descriptive method, based on observation. In short, he firmly believes that it is possible to arrive at the formulation of laws, expressed in terms of cause and effect, that explain the behavior and social interactions between the members of a society.

In addition to this profession of faith in causality, he uses two other methodologies. On the one hand, he uses a comparative approach, i.e. he observes and compares different societies in order to better identify the single cause or the multiple reasons that have determined a specific social phenomenon. On the other hand, he uses a historical analysis of certain phenomena in order to explain which causes have been decisive for the evolution of a society over time.

1.2.2 Theories of Social Change and the Development of Societal Organizations

The second important sociological contribution that Dobruska has left us concerns the theory of social change. As a member of the Jacobin *élite* and witness to an important phase of the French Revolution, he wonders what social and cultural processes can explain the collapse of the social order of the *Ancien Régime*. How will it be possible to rebuild a new society, one that is democratic and that makes its citizens happy? How have social organizations evolved over time, since ancient times, and what forms of thought support and justify the social order?

To answer these questions, Dobruska formulates two important hypotheses: on the one hand, the theory of social disorganization and reorganization, and on the other, the theory of the historical development of social organizations and their systems of thought, which have justified the constituted social order.

According to the first theorization, radical change, which leads to the transformation of a social organization based on a specific order to another, inspired by different principles, is only possible if there are two phases: the first is that of "social disorganization", in which the order is deconstructed and dismantled.

The second phase is that of "social reorganization", in which the structure of society is reconstructed on new cultural bases.

The *Philosophie sociale,* however, goes beyond the observation, albeit theoretically new and influential, of the dynamics of deconstruction and reconstruction of society. One of the questions the book tries to answer concerns the "deep causes" of change, both disorganization and reorganization.

According to Dobruska, the reasons for the collapse of the *Ancien Régime* are both social, political and cultural. In the *Philosophie sociale*, these elements of decay and disintegration are called *mélanges monstreux,* "monstrous mixtures": the great oppression exercised against the rest of the population by certain social groups, such as the nobles and the clergy, the lack of freedom for the individual and the lack of recognition of individuals as citizens with equal rights. The decisive impulse to radical change came from the *savants*, i.e. the *philosophes*, who enlightened the people with their thoughts; they showed the social abuses and abuses of power, and the lack of freedom in which the majority lived under the absolutist monarchy.

The great thinker, who tried in every way with his own writings to awaken consciences during the *Ancien Régime,* was Jean-Jacques Rousseau: first with his *Address on the Origin of Inequality* (1754) and then with his celebrated *Social Contract* (1762):

> Man is born free; and everywhere he is in chains. One thinks himself the master of others, and still remains a greater slave than they. How did this change come about? I do not know. What can make it legitimate? That question I think I can answer.[18]

Dobruska praises and pays tribute to Rousseau as "the one who provoked and determined the French Revolution".[19]

Once "the old order of things has been disorganized"[20] we need to reorganize it. And once again, what causes the change is the intersection of social and cultural factors, so that the *savants* are attributed a role as fundamental as that of disorganization. The specific recipients of the *Philosophie sociale* are *les gens de bien*, those who, free from superstitions, love knowledge and strive to follow the path of truth. Their task is to show the new values – universal citizenship, equal rights, freedom – so that we can arrive at the Constitution, which the

---

18 Jean-Jacques Rousseau, *Du contrat social. Ou, Principes du droit politique* (Amsterdam: Chez Marc-Michel Rey, 1762), I. 1. 3. See also below, 3.12. Idem, *The Social Contract, and Discourses,* introduction by George Douglas Howard Cole (London: J.M. Dent & Sons, Ltd, 1910), 5.
19 Dobruska, *Philosophie sociale*, 5: [Donc, en rendant à Rousseau l'hommage que nous devons à celui qui a provoqué et déterminé la Révolution françoise].
20 *Ibidem*, 27.

legislators must adopt. The prerequisite of the Universal Constitution is a common intellectual space, based on the principles that arise from a deep knowledge of human beings and society.

The second theorization of social change, elaborated by Dobruska, concerns the development of social organizations from ancient times to the present day. It is a theory that partly recalls what Giambattista Vico (1668–1744) had written in his *Scienza nuova* of 1725,[21] although with differences in focus and approach. Dobruska associates different systems of thought with the phases of the development of humanity, each of which supports and justifies its respective social order. In the first phase, the social order is marked by a theological system of thought. Sovereigns are considered to be representatives of the gods, and society is entrusted to theocratic governments. Theological power is closely linked to political power. This first phase is followed by a second, in which the constituted order is governed by a system of thought of a metaphysical nature. Humanity then evolved, until it reached the last phase, which Dobruska considers revolutionary, and still in progress as he writes, based on the scientific knowledge of nature and physics.

We will see in the final chapter how this scheme influenced first the thought of Saint-Simon, and then that of Auguste Comte.

One cannot fail to notice how the theories on social change, elaborated by Dobruska, highlight cultural factors (systems of thought, ideas, values, and beliefs) and social factors above all as factors of change, almost completely leaving aside economic ones. This lack of attention to economic determinants reflects not only his class appurtenance but also the wider revolutionary cultural context.

Cultural change must undoubtedly be considered an important factor in the French Revolution. It is an independent variable, alongside the economic and social variables, and not a dependent variable, caused by social unrest and economic transformation. As the historian Patrice Higonnet rightly pointed out, the revolutionary *élite*, and in particular the Jacobin faction, was made up both of bourgeoisie, often professionals and mostly lawyers, and of nobles, such as La Fayette (1757–1834), Talleyrand-Périgord (1754–1838), Condorcet (1743–1794), and Barras (1755–1829),[22] to name but a few, and certainly not of farmers or the poor. Let us remember that Dobruska himself had managed to achieve, before reaching Paris, a striking social climb. Thanks to his conversion, he had obtained the title of nobility, which had opened the doors of the Habsburg court to him.

---

21 See below, 7. 3. 3.
22 Patrice Higonnet, "Sociability, Social Structure, and the French Revolution," *Social Research* 56 (1989), 116.

Many members of the revolutionary élite lived in economic comfort – if not in luxury – and were certainly not motivated in the first instance by material needs and the hope for an improvement in their socio-economic conditions. They were driven to fight for a radical transformation of the *Ancien Régime* by the abuses of power and the privileges of the ruling classes – the aristocracy and the clergy. Important triggers of the Revolution were the lack of individual freedom of expression – for example, the limitations on religious freedom (think of the discrimination, in France, against Jews and Protestants) – and the lack of recognition of equality of all before the law.

1.2.3 Theories of Man in Society and Social Interactions

The third important sociological contribution of the *Philosophie sociale* concerns the analysis both of the man who lives in society with his fellow human beings, and of society as a whole.

The analysis of the individual in society from which Dobruska initially departs, and from which he then detaches himself, must be understood within the broader conceptual framework of naturalistic legal philosophy, which found expression in Montesquieu's *The Spirit of the Laws*. Dobruska distinguishes between a man who lives in the "state of nature" and one who lives in the "state of culture or society". The state of nature is conceived in line with most naturalistic legal thinkers as a pre-social condition, not historically and geographically determined.

In opposition to Hobbes,[23] and in consonance with Montesquieu, Dobruska believes that, in the state of nature (*im Naturzustand*[24]), man is not belligerent and in constant conflict with his fellow men. Rather, in this natural state, men are free, autonomous, and able to look after their own self-preservation without the help of others. They don't care about relationships with others, because they don't need them for their livelihood. In further opposition to Hobbes, Dobruska argues that men in the state of nature have different skills and abilities, and thus agrees with the diversity postulated by Montesquieu[25] and the physical inequality in which Rousseau also believed.[26]

---

23 Thomas Hobbes, *Leviathan* (London: Crooke, 1651), 61. See below, 4.2.
24 When available, I'll refer to the German terms used by Dobruska in the first draft of his *Philosophie sociale*. See below Appendix 3.
25 Aron, *Les étapes de la pensée sociologique*, 81. See also below, 4. 2.
26 Jean-Jacques Rousseau, *Discours sur l'origine et les fondements de l'inégalité parmi les hommes* (Amsterdam: Chez Marc-Michel Rey, 1755), 1–2.

Although they differ in their abilities, men enjoy the most perfect equality in natural rights, the same access to resources; they are not subject to abuse of power as far has no one enjoys special privileges.

Like Hobbes and Rousseau, Dobruska believes that a social contract is required to join society. With the transition to the state of culture, men lose their autonomy and their ability to self-preserve themselves, and therefore become dependent on other members of society for their livelihood.

The drive to sign the social contract does not derive, as for Hobbes, from the need to tame the social conflict and to guarantee the stability of the State. Rather, it originates, in the negative, from the lack of self-sufficiency of the individual in the state of culture and, in the positive, from the opportunity to develop one's own material and intellectual abilities, until reaching the highest perfection.

Dobruska makes a clear departure from an atomistic conception of men, which considers them as rational actors who maximize their preferences and advantages thanks to rational calculations. This is the approach of utilitarian economic thought of the late eighteenth century – think for example of Smith and Bentham.

He develops a sociological conception instead, which starts from the individual (methodological individualism) and from his multiple needs, his desires, and his ability to perfect himself (micro level of analysis).

At the same time, Dobruska believes that man is inserted in social bonds, which he needs both for his own survival (level of meso analysis), and that he should also be embedded in the broader cultural and social context (levels of macro analysis).

From these premises, he elaborates an interesting theory of the importance of the reciprocity of bonds, which we know will become a central theme in the sociological thought from the nineteenth century up to the present day. For Dobruska, reciprocity performs important functions for social organization: it guarantees the preservation of both the individual and social self, it allows the satisfaction of the multiple needs (*besoins multiplies*) of individuals, it represents an antidote to the immorality of the individual and that of the State, and it makes social cohesion and stability possible in a society over time.

Although Dobruska starts from the assumption that the individual is able to act in the social context in which he lives and can pursue his own goals, related to his personal development and the achievement of happiness, he clearly theorizes how the behaviors and daily habits of individual actors are influenced by the socio-cultural context in which they are "socialized", as we would say today. He shows how, in societies regulated by different legislators and by different systems of values and standards, behaviors, customs, and lifestyles are completely different. Dobruska gives us the example of people born and raised in a predominantly Muslim society. As far as sexuality and culinary habits are concerned, such individuals have different lifestyles than those born in a predominantly Christian society. The former love polygamy and are not allowed to drink alcoholic beverages, while Christians are required to practice monogamy but can enjoy the delicacies of wine.

If, on the one hand, society binds the social action of the individual through its "legislator" and its normative corpus, on the other hand society itself supports and allows the development of the intellectual faculties of its members (their *perfectibilité*) through the "social treasure" (*trésor social*).

The sociological thought that Dobruska elaborates in the *Philosophie sociale* underlines in a very articulated way the interactions and the mutual influences between the individual actor (*moi individuel*) and society (*moi social*).

1.2.4 Theories About Happiness and Its Cultural, Social, and Political Determinants

The fourth area of sociological reflection concerns happiness, a theme that impassioned the *philosophes* and men (and women) of letters of the eighteenth century. Dobruska never defines happiness in general, because he assumes that individuals are different and have different desires and goals – those who are more materialistic will aim to increase their economic wealth, those who are driven by spiritual satisfaction will be content with a more modest lifestyle. As a good liberal, he does not think that defining the happiness to which everyone should aspire is the task of society, let alone of the State. As a good sociologist, however, he highlights both the political, legal, and cultural determinants of happiness and the barriers that prevent both the individual and society from reaching it.

At the political level, happiness is made possible by democratic regimes, based on the freedom of rights for all citizens. Despotic regimes, in contrast, do not guarantee the right to equality and freedom, and are characterized by the abuse of power by one social group over others.

Legal factors that promote happiness also allow the application and realization of the Universal Constitution.

Education is a crucial element among the cultural determinants that increase the state of well-being of individuals; false morality, which distances itself from the fundamental principles of the Universal Constitution, instead prevents well-being.

Finally, Dobruska does not deny that there is a link between happiness and economic and social resources. He does not believe, like Montesquieu, that the achievement of happiness is a subjective factor, to be found in the convictions and attitudes of the soul. *Philosophie sociale* supports a hedonistic and material-istic view of life. Material riches and luxury are anything but condemnable, since they increase the pleasant sensations of life. Dobruska also does not argue that a fair redistribution of economic resources can increase happiness. On the con-trary, it could represent an obstacle to everyone's drive to improve their living conditions.

1.2.5 Political Sociology: Citizens, Governance Models, and Recruitment of Civil Servants

In the *Philosophie sociale* we also find a political sociology, focused on models of government and recruitment of public employees.

Dobruska distinguishes between society and the State but, unlike Hobbes, does not believe that society is subordinate and marginalized in relation to the State. As I have already pointed out, Dobruska starts with an analysis of society, and then considers which political system is best suited to ensuring the happiness of its citizens.

According to the *Philosophie sociale*, only the representative democratic state is suitable for this purpose, whatever the size of its territory. In this regard, Do-bruska criticized Jean-Jacques Rousseau, who had argued in the *Social Contract* of 1762 that democracy was onlysuited to small states.[27]

Dobruska's thesis, in support of representative democracy, is articulated. First of all, it is only in a democracy that all members of society are also citizens with equal rights. Moreover, representative democracy is the only regime that al-lows individuals to be given a portion of "food equal to their needs", so that they achieve the desired welfare.

Finally, since the general well-being of a State is the sum of happiness of individual citizens, representative democracy brings universal happiness to its fullest possible fulfillment.

The second theory, which we could define as political sociology, concerns the role of education in training citizens and in making it possible to recruit public officials. The educational process ensures that only the most deserving and capa-ble can be chosen, that is, those who have understood the principles of the Uni-versal Constitution not only with rationality but also with their feelings. Dobruska, who agrees with Montesquieu on this, believes that this educational process

---

27 Dobruska, *Philosophie sociale*, 25.

should begin in the family, courtesy of parents who are themselves already educated in the principles of the Constitution.[28] The Constitution itself is, in the *Philosophie sociale*, the primary source of social education.

1.3 Moses Dobruska, or the Social Philosopher *Ante Litteram*

Together with sociological thought, Moses Dobruska elaborates an acute philosophical-social thought. As we shall see, some of the qualifying points of the *Philosophie sociale* partly anticipate social philosophy, especially German social philosophy, up until the present day.[29]

How does Moses Dobruska's social philosophy fit into the cultural and intellectual context of the eighteenth century? Which thinkers have most influenced his work? Finally, what are the salient features of the Dobruskian approach? These are the questions I want to answer in the continuation of this chapter.

Let us recall how the term "social philosophy" was used for the first time, not by Thomas Hobbes as some have argued, but by an abbot, Jean-Baptiste Durosoy (1726–1804), who in 1783 published a work entitled *Philosophie sociale ou essai sur les devoirs de l'homme et du citoyen*.[30] Beyond the title, rather than a real "social philosophy", Durosoy's work proposes a practical moral philosophy, consisting of a copious collection of ethical-moral precepts to be able to live "well" in society (without this good being specified).

It is therefore with Dobruska that social philosophy, in the modern sense, makes its entrance into the intellectual debate. The philosophical-social approach of our author can be summarized in four fundamental elements.

The first characteristic, which more clearly intersects with his "sociological thinking",[31] concerns the focus on the social, on life in society, and on social relationships. In short, it is a specific choice of field, which differs from reflections centered on the State or on ethics.

The second characteristic concerns the theorization of the social and political phenomena that led to the collapse of the absolute monarchy of Louis XVI

---

28 *Ibidem*, 214.
29 See Franck Fischbach, *Manifeste pour une philosophie sociale* (Paris: La Decouverte, 2009).
30 Jean-Baptiste Durosoy, *Philosophie sociale ou essai sur les devoirs de l'homme et du citoyen* (Paris: C.P. Berton, 1783). See below, 3. 2.
31 See Silvana Greco. "Soziologie des Judentums in Deutschland. Markante Felder, Perspektiven und Methoden," in *Ein halbes Jahrhundert deutscher Forschung und Lehre über das Judentum in Deutschland*, ed. Andreas Lenhardt. (Berlin: De Gruyter, 2017),147–148.

and its social disorganization. This is not a neutral description, but rather a critical assessment of the dysfunctionality and injustice of the *Ancien Régime*.

These are serious social questions, or *mélanges monstreux*, in the language of the *Philosophie sociale*[32] conceptually similar to what the social philosopher Axel Honneth calls "social pathologies". The causes of these dysfunctions are, for Dobruska, the division of men into different social classes and the lack of recognition of citizenship for members of certain social groups, tyranny, disregard for the common good and, finally, the lack of freedom.

Dobruska makes very clear value judgments, having in mind a better ethical and regulatory model for the future democratic society. The hypothesis from which he starts is that human beings are the bearer of many needs and have the desire to develop their intellectual and material faculties. This can only happen in a society in which everyone is a citizen and enjoys the same rights, primarily freedom. It is precisely because of this lack of freedom and the abuse of power that social philosophies view the previous order so negatively.

If, as a sociologist, Dobruska knows how to define and circumscribe these critical points, we owe the evaluative judgment, built on the basis of a more equitable and functional "must be", to the social philosopher within him.

After having identified "all that was wrong" in Louis XVI's regime of absolute monarchy, Dobruska's social philosophy – and here we come to the third characteristic, the normative and teleological one – defines the social and political conditions necessary to overcome social disorganization and achieve happiness. These range from the separation of religious and political power to the establishment of a representative democratic society based on the "Universal Constitution" which guarantees all citizens the same rights.

Finally, the last feature of Dobruska's social philosophy is the ability to define which recipients to turn to – to identify those who can share the worldview expressed in the *Philosophie sociale*, who can understand the principles that govern social life, and who know how to begin a process of change in society. The *Philosophie sociale* is aimed at two different recipients: on the one hand, a collective recipient, namely the French people, and on the other, the so-called "decent people" (*les gens de bien*). As a good social philosopher, Dobruska needs to recruit intellectual and civil forces for social change.

---

32 Durosoy, *Philosophie sociale ou essai sur les devoirs de l'homme et du citoyen*, 40.

1.4 The Structure of the Present Study

Having illustrated the objectives of the *Philosophie sociale* and its two "souls" – the sociological one and the other more properly philosophical-social – I will now outline the structure of the present study.

The first chapter is dedicated to the intricate, adventurous, surprising biographical journey of Moses Dobruska, the son of a wealthy and cultured Jew named Solomon Dobruska and Schöndl of Prossnitz, a beautiful, clever, and charismatic woman, who was close to the heretical sect of the Sabbatians. Moses was born on July 12, 1753 in Brno, Moravia, the second-born of twelve children. After leaving Moravia, he married in Prague in 1773, and became a father the following year. Although he was a well-educated man and had already published some poems and essays, both in Hebrew and in German, he was also ambitious and enterprising. To overcome the many restrictions to which Jews were subjected in the Habsburg kingdom, in 1775 he converted to Catholicism, with the name Franz Thomas Schönfeld. The conversion was followed by a license of nobility, granted by Maria Theresa, and a considerable social climb, which took him to the imperial court of Vienna, with which he also entered into fruitful business contracts. The reign of Joseph II marks the moment of his greatest ascent, while the succession of Leopold II marked the beginning of a decline, if not a serious misfortune. Perhaps because of problems related to his position in Vienna, as well as ideological reasons, Moses arrived in Strasbourg in 1792 where he began to participate with passion in the political life of revolutionary France. In June of the same year he moved to Paris. As a convinced Jacobin, he began to write feverishly his great work, the *Philosophie sociale,* which he published in June 1793. Accused of conspiring against the Revolution, he was arrested in November. On April 5 of the following year, his revolutionary fervor and his action "to do good" came to a dramatic end: he was guillotined together with his brother, Emmanuel, and Danton.

The second chapter will go into the *Philosophie sociale* of Moses Dobruska, *alias* Junius Frey. I will first survey the aims, structure, and recipients of the book. I will then outline the theoretical framework of Dobruska's thought and analyze in detail his important ideas on social change – the theory of social disorganization and reorganization – to arrive at the Universal Constitution, the essence and form of which I will outline.

In the third chapter we will see how Moses Dobruska conceives man, after he has left the state of nature and has achieved, by virtue of the social contract, the state of culture or society. The *Philosophie sociale* starts from the individual, seen as a dynamic being in continuous evolution, able to develop his own material and intellectual faculties until reaching perfection. At the same time, Dobruska demonstrates how deeply rooted the individual is in his socio-cultural context, how influenced he is by the system of norms and values in force in that environment, and how much he also needs the other members of society for survival. I will highlight the different forms of social interaction – from selfishness to reciprocity – that characterize this state of fluid participation by the individual in the lives of his fellow human beings. The chapter will continue with the Dobruskian reflection on society and its rights and duties towards citizens.

In the fourth chapter I will focus on the different political regimes outlined in the *Philosophie sociale*: aristocracy, monarchy, and democracy. According to Dobruska, only representative democracy can guarantee happiness for citizens. The role and functioning of the three powers which for Dobruska, drawing from Montesquieu, uphold a democracy – legislative, executive and judicial power – will be examined in greater depth. In conclusion, the recruitment of civil servants and their education in constitutional principles will be studied.

In the fifth chapter I will focus on the ultimate goal of the new democratic society outlined in the *Philosophie sociale*: individual happiness and the happiness of society as a whole. With a fine analysis, anticipating sociology, Dobruska highlights which economic, social, cultural and legal factors allow the achievement of the state of happiness and which instead hinder it.

In the sixth chapter I will outline the reception of the *Philosophie sociale* by contemporaries of Dobruska and up to the present day. In particular, I will show how the work was read by François Chabot (1756–1794), Jacobin parliamentarian and friend and brother-in-law of Dobruska (he married his sister Léopoldine), and by the great German philosopher Immanuel Kant (1724–1804), for whom Dobruska had deep admiration. I will also mention the rather *tranchant* judgment of Maximilien de Robespierre (1758–1794), the main protagonist of Terror, and the indirect use of Dobruska's ideas by the German philosopher Johann August Eberhard (1739–1809), a critic of Kant.

I will show the influence of the *Philosophie sociale* on the work of Henri de Saint-Simon (1760–1825) and on that of Auguste Comte, considered the "father" of sociology. In particular, I will highlight the significant impact that Dobruska's thought had on the young Comte – from the theory of social disorganization-reorganization to the law of the three stages of human progress. The biographical-intellectual profile that Gershom Scholem has traced of Dobruska, and specifically the part that directly concerns the *Philosophie sociale*,[33] will then be briefly discussed, concluding with occasional references to Dobruska in the sociological and philosophical research of the twenty-first century.

---

33 Scholem, *Du Frankisme au jacobinisme*. See below, 7. 4.

A chapter summarizing the work carried out and the new perspectives resulting from it will follow. The *Philosophie sociale* is by no means a mere draft Constitution, but a pioneering essay on sociology and social philosophy. From Dobruska's ideas, widely used between the late eighteenth century and the first decades of the nineteenth century without giving credit to the author, come some key concepts of social disciplines, as we know them today. An enthusiastic and unfortunate initiator, and sometimes a brilliant theorist, Moses Dobruska deserves a role of his own in the history of social thought.

2 Moses Dobruska: Rise and Fall of an Alternative Hero

2.1 The First Years: From Brno to Vienna

Throughout his life, Moses Dobruska took on a number of different names. Each change of name corresponded to a transformation, even an abrupt one, in his environment and social status. Born on July 12, 1753 into a Jewish family based in Brno,[34] Moravia, Moses was educated in the Hebrew language. Of course, he also learned Yiddish, which was used at the time among Ashkenazi Jews in everyday life. His parents, Solomon and Schöndl, née Hirschel, enjoyed considerable economic prosperity, and allowed him to have a private teacher. A relatively unusual case among the Moravian Jews of the time, he also received a good education in European languages and literatures. He began to write poems in German very early, and even published his first literary attempt at the age of twenty, after which many more compositions followed. His first collection of verses, *Etliche Gedichte zur Probe,* was judged quite harshly by the learned reviewer Johann Enrich Biester, but Moses eventually made a name for himself gained a reputation among German literati, with some of his poems still being included in anthologies as late as 1812.[35]

In 1775, Moses published the *Sefer sha'ashua',* a commentary in Hebrew on the first part of *Sefer Behinat 'olam* by Jedaiah ben Abraham Bedersi (1270–1340).[36] In this work, he quotes extensively from rabbinic and philosophic literature and repeatedly quotes Moses Mendelssohn. The *Sefer sha'ashua'* is dedicated, with

---

34 The first to settle in Brno, from his native town Dobruška, in northeastern Bohemia, was Jacob Moyses, the grandfather of our Moses. On him see Bruno Mauritz Trapp, "Dobruschka – Schönfeld – Frey," *[Brünner] Tagesbote,* (January 16 1928): 5; Josef Karniel, "Jüdischer Pseudo-messianismus und deutsche Kultur. Der Weg der frankistichen Familie Dobruschka-Schönfeld im Zeitalter der Aufklärung," in *Gegenseitige Einflüsse deutscher und jüdischer Kultur von der Epoche der Aufklärung bis zu Weimarer Republik,* ed. by Walter Grab (Tel Aviv: Nateev-Printing and Publ. Enterprises, 1982): 33–34; Dušan Uhlíř, "Juden in Mähren und das Mährische Zentrum des Frankismus im ausgehenden 18. Jahrhundert," *Aufklärung, Vormärz, Revolution* 4 (1999): 46–47.
35 Ladislaus Leopold Pfest, *Die Jahreszeiten. Eine Liederlese für Freunde der Natur* (Salzburg: Salzburg: Mayr'schen, 1812), 460 (Der Winterabend).
36 The Italian Hebraist Giovanni Bernardo De Rossi, who quotes the booklet by Dobruska in his *Dizionario storico degli autori ebrei e delle loro opere,* 3 vols. (Parma: Stamperia Reale, 1802), vol . 1, 167: "Mosè Dobruski stampò nel 1775 in Praga una nuova esposizione del I capitolo [of the *Behinat 'olam*] col titolo di *Libro delle Delizie*".

high praise, to Hayyim Popper of Bresnitz, or Joachim Popper, later ennobled as Edler von Popper.[37] Such an enthusiastic dedication was motivated by the fact that Dobruska had married Popper's stepdaughter Elke (Elkele) Joß on May 20, 1773. Popper was a wealthy merchant and banker, and his adopted daughter Elke was "probably the best Jewish match in the Czech lands".[38]

Soon, however, the young couple, who had in the meantime moved to Prague, converted to Christianity, together with their little daughter Maria Anna on December 17, 1775, in St. Vitus Cathedral. As Popper, who opposed the baptism, decided to withdraw the donations he had made to Elke, a lawsuit followed, which went on for quite a long time. In 1778, Moses and his wife signed an agreement in which they renounced any further claim, having been satisfactorily compensated.[39] This was the first fundamental break in the life of Moses Dobruska, which allowed him to leave the Jewish environment in which he was born and to begin a long, fruitful social ascent. It must be said that Moses' mother, Schöndl, certainly belonged to the sect of the Sabbatians, a heretical movement that had developed in the mid-seventeenth century around the pseudo-messiah Sabbatai Zevi. In 1666, Zevi was forced to convert to Islam by the Ottoman sultan. However, despite this conversion, which was justified in cabbalistic terms, the Sabbatians, in opposition to rabbinical orthodoxy, honored Zevi as the true messiah and believed in his reincarnation.[40] Schöndl was a cousin of Jacob Frank, a protagonist of Sabbatianism in the eighteenth century, who presented himself as the messianic heir of Zevi. The documents of the time attest to the commitment of Moses' mother to support the cause of the Sabbatians,[41] and it is likely that her husband, Solomon, also shared Sabbatian views. In Sabbatian circles, at the confessional margins of Judaism, conversion, more or less instrumental, was very frequent. As early as 1764, Moses' eldest

---

37 Popper was the first Jew to be ennobled by the Austrian Emperor, 1790, without having converted to Christianity. See Samuel Kraus, *Joachim Edler von Popper. Ein Zeit- und Lebensbild aus der Geschichte der Juden in Böhmen* (Wien: Selbstverlag, 1926).

38 Pawel Maciejko, *The Mixed Multitude. Jacob Frank and the Frankist Movement, 1755–1816* (Philadelphia: University of Pennsylvania Press, 2011), 195.

39 Samuel Krauss, *Joachim Edler von Popper*, 76–77.

40 For a masterly study of Sabbatianism see Gershom. Scholem, *Sabbatai Sevi. The mystical Messiah* (Princeton-London: Routledge 1973) (Heb. ed. 1957).

41 I have dwelt on these documentary aspects in my article *Heresy*, "Apostasy, and the Beginnings of Social Philosophy. Moses Dobruska reconsidered," *Materia giudaica* 20–21 (2015–2016): 439–464.

brother Carl, born in 1751, left home against the will of his parents.[42] He then took baptism, entered the military service, and became an officer in the Imperial army. Carl was also the first Dobruska to adopt the name Schönfeld. His example influenced his brothers and sisters: on November 17, 1775, two younger brothers of his, Blumele and Gerson, were baptized in the Vienna Cathedral of Saint Stephen, in a lavish ceremony. Blumele, aged sixteenth, was named Theresia Maria Josepha and Gerson, who was eighteen, became Joseph Carl.

Three further brothers – Jacob Naftali, Josef and David[43] – went to the baptismal font a few hours before Moses, in a separate ceremony. Within a couple of months, six members of the younger generation had abandoned Judaism. Thanks to Carl's efforts, the young converts, including Moses, obtained a license of nobility from Maria Theresa.[44]

While Carl had been crucial in obtaining the collective ennoblement, Moses, now Franz Thomas Schönfeld, had also contributed to the reputation of the family. Among other things, heproduced a German translation of the *Exercices de l'âme*, a book of devotion written in French by the Jesuit Denis-Xavier Clément (1706–1771) and first published in 1758.[45] Dobruska's translation, the only translation of the text into German, opens with a dedication to Maria Theresa, and a short preface, signed "Schönfeld".[46]

During the first years following his conversion, Dobruska managed to be appointed at the Garellian library in Vienna and even worked as a censor for books, first in Prague and then in Vienna.[47] He was also actively involved as an entrepreneur in various fields: tobacco manufacture, army supplies, banking. He did invest in his own name, but mostly he did so in partnership, his best partner being his mother Schöndl. The Austrian National Archives in Vienna

---

42 According to his own report in his request of ennoblement to Empress Maria Theresa dated October 17, 1777: "nachdem [ich] als ein Knab von 14. Jahren aus eigenem Trieb meine Eltern verlassen, und das Licht des wahren Glaubens angenommen . . . ", quoted by Susanne Wölfle-Fischer, *Junius Frey (1753–1794). Jude, Aristokrat und Revolutionär* (Frankfurt a. M.: Peter Lang, 1997), 45.
43 They were called Maximilian Friedrich, Leopold Prokop, and Emanuel Neopomuk, respectively.
44 Joseph, Maximilian, Leopold, Emanuel, and Maria Theresia.
45 Denis-Xavier Clément, *Exercices de l'âme pour se disposer aux sacrements de pénitence et d'eucharistie* (Paris: Guerin, 1758).
46 *Seelenübungen zur Vorbereitung zu den Sakramenten der Buße und des heiligen Abendmahls*, Wien 1778 (a copy of the book is preserved at the Austrian National Library in Vienna: see Greco, *Heresy, Apostasy, and the Beginnings of Social Philosophy*, 449–450).
47 Wölfle-Fischer, *Junius Frey*, 77.

preserve several business proposals Dobruska addressed to the administration and to the Court, some of which were rejected while a few were approved. It is clear that our Dobruska/Schönfeld was highly regarded within the most powerful circles of the Habsburg court.

2.2 Freemason in Vienna (and around Europe)

The social rise of Dobruska, and his inclusion in the elitist circles of imperial Vienna was certainly helped by his commitment to Freemasonry, which he entered while he still young, probably immediately after his conversion to Catholicism. Maria Theresa had initially opposed the Masonic phenomenon and had forced the closure of the Vienna Lodge in 1745. In the following decades, however, Freemasonry had gradually gained influence and established itself as an important social and cultural factor.[48] In 1781, the Bavarian nobleman Hans Heinrich von Ecker and Eckhofen founded the order of the "Asian brothers", and Dobruska played an important role in shaping its Kabbalistic-esoteric background. Jacob Katz and Gershom Scholem have meticulously compiled the scattered evidence of Dobruska's involvement, a task made more difficult by the use of multiple secret names. It seems that he began his Masonic activity among the Asian brothers as Scharia, then switched to Nachem, and finally adopted the alias Jacob ben Josef (or Josef ben Jacob). At some point, however, Dobruska withdrew from active membership, while maintaining some kind of "silent" role in the organization.[49] Although the reason for this decision

---

48 See Helmut Reinhalter, *Joseph II. und die Freimaurerei im Lichte zeitgenössischer Broschüren* (Wien, Köln, Graz: Böhlaus, 1987); Karl Gutkas, *Kaiser Joseph II* (Wien-Darmstadt: Zsolnay, 1989) 326–329; Andreas Önnerfors, "Freemasonry and Civil Society: Reform of Manners and the Journal für Freymaurer (1784–1786)," in *The Enlightenment in Bohemia: Religion, Morality and Multiculturalism*, ed. Ivo Cerman, Rita Kruger and Susan Reynolds (Oxford: Voltaire Foundation 2011), 111–128.

49 Jakob Katz, *Jews and Freemasons in Europe. 1723–1939* (Cambridge (Mass.): Harward University Press, 1970); Scholem, *Du Frankisme au jacobinisme*, 27–42. According to Scholem, *ibidem*, 30, Dobruska is the author of the partial German translation – more precisely an abridged paraphrase – of the Sabbatian kabbalistic work *Wa-avo ha-yom el ha-ayin*, published in *Die Brüder St. Johannis des Evangelisten aus Asien in Europa oder die einzige wahre und ächte Freimaurerei nebst einem Anhange, die Fesslersche Kritische Geschichte der Freimaurerbrüderschaft und ihre Nichtigkeit betreffend* (Berlin: Schmidt, 1803), 265–276. For the original Hebrew text see Jonathan Eibeschütz, *And I Came this Day unto the Fountain*, critically edited and introduced by Pawel Maciejko (Los Angeles: Cherub Press, 2014) 16–40 (Heb.)

remains uncertain, Dobruska's withdrawal was very timely, as in December 1785 Emperor Joseph II limited by decree both the number of Masonic lodges and their activity, which led to the relocation of the Asian brothers to northern Germany and Denmark. In the following years, Dobruska occasionally played the role of covert adviser, and was in close contact with Ephraim Joseph Hirschfeld, who had inherited leadership in Kabbalistic matters among the Brothers. It is worth mentioning that Hirschfeld accompanied Dobruska to Strasbourg in 1792, as the latter went to Alsace and began to participate in French political life. Here they separated: Hirschfeld returned to Germany while Dobruska moved to Paris.[50] We have no other evidence of his relationship to Freemasonry during the last two years of his life. Although he probably also took advantage of his connections with the French capital, he must have done so very covertly.

2.3 The Plunge into Revolution

In March 1792, Moses Dobruska arrived in Strasbourg, France, together with his brother Emmanuel and their younger sister Léopoldine. Since Moses was the predominant figure among them, it is to him that we must attribute the abrupt decision to change both place and lifestyle. Perhaps it was a decision influenced by changes at the court of Vienna, after the death of Joseph II on February 20, 1790, and the rise to the throne of his brother, Leopold. It seems that Dobruska lost, at least in part, the favor he enjoyed in the highest circles of the empire, and therefore tried to transfer his economic interests elsewhere, choosing revolutionary France, where it seemed possible, in the excitement of the time, to conduct remunerative speculation and ambitious economic enterprises. It is certain, however,

---

50 Scholem, *Du Frankisme au jacobinisme*, 54. On Hirschfeld see also idem, "Ein verschollener jüdischer Mystiker der Aufklärungszeit. Ephraim Josef Hirschfeld," *Leo Baeck Institute Yearbook* 7 (1962): 247–279; Jakob Katz, "Moses Mendelssohn und Ephraim Josef Hirschfeld," *Bulletin des Leo Baeck Institutes* 28 (1964) : 295–311; Yves Dangers, "Ephraim Josef Hirschfeld et les Frères de l'Asie," *Le Symbolisme* 375–376 (1966), 41–359; Giuseppe Veltri, Gerold Necker and Patrick Koch, "Die versuchte Wiederaufnahme des jüdischen Freimaurers geheimer Rapport," *Judaica* 68 (2012): 129–155; Patrick Koch, "Ein verschollener jüdischer Mystiker? Gershom Scholems Nachforschungen zu Ephraim Joseph Hirschfeld," in *Gershom Scholem in Deutschland*, ed. Gerold Necker, Elke Morlok und Matthias Morgenstern (Tübingen: Mohr Siebeck, 2014), 219–242.

that Moses Dobruska had deep revolutionary sympathies, which led him to commit himself, body and soul, to political life, although this would prove disastrous for him in the end. France, which he described in a letter to his friend Voss as a "paradise",[51] would become his tomb.

The question that hovered over him from the beginning of his activities in France concerned his true origin and his "sincere" goals. Doubts were raised quite soon, but it was only in late 1793 that the doubting party took the lead and eventually caused him to be arrested and put to death.

When Moses Dobruska arrived in Strasbourg, the city was plagued by social tensions and libertarian turmoil. Situated at the border between two cultures and traditions, Strasbourg was equally divided between the French-Catholic and German-protestant populations.

Since the beginning of the Revolution, quite a number of intellectuals had flocked from German-speaking countries to Alsace, driven by the dream of liberty. The inner-French and the German immigrants had even taken the lead within the revolutionary movement, pleading for radical views and reforms.

While a pronounced cosmopolitanism thrived within the Strasbourg Jacobinists, the local *élite* was inclined to oppose the newcomers and to defend its privileges. Head of the moderate party was the mayor of Strasbourg, Philippe-Frédéric de Dietrich. A scion of an old and notable family, Dietrich played a pivotal role in the new political system after having held high offices under the *Ancien Régime*. A baron by birth and a distinguished scientist in his own right, Dietrich was a friend of General La Fayette.

The radical faction was led by Jean-Charles Laveaux[52] and Eulogius Schneider, both of whom arrived from Germany in 1791. Laveaux, a native to France, had lived in Basel and Berlin, and held a chair for French literature in Stuttgart; Schneider had entered the Franciscan order before becoming a preacher at the Court in Stuttgart and a professor at the University in Bonn. In Strasbourg, Laveaux founded the "Courier of Strasbourg", while Schneider directed "Argos oder der Mann mit hundert Augen". Besides being involved in a hectic trade as a journalist, Laveaux was elected president of the Societé des amis de la constitution after the moderate wing had left it in February 1792.[53]

---

51 Letter dated Strasbourg, April 8, 1792: cf. Wölfle-Fischer, *Junius Frey*, 88.
52 Hugh Gough, "Jean-Charles Laveaux (1749–1827). A Political Biography" (PhD. diss., Oxford: University of Oxford, 1974).
53 Daniel Schönpflug, *Der Weg in die Terreur. Radikalisierung und Konflikte im Straßburger Jakobinerklub (1790–1795)* (München: Oldenbourg, 2002), 114.

It was only natural that Dobruska, imbued with German culture, entered France from its eastern gate in Alsace. What might seem less obvious is the fact that a high-profile businessman like him, who even had been the fixer in some substantial deals involving the Court of Vienna, could support wholeheartedly the radical wing against his wealthy opponents.

Dobruska, or Junius G(ottlob) Frey, as he used to identify himself in Strasbourg, spared no effort in sustaining Laveaux. In April the conflict between the two factions escalated, and Dietrich had Laveaux arrested (April 22, 1792)[54] with the charge of sedition. Frey vociferously supported his friend in jail and offered a sizeable amount of money in order to assist him during detention. As Laveaux was freed on May 17,[55] our former Austrian baron minted a commemorative medal that he had carefully conceived for the occasion.

But Strasbourg, with its provincial framework, was not enough for our ambitious Moses. It was time to make the great leap, and to aim for the nerve center of the Revolution and of French economic and cultural life. The road to Dobruska now turned decisively towards Paris.

2.4 From Jacobin Fervor to the Guillotine

On June 2, 1792, at the end of a meeting of the Strasburg Jacobin club, Dobruska presented a precious sword to prince Carl von Hessen-Rheinfels-Rotenburg (1752–1821), a German noble who served in France as a General during the Revolution.[56] Immediately afterward, he left Alsace for Paris, together with Laveaux. On June 10, the latter gave a short speech at the Parisian assembly of the Jacobins, excusing himself for being tired because of the long trip.[57] Dobruska also attended this meeting,[58] which was chaired by François Chabot (1756–1794), a

---

54 Gough, *Laveaux*, 134.

55 *Ibidem*, 43.

56 *Les sociétés politiques de Strasbourg pendant les années 1790 a 1795. Extraits de leurs procès-verbaux publiés par Friedrich Carl Heitz* (Strasboug Fréderic-Charles Heitz, 1863), 216 (Juin 2, 1792): "A la clôture de la séance, le citoyen Frey offre au Général patriote un sabre d'honneur de la valeur de cent louis d'or".

57 François A. Aulard, *La Société des Jacobins. Recueil de documents pour l'histoire du club des Jacobins de Paris*, vol. 3, *Juillet 1791 à juin 1792* (Paris: Joaust – Noblet – Quantin, 1892), 674, nr. CCXXXVII (Séance du dimanche 10 juin 1792) : [Laveaux monte à la tribune, au milieu des applaudissements universels, et s'excuse sur la fatigue que lui a fait éprouver le voyage de donner aujourd'hui les détails de son arrestation et de sa délivrance".

58 See "Le Courrier des LXXXIII departemens], Juin 11, 1792 – Léon Kahn, *Les Juifs de Paris pendant la révolution*, (Paris: Paul Ollendorf, 1899), 25.

politician whose fortune and, later, disgrace, was going to be ominously linked with Dobruska's fate. Our Austrian émigré, now universally known as Monsieur Frey, first rented accommodation in Rue Traversière St. Honoré[59] and then moved to a luxurious mansion in Rue d'Anjou-Saint-Honoré, No 19.[60] Together with his brother Emmanuel, he took part in the assault on the Tuileries palace on August 10, 1792[61] and became increasingly involved in the political life of the capital. In late 1792, he began writing his *Philosophie sociale*, which appeared in print in June 1793 and gained him a reputation as a revolutionary thinker. In summer 1793, a second work by Dobruska was published, under the title *Les aventures politiques du père Nicaise*.[62] Parallel to his political involvement, Dobruska engaged in intense business activity, which ostensibly brought him substantial profits. He later declared to have invested the sums his wife had sent him from Vienna, while his opponents suspected that he was provided with

---

59 Among the documents confiscated to Dobruska and now kept at the Archives nationales de France, see the card by Laveaux addressed to "Monsieur S. G. Frey logé prés Madame de la Seïne, Hotel du grand Balcon No 19, rue Traversière St. Honnoré [sic]". It is surely no coincidence that three representatives of the "Departement du Bas Rhin" at the National Convention (Laurent, Louis, Simond) were domiciled at the same address *The Political State of Europe for the Year 1793*, vol. 3 (London: J.S. Jordan, 1793), 26.

60 Alexandre Tuetey, *Répertoire général des sources manuscrites de l'histoire de Paris pendant la Révolution française*, 12 vols., (Paris: Imprimerie Nouvelle (Association ouvrière) 1890–1914) vol. 11, 236, No 757; cf. Gustave Bord, *La fin de deux légendes. L'affaire Léonard, le baron de Batz* (Paris: Daragon 1909), 94; Albert Mathiez, "L'arrestation de Trenck," *Annales révolutionnaires* 7 (1914), 101–105.

61 Tuetey, *Repertoire*, vol. 11, 232, No 742 : [18 août 1792 [. . .] Attestation de l'Assemblée générale des fédérés, séante aux Jacobins, constatant qu'Emmanuel – Ernest Frey, cadet, s'est trouvé en personne à l'affaire du 10 août, qu'il s'y est conduit avec bravoure et fermeté, et qu'il a constamment donné des preuves du patriotisme le plus pur]; ibidem, No 743 : same attestation concerning "Sigismond-Gottlob Junius Frey", dated August 20, 1792.

62 [Moses Dobruska *alias* Junius Frey], *Les aventures politiques du père Nicaise, ou l'Anti-fédéraliste* (Paris: l'imp. De J. Grand, 1793) (fol. 1b : [A Paris, CE 20 juillet, l'an deuxième de la République française une et indivisible]. The booklet is anonymous, but is clearly ascribed to Dobruska, alias Frey, by François Chabot, in *Gazette nationale ou le Moniteur universel*, No 19, October 10, 1793, 75: [Junius Frey, homme de lettres estimable, connu par deux ouvrages très patriotiques, l'*Anti-fédéraliste* et la *Philosophie sociale*]. Already on August 4, 1793, Chabot had praised both works by Dobruska, even if the name of the author is not mentioned in the record of Chabot's speech in the *Journal des débats et de la correspondance de la Société des Jacobins* 464, August 6, 1793, 2 (also in *Journal de la Montagne* 66, August 6, 1793, 424): see below, 7. 1. 1.

money by the Habsburg government in order to act as an undercover counter-revolutionary agent.[63] In fact, a few documents, hitherto unnoticed, prove that, during his stay in Paris, his house in Vienna was forcibly auctioned for unpaid debts.[64] Were such losses carefully staged? It seems hard to believe it, even if we already know Dobruska's lack of scruples and his ability in adapting himself to new situations. As had been the case in Strasbourg, where he lavishly spent in order to gain the favor of the Jacobin party, Dobruska kept mixing business affairs and politics, and probably rose through Parisian public life through bribery. The most daring attempt of social ascent he made involved the already mentioned François Chabot, a former Capuchin friar who had become a powerful member of the National Convention. In summer 1793, Dobruska offered to Chabot, who gladly accepted, the hand of his sister Léopoldine, a woman of reputed beauty, together with a remarkably high dowry. Glamorous as it was, the marriage proved fatal for both parties.[65] In November 1793, Chabot was accused of

---

63 Dobruska refers to the money coming from his wife during his trial for conspiracy, in April 1794. See *Bulletin du tribunal révolutionnaire* s. 4, No 26, 1794, 102: [Mes revenus m'ont été arrêté pendant plusieurs années; mais ma femme, fille adoptive d'un homme opulent, avoit à sa disposition des fonds pour près de deux millions, et m'envoyoit de l'argent à mesure que je lui en demandois, ce qui doit prouver que je n'étois point l'agent de l'empereur, c'est que j'ai été chassé de Berlin comme émissaire de la propagande des jacobins].

64 See *Wiener Zeitung*, No 589, March 7, 1792, 617: "writ of summons by the Tribunal of Vienna, to which the present domicile of Thomas von Schönfeld is unknown ("das Gericht, dem der Ort seines [i.e. of Schönfeld] Aufenthalts unbekannt [ist]"), regarding a debt of 5,187.10 florins towards "Baptist Malfatti"; *ibidem*, No 1113, April 25, 1792, 1151, writ of summons by the Tribunal, regarding a debt of 6,000 florins towards "Nathan Adam Arnsteiner"; *ibidem*, No 2525, September 15, 1792, 2,547: forced sale auction of a house belonging to Schönfeld in Vienna, "Rittergasse zu Erdberg No 25", because of an unpaid debt of 6,000 florins towards "Anton Petziger von Weissenberg". These legal lawsuits seem to have remained unknown to all previous biographers of Dobruska.

65 Chabot announced his marriage to Léopoldine Frey at the meeting of the Société des jacobins on October 5th, 1793 (*Gazette nationale ou le Moniteur universel*, No 19, October 10, 1793, 75). While in jail, after having been accused of corruption, he gave his own lengthy justification of the marriage in a handwritten memorandum, dated January 26, 1794, published by Albert Mathiez, "Histoire véritable du mariage de François Chabot avec Léopoldine Frey en réponse à toutes les calomnies que l'on a répandues à ce sujet," *Annales revolutionnaires* 7 (1914), 248–254 (see also Tuetey, *Repertoire*, vol. 11, 218, No 685). Cf. Ruth Graham, "Les mariages des ecclésiastiques députés à la Convention," *Annales historiques de la Révolution française* 262 (1985) : 480–499.

corruption while Dobruska was arrested for having corrupted him and for conspiring against the Revolution in favor of foreign powers.[66] On April 5, 1794, Moses Dobruska, his brother Emanuel and François Chabot were guillotined in Paris, together with a host of other politicians, the most illustrious among them being Georges Jacques Danton.

---

66 Moses was arrested, together with his brother, on November 23 1793: Tuetey, *Repertoire*, vol. 10, p. 187, No 973. For the official act of accusing against the two, dated "8 germinal an II (March 28, 1794), see *ibidem*, vol. 11, 250, No 822: "Acte d'accusation de Fouquier-Tinville, accusateur public du Tribunal révolutionnaire, contre [. . .] les frères Junius et Emmanuel Frey, beaux-frères de Chabot [. . .] ex-barons étrangers, agents de l'Angleterre et du cabinet de Vienne, masqués du voile du patriotisme, que Chabot prétend avoir été pendus en effigie, afin de faire croire à leur amour pour la Liberté, et malgré la confiscation de leurs biens, trouvant le moyen de donner à leur sœur une dot de 200,000 livres, corrupteurs et conspirateurs, qui ont ourdi leurs trames avec autant d'audace que de scélératesse [. . .] les individus en question prévenus d'avoir cherché à détruire par la corruption le gouvernement républicain, en achetant et trafiquant de l'opinion de Chabot, Basire, Julien de Toulouse, Delaunay d'Angers et Fabre d'Eglantine, en devenant auteurs et complices des manœuvres et intelligences pratiquées à prix convenu pour opérer la suppression et la falsification du décret du 27 vendémiaire concernant la Compagnie des Indes, à l'effet d'y substituer un faux décret, promulgué sous la date du même jour, ce qui est contraire à la loi du 16 ventôse, avec ordre d'écrou de Gusman, d'Espagnac et Frey, frères, en la Conciergerie". On the supposed conspiracy in which the Dobruskas were involved see Albert Mathiez, *La révolution et les étrangers. Cosmopolitisme et défense nationale* (Paris: Renaissance du Livre, 1918); Arnaud de Lestapis, *La 'Conspiration de Batz' (1793–1794)* (Paris: Société des études robespierristes, 1969); Michel Benoît, *1793 La République de la tentation. Une affaire de corruption sous la Ière République* (Précy-sous-Thil: Éd. de l'Armançon, 2008).

3 The *Philosophie Sociale* of 1793: A New Thought

3.1 The Philophie Sociale of 1793

In this second chapter I will delve into the *Philosophie sociale*, on which Moses Dobruska began to work feverishly, in Paris, towards the end of 1792. In all likelihood, Dobruska wrote the first version of the opus in German. Of this *Urauffassung* only a few sheets remain: these were among the papers seized from the author at the time of his arrest in November 1793 and were then deposited at the *Archives nationales* of Paris. The German text, which I am publishing for the first time here in the appendix, and which I will quote where the pages are available, although limited to a small part of the work, is very significant. It shows us how much Dobruska was deeply immersed in the German culture of his time, and how the *Philosophie sociale*, composed in France and so closely linked to French politics and the Revolution, has a fundamental German intellectual component.

3.2 The Title

First and foremost, the title deserves our attention. Although he is not the inventor of the expression "social philosophy",[67] Dobruska certainly has a good claim to be considered the first great promoter of the union between philosophy, the symbol of Enlightenment, and the social sphere. As I already mentioned, Jean-Baptiste Durosoy, a Jesuit from Belfort, in Bourgogne-Franche-Comté, had already published a work entitled *Philosophie sociale ou essai sur les devoirs de l'homme et du*

---

[67] Axel Honneth's statement that Thomas Hobbes coined the term "social philosophy" does not seem to be justified: "Wenn es auch Thomas Hobbes war, der an der Mitte des 17". *Pathologien des Sozialen. Die Aufgaben der Sozialphilosophie*, ed. Axel Honneth (Frankfurt am Main: Fischer, 1994), 11, which in note – ibidem 63 – refers to *Leviathan*). In *Leviathan* Hobbes speaks only of "civil philosophy", in reference to ancient philosophy, from which he distances himself: "and for their moral and civil philosophy, it hath the same or greater absurdities", see Thomas Hobbes, *Leviathan* (London: Crooke, 1651), 455.

https://doi.org/10.1515/9783110758825-003

citoyen in 1783.[68] This book was reprinted several times (1822, 1843) and was also translated into German in 1852.[69]

The assumption from which Durosoy starts is that the human being was born for society, to be together with his fellow human beings. There are no human beings who live isolated as individual atoms. Not only does man seek the company of his fellow human beings, but he also wants to set a "good example" for them, even though there are people whose way of relating to others does not represent a good example to follow.

Durosoy mentions, among these negative cases, individuals who give themselves to luxury, the corrupt, the spouses who never exchange affection, the fathers who do not take care of their children, etc., as well as those who do not take care of their children. The objective of his social philosophy is to provide a well articulated mapping of duties and rules of conduct to be followed in relation to society and its members. In addition, Durosoy identifies a list of specific

---

68 Jean-Baptiste Durosoy, *Philosophie sociale ou essai sur les devoirs de l'homme et du citoyen* (Paris: C.P. Berton, 1783). According to the frontispiece, Durosoy was "abbot, professor of philosophy, doctor and professor of theology, ecclesiastical advisor of his Highness the Prince-Bishop of Basel". Some details about Jean-Baptiste Durosoy in Jean Joseph C. D[escharrères], *Essai sur l'histoire littéraire de Belfort et du voisinage* (Belfort: J. P. Clerc, 1808), 16–18; *Note de la Direction* at the foot of the "Vie de Monseigneur Casimir-Fréderic des Baraons de Rathsamhausen", also written by Descharrères, in *Revue d'Alsace* 10 (1859), 347–348. I drew attention to the antecedent, represented by Durosoy's *Philosophie sociale*, for the first time in Silvana Greco, *Heresy, Apostasy, and the Beginnings of Social Philosophy. Moses Dobruska reconsidered*, in "Materia giudaica" 20–21 (2015–2016), pp. 439–464, esp. 14. Franck Fischbach, *Manifeste pour une philosophie sociale* (Paris: La Decouverte 2009), 19, was not aware of it when he wrote that the expression "social philosophy" was first used by our Dobruska/Frey (see also the German version: Idem, *Manifest für eine Sozialphilosophie*, transl., Lilian Peter, with an afterword by Thomas Bedorf und Kurt Röttgers (Bielefeld: Transcript, 2016), 20. *Ibidem*, 141 – the two editors of the German edition, correcting Fischbach, cite Durosoy and refer to "recent research" for clarification, without explicitly naming their source: "Das [i.e. the *Philosophie sociale* of Dobruska / Frey] ist zwar nicht die erste Erwähnung, die erste war eine quasi-rousseauistische "Ethik" des elsässischen Abbé Durosoy, wie jüngere Forschungen ergeben haben").
69 Jean Baptiste Durosoy, *Der christliche Weltbürger oder Grundsätze des socialen Lebens ein Versuch über unsere Pflichten als Menschen und Staatsbürger* (Münster: Theissing, 1852). Cfr. anche Adolph L. H. Geck, "Die Aufgaben einer Christlichen Gesellschaftslehre als einer Wissenschaftlichen Disziplin," *Jahrbuch für christlichen Sozialwissenschaften* 11 (1970): 262, which, however, gives, for the original French edition the date 1793, clearly confusing the work of Abbé Durosoy, published in 1783, with that of our Dobruska.

duties that man should follow in the various stages of the cycle of his life in which he assumes different social roles, such as that of spouse and family man.[70]

In fact, the book by Durosoy doesn't propose a veritable "social philosophy", as Dobruska began to characterize it and as it was later developed from the nineteenth century until today, especially in the German context. What's more, Durosoy's work is an extensive collection of ethical precepts meant to be useful in living "well" in society, without, however, specifying this well-being more clearly.

3.3 Purposes and Structure

The *Philosophie sociale* has three core purposes.

First, Dobruska wants to deepen our knowledge, which he hopes will become scientific in the future, of the individual and society. It is the society of the *Ancien Régime*, but also the democratic one, still in the making. As he intends it, the future democratic society must aim to achieve the happiness of individuals and the community.[71] Only a deep understanding of human nature, of acting in society and of the social structure as a whole, allows us to define concepts such as "individual", "society", "freedom", "equality", etc., and to elaborate, on the basis of them, rules and norms of action, termed "principles" (*principes*) by Dobruska.

Secondly, the *Philosophie sociale* intends to propose a philosophical and critical reflection on the society of the *Ancien Régime*, underlining the "monstrous mixtures" (*mélanges monstreux*) that must be overcome through a process of "social disorganization". As I already pointed out, in the parlance of today's scientific investigation we could match Dobruska's *mélanges* to the "social pathologies" of Axel Honneth.[72]

Thirdly, the book draws up a universal constitution for the French people, which contains seventy principles, to be understood as rules and standards of action, for the formation of a representative democratic society.

---

70 Durosoy, *Philosophie sociale ou essai sur les devoirs de l'homme et du citoyen*, 1–6.
71 Dobruska, *Philosophie sociale*, vi.
72 Honneth, *Pathologien des Sozialen*, 51: [Was als sozialer Mißstand gilt, liegt demnach nicht einfach auf der Ebene der Verletzung von Gerechtigkeitsgrundsätzen; vielmehr sollen Störungen kritisiert werden, die mit psychischen Krankheiten die Eigenschaft teilen, daß sie die Lebensmöglichkeiten einschränken oder deformieren, die als ‚normal' oder ‚gesund' vorausgesetzt werden].

These principles concern, on the one hand, man, his intellectual and moral faculties, his way of relating to other members of society, and his rights, as well as his duties towards other citizens and towards society and the State. On the other hand, the principles are addressed to society, its property, its rights and duties towards citizens, and the powers of the State, necessary to govern society itself (see Appendix 2).

It will be the task of the representatives of the French people to draw up the body of legislation and define the institutions and their regulations, on the basis of the principles contained in the first part of the Constitution. This process of applying the principles constitutes the second part of the Constitution.

Dobruska himself indicates three parts into which his work is divided.

The first part of the essay is what he calls the "revolutionary" one – at once a critique and a predictable target of criticism:

> so that I could establish and build, it was necessary for me to overturn and secure some land on which to erect my building. I could define this first part of my work as the revolutionary part, which will certainly be the subject of more or less philosophical counter-revolutionary criticism.[73]

The second part focuses on the "essence and form" of the Constitution of the nascent democratic society, after the collapse of the *Ancien Régime*. Dobruska would like to point out that this part of the reflection is often neglected in philosophical treatises. It is precisely in order to remedy this shortcoming that *Philosophie sociale* is spreading about the ethical principles and social and institutional practices on which the Constitution must be based.

The third and final part of the work is the constituent one, in which the fundamental themes to be contained in the Universal Constitution and its principles are elaborated.[74]

This is the succession of the three parts (see Fig. 1):

Part One: Research on some of the main themes of social philosophy

Part Two: On the essence of a Constitution and its form

Part Three: Universal Constitution

---

73 Dobruska, *Philosophie sociale*, XII: [La première partie de cet ouvrage est une discussion abrégée de quelques préjugés de cette espèce; car avant de bâtir et de construire, il a fallu que je renversasse et que j'assurasse en quelque sorte le terrain sur lequel je voulois élever mon édifice. Je pourrois nommer cette pre-mière partie, la partie révolutionnaire de mon ouvrage, qui s'attend, à coups sûrs, à des chocs contre-révolutionnaires plus ou moins philosophiques].
74 *Ibidem*.

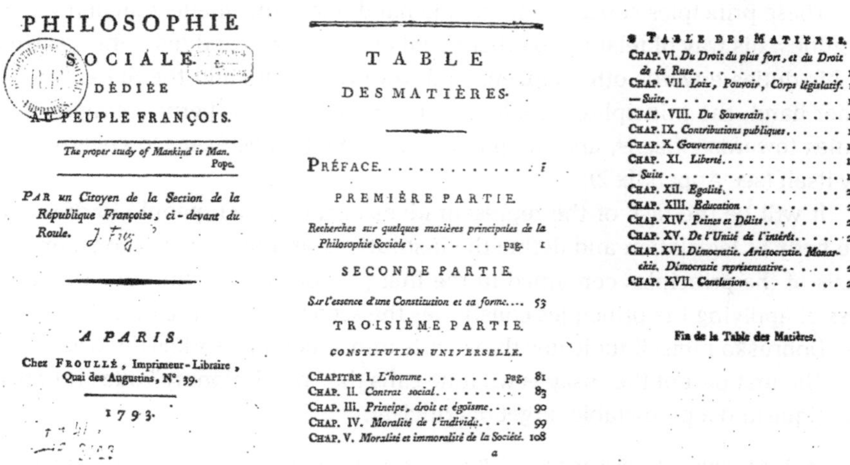

PHILOSOPHIE SOCIALE DÉDIÉE AU PEUPLE FRANÇOIS.

The proper study of Mankind is Man. Pope.

PAR un Citoyen de la Section de la République Françoise, ci-devant du Roule.

A PARIS,
Chez FROULLÉ, Imprimeur-Libraire, Quai des Augustins, N°. 39.

1793.

TABLE DES MATIÈRES.

Fin de la Table des Matières.

Fig. 1: Frontispiece and Table of Contents of the *Philosophie sociale, dédiée au peuple françois* (1793).

3.4 Recipients of the *Philosophie Sociale*

As we begin to flip through the book, we can ask ourselves who the recipients are. There is one collective recipient, namely the French people, and one more particular one, namely the so-called "decent people".

The full title of the book is revealing: *Philosophie sociale dédiée au peuple françois* (Social philosophy dedicated to the French people).

The principal addressees of the work are, however, *les gens de bien*, i.e. people who are capable of critical thinking, of judging with their own rational faculties, who do not recognize any other authority, in the republic of letters, outside the truth and who are not seduced by superstition or even less by prejudices. This is the tone of the dedication at the beginning of the volume:

> I dedicate this work to all good people, exempt from all literary glory, who are not prevented prejudiced,and who are without school superstition. I dedicate it to the tribunal of men, who think and judge for themselves and who do not recognize any authority in the republic of letters outside the truth; and who love the truth for the truth, no matter the book in which they find it; no matter the licenses and vigor with which prejudices are broken down, supported by the powerful protection of great men; for there are profound

and erudite prejudices but also superficial prejudices, foolish and vulgar, which seduce and fascinate the heart.[75]

3.5 Distinction Between State and Society

From this synthetic scheme, one can already understand how Dobruska's thought cannot be reduced to a mere "political philosophy" and, in particular, to a simple draft of a Constitution, necessary after the French Revolution, as was until now supported on the basis, I believe, of only a shallow examination of the *Philosophie sociale*.[76]

The fact that this is not just a simple political philosophy can be seen not only from the wealth of topics covered but also from the more general theoretical approach.[77]

In a broad sense, the object of study of classical political philosophy, from Greek thinkers to, one can say, today, is "political life", as an expression of the dynamics between groups confronting each other to gain power within a community. In a narrower sense, political philosophy deals with so-called "political foundations" which are made up of two types of categories, according to Leo Strauss' acute definition. On the one hand, the "nature of political things", that is, the laws, institutions, actions, decisions, programs, and desires of human beings as political actors. On the other hand, the categories of the second type concern the best or fairest political order.[78]

Especially in the tenth and sixteenth chapters of the third part, Dobruska reflects on which is the best and most suitable political regime for the society that is emerging from the French Revolution.[79] But the primary object of the

---

75 Dobruska, *Philosophie sociale*, XI–XII: [J'adresse mon ouvrage à tous les gens de bien, exempts de toute gloriole littéraire, sans prévention et sans superstition scholastique; c'est au tribunal des hommes, qui pensent et qui jugent par eux-mêmes, qui ne reconnoissent aucune autorité dans la république des lettres que la vérité, et qui ne l'aiment que pour elle, n'importe le livre où ils la trouvent, n'importe avec quelle franchise et quelle vigueur on y terrasse des préjugés soutenous de la puissance protection des grands hommes, et devenus chers à l'esprit du siècle; car il y a des préjugés profonds et érudits, qui séduisent et captivent l'esprit, comme il y a des préjugés superficiels, sots et vulgaires, qui séduisent et captivent le cœur].

76 Thomas Bedorf and Kurt Röttgers, "Einleitung," in *Einführung in die Sozialphilosophie*, by Franck Fischbach (Hagen: FernUniversität in Hagen 2017), 1–12.

77 Rahel Jaeggi and Robin Celikates, *Sozialphilosophie. Eine Einführung* (München: Beck, 2017), 7–10.

78 Leo Strauss, "On classical political Philosophy," *Social Research* 12 (1945): 98.

79 Dobruska, *Philosophie sociale*, 31–235.

Philosophie sociale is society and, consequently, the reorganization of a new democratic society in which citizens can be happy. With the French Revolution there came "social disorganization", and it was therefore necessary to think about "social reorganization", to reflect on how to rebuild a society, and not simply structure a state. Reconstruction and integration is, moreover, one of the recurrent themes of both social philosophy[80] and sociological thought.

As noted by Rahel Jaeggi and Robert Celikates, it was precisely with the birth of modernity and the development of capitalism that modern social philosophy and attention to social issues arose. In fact, before the French Revolution, the social order was justified and legitimized as being of a divine nature. The absolute monarchy was the legitimate representative of that order. It is only with the fall of absolutism that man regains a central place in society and places himself as the creator of his own destiny.

But it is not only a different and wider object of study that distinguishes social philosophy from political philosophy. There is, in the former but not in the latter, the desire to carry out "a socio-theoretical and socio-ontological analysis of the structure and dynamics of societal circumstances".[81]

This desire for analysis, in which the emphasis is placed on society, on life in society and, in particular, on individuals who live and interact with each other in different social spheres, is grasped from the very beginning of Dobruska's work.

In short, there is a reversal of perspective with respect to political philosophy. It is the analysis and understanding of social reality – from individuals and their interactions to society in general – that determines the content of the Constitution, the principles of its laws, the political institutions necessary for the new society. We do not start from politics to reach society, but vice versa: social interactions determine the political structure. To use a contemporary expression, Dobruska embraces a "bottom up" vision of politics, not a "top down" one. Political institutions are a cultural and social product; they are determined by social life.

It is no coincidence that, at the very beginning of the work, Dobruska argues with Jean-Jacques Rousseau's thesis according to which the form of government best suited to a nation is also determined by its territorial dimension.

Dobruska replies that the human being always remains the same, both in a large territory and in a smaller one. As a good liberal, in fact, Dobruska embraces

---

80 Cf. Alessandro Ferrara, "The Idea of a Social Philosophy," *Constellations* 9 (2002): 422.
81 Cf. Jaeggi, Celikates, *Sozialphilosophie*, 11: [eine sozialtheoretische und sozialontologische Analyse der Struktur und Dynamik gesellschaftlicher Verhältnisse].

methodological individualism. It is from the analysis of the individual and from the understanding of the individual understood as a social being and as a citizen (holder of rights) that one must start in order to be able to reorganize society. Political institutions are only instrumental to this broader vision of society.

3.6 The Need for a Scientific Reflection on Social Issues

From the very first pages of his work, Dobruska condemns the pre-existing social philosophy. "A science of rulers to betray the governed"[82] is no longer acceptable. Now is the time for a radical change in thinking, which should focus primarily on social reality and only secondarily on political institutions. In other words, we must consider the "governed", their needs and their social interaction, if we do not want to "betray" them.

Social philosophy had until then been nothing more than a poor political philosophy. To change, it is necessary to adopt not only new content, but also a different method of investigation.

In its *pars destruens*, the new social philosophy of Dobruska has the task of understanding and highlighting everything that did not work in the society of the *Ancien Régime*. In its *pars construens*, it aims at defining the principles capable of regulating a society in which individuals can be happy.

To achieve this ambitious goal, however, it is necessary to know the nature of human beings: "the general order of nature, the immense system of created beings".[83] Therefore, Dobruska investigates not only the physical and socio-cultural context in which individuals live, as social beings, but also the way in which they interact with each other. But Dobruska does not stop there – he digs deeper into the human soul because he wants to understand its desires, motivations, and ethical and moral demands.

What do men want? How do they behave and how do they interact with each other as individuals and as members of a society? What are their moral abilities? Why are some rich and others poor? What makes man happy and what makes society as a whole happy? How have societies evolved over time?

These are the main questions that Dobruska wants to answer, elaborating a thought that he himself defines as "social art" (*art social*), of which we see two strands. One is properly philosophical-social, while we can rightly define the second

---

82 Dobruska, *Philosophie sociale*, VI: [*La science des gouvernans pour tromper les gouvernés*].
83 *Ibidem*, 53 : "l'ordre général de la nature, dans l'immense système des êtres créés".

strand as sociological. Social art must be rethought, down to its fundamentals, and stripped of the "miserable rags" with which it has covered itself in the past:

> I decided to go down from an illusory height, to start studying again, to meditate first of all on definitions, to ask them to nature itself, to go back to that primitive source of social art, to erase from my spirit everything I had read in books, to strip myself of all those miserable rags of a wrong and pedantic politics, of an illusory and destructive social art.[84]

Proud of his new clothes, which replace the theoretical "rags" of the past, Dobruska's social thinking seeks to understand the motivations of men, their behaviors and the development of society, not as *they should be* but as *they are* and *as they have been realized historically:* social reality must be explained in the same way as the natural world, taking inspiration from the laws and natural principles (that is, laws of cause and effect).

Dobruska's is a fundamental transformation of the "reflection on the social", from the metaphysics that it was, into a true science:[85]

> Social philosophy in the state in which it finds itself cannot yet strictly speaking be called a science [. . .] It was only after the successful demonstration of the *equilateral triangle* that mathematics rose to the level of *science*, and to this dignity of a safe and firm march. It is only after the happy discoveries of *Galileo, Toricelli* [sic] and *Stahl*, that physics and chemistry began to deserve the name of sciences, which opened a certain way for centuries to come.[86]

As in mathematics, physics, and chemistry, "social art" must discover the laws of cause and effect of its object of study. It aims to understand that truth that remains hidden from most, which has nothing to do with the opinions of individuals. In other words, Dobruska believes that "the social world, like the natural world, is governed by laws. And the former, like the latter, can be studied

---

84 *Ibidem*, VIII: [Je me suis donc déterminé à descendre d'une hauteur illusoire, à commencer à étudier de nouveau, à méditer avant tout sur les définitions, à les demander à la nature elle-même, à remonter à cette source primitive de l'art social, à effacer de mon esprit tout ce que j'avais lu dans les livres, et à me dépouiller de tous ces haillons misérables d'une politique fausse et pédantesque, d'un art social illusoire et destructeur].

85 *Ibidem*, IV–V.

86 *Ibidem*, IV–V, XIV: [La philosophie sociale dans l'état où elle se trouve, ne peut pas encore être nommée strictement et proprement une science [. . .] Ce n'est que depuis la première démonstration heureuse du *triangle équilatéral*, que les mathématiques se sont élévées à la hauteur d'une *science*, et à cette dignité d'une marche sûre et ferme. Ce n'est que depuis les heureuses découvertes de *Galilei*, et *Toricelli* et de *Stahl*, que la physique et la chymie ont commencé à mériter le nom de sciences, qu'elles ont frayé une route certaine aux siècles avenir].

objectively with the same logic of investigation and the same method".[87] This is a prescient intuition, which anticipates the assumptions of positivist sociology. The study of society finally carried out using scientific methods: this is the social art of Dobruska. In the chapter on the posthumous fortune of the *Philosophie sociale*, we will see how, from these intuitions, Comte's "social physics" is born.

In order to arrive at the truth to which it aspires, social reflection must follow a "safe path", that is, it must adopt the tools and techniques of the natural sciences, from the formulation of definitions (which today we would call hypotheses) to the questioning of "nature", observing natural facts in order to succeed in arriving at a law, by inductive means, from the particular to the universal.

Dobruska certainly lays rudimentary foundations for what would become known in the literature in the following centuries as the positivist paradigm of the social sciences, namely "the study of social reality using the conceptual apparatus, the techniques of observation and measurement, the instruments of mathematical analysis, the procedures of inference of the natural sciences".[88]

We have talked about rudimentary traits of Dobruska's works, and this is a judgment that concerns the lack of in-depth study of the criteria of scientificity. Although Dobruska believes that a scientific approach is necessary to know the social world, he does not devote a single chapter of his work to scientific methodology. In short, his declaration of scientificity is more of a declaration of principle, however brilliant, than an articulation of an adequate scientific methodology.

Having said that, a careful analysis of his *Philosophie sociale* reveals a methodological path which the author follows to reflect on human behavior and society in a "scientific" way. It is the way he travels in search of the social principles and rules with which to build a democratic society, in which people can be happy.

Reading between the lines we can identify three different methodological approaches, which the sociologists of the nineteenth century would go on to develop in their own writings- think first of Auguste Comte in his *Cours de philosophie positive* – Dobruska uses an empirical-descriptive method based on observation, a comparative method, and, finally, a historical method.

Dobruska, as a forerunner of the positivists of the nineteenth century, from whom those of the twentieth century would differ,[89] implicitly postulates, on

---

87 Piergiorgio Corbetta, *Metodologia e tecnica della ricerca sociale* (Bologna: Il Mulino, 1999), 25.
88 Corbetta, *Metodologia e tecnica della ricerca sociale*, 24.
89 *Ibidem*, 23.

an ontological level, a rather simplistic realism, whereby the social world is considered real and knowable in exactly the same way as the natural one.[90] Social relations are treated as if they were "things".[91]

On the epistemological level, however, our author implicitly adheres to the idea, also developed by nineteenth-century positivists, of an objective separation between social reality and the researcher who studies it. The aim is to produce knowledge that takes the form of "laws, based on categories of cause and effect. They exist in the external reality independently from the observers and supervise it ('natural laws'): the task of the social scientist is to "discover them".[92]

And here we see how much Dobruska's thought is influenced by Montesquieu and, in particular, his work *The Spirit of the Laws*. Already Montesquieu seeks to observe social reality and to infer from it laws in the form of cause and effect. He seeks to extract the causes of social phenomena.

To illustrate this, I will cite some initial and clarifying phrases from the preface of *The Spirit of the Laws*:

> I have first of all considered mankind; and the result of my thoughts has been, that, amidst such an infinite diversity of laws and manners, they were not solely conducted by the caprice of fancy. I have laid down the first principles, and have found that the particular cases apply naturally to them; that the histories of all nations are only consequences of them; and that every particular law is connected with another law, or depends on some other of a more general extent.[93] [. . .] I have not drawn my principles from my prejudices, but from the nature of things.[94]

---

90 *Loc. cit.*

91 It was the French sociologist Emile Durkheim, in the *Rules of the sociological method* (*Les règles de la méthode sociologique*), which appeared in 1894 in the *Revue philosophique*, and in book form the following year (Paris 1895), who stated that the social scientist, in particular the sociologist, should consider social facts as things: "En second lieu, notre méthode est objective. Elle est dominée tout entière par cette idée que les faits sociaux sont des choses et doivent être traités comme telles" (Durkheim, *Les règles*, 175).

92 Corbetta, *Metodologia e tecnica*, 27.

93 [Charles -Louis de] Montesquieu, *Tutte le opere 1721–1754*, ed., Domenico Felice (Milano: Bompiani, 2014), 896–897: [J'ai d'abord examiné les hommes, et j'ai crû que dans cette infinie diversité de loix et de mœurs, ils n'étoient pas uniquement conduits par leurs fantaisies. J'ai posé les principes, et j'ai vû les cas particuliers s'y plier comme d'eux-mêmes, les histoires de toutes les nations n'en être que les suites, et chaque loi particulière liée avec une autre loi, ou dépendre d'une autre plus générale]. Idem, *The complete Works of M. de Montesquieu*, Volume the First, Dublin: W. Watson, 1777, xxxvii.

94 *Ibidem*, . 898–899: [Je n'ai point tiré mes principes de mes préjugés, mais de la nature des choses]. Idem, *The complete Works of M. de Montesquieu*, Volume the First, Dublin: W. Watson, 1777, xxxviii.

The objective already set by the Montesquieu sociologist is partly taken up and elaborated by Dobruska, who makes use of the observation of social reality in a detached and objective way and then, in an inductive way, inferring from the particular to the general, arrives at the formulation of the law.

Let's look at two examples from his work to better clarify this "scientific procedure".

The first example concerns the law on the morality of the State, elaborated in the fifth chapter of the *Philosophie sociale*. On this, Dobruska states: "The morality of the State is the consequence of individual morality".[95] Notice how this law has been formulated in terms of cause (individual morality) and effect (the morality of the State).

He himself explains to us in the following how he came to this theory, starting from the observation of the particular and arriving at a generalization. In the philosophical-scientific literature of the eighteenth and nineteenth centuries, the process is still fundamentally inductive, that is, "the passage from the details to the universal, the process by which from empirical observation, from the identification of regularity and recurrences in the fraction of reality empirically studied, one reaches generalizations or universal laws".[96]

Dobruska says:

> Let me explain: if an individual has saved another from the clutches of a fierce beast, if he has saved him from the flames, if he has prevented him from being swallowed by the force of a strong wave; finally, if he has preserved his days from any imminent danger. And if society rewards this individual for this particular voluntary act, then this reward represents a moral act of the state society.[97]

The second example concerns his conceptualization of man. He observes that in nature all men are equal, albeit with different attitudes and abilities. It therefore makes no sense to distinguish between a social man, a political or a civil man, as the absolutist regime of Louis XVI did. In a democratic society, every man must be a citizen. The deepest motivation of every human being is the desire to achieve certain material or intellectual goals, to develop his ingenuity

---

95 Dobruska, *Philosophie sociale*, 108: [La moralité d'état est *la conséquence de la moralité individuelle*].

96 Corbetta, *Metodologia e tecnica*, 25.

97 Dobruska, *Philosophie sociale*, 108: [Je m'explique: si un individu en a sauvé volontairement un autre des griffes d'une bête féroce, s'il l'a arraché aux flammes, s'il l'a empêché d'être englouti sous les flots d'une onde couroucée [sic]; enfin, s'il a préservé ses jours de tout autre péril éminent, et que la société récompense cet individu de cet acte de relation volontaire particulière, cette récompense est un acte moral de la société d'état].

and his faculties to the highest levels. "Man" – he says – "is a living being, whose instinct is susceptible to the widest development and the greatest perfection".[98]

Although Dobruska aims to use a scientific procedure, the way he conceives of this procedure is still very rudimentary. As is obvious, given his time, he does not use empirical data collection techniques as we know them today, accustomed as we are to questionnaires on representative samples of the population under investigation.

However, Dobruska uses two other methods to obtain "empirical data" on which to base his knowledge of human beings as social beings. On the one hand, he uses comparison of different societies while, on the other hand, he also provides a historical analysis of certain phenomena, i.e. how they have evolved over time.

The comparison used by Dobruska does not draw contrast between the animal level and the level of men, but between different societies in a given historical period. This allows Dobruska the sociologist to better focus on certain social phenomena and arrive at the formulation of certain laws that, as we have seen, are always based on the principle of cause and effect.

As an example, in the chapter on freedom, Dobruska tries to explain why, in societies that develop in the same natural climate, there can be such varied customs regarding the sexual habits of men and women and such varied drinking customs. In societies where the inhabitants are predominantly Christian, men "limit themselves to the pleasure of a single hymen and drink unscrupulous wine, while in societies where the inhabitants are predominantly Muslim, they abandon themselves to polygamy and refrain from this intoxicating liqueur".[99]

Dobruska shows that the cause of these differences in sexual and culinary customs in peoples is not due to climatic factors but to two social-cultural and political factors: the type of legislation and the content of the constitution.[100]

Before the French Revolution, societies, without any distinction between political and religious power, were essentially teleological. The social order was justified by a divine principle.

---

98 *Ibidem*, 82: [L'être-homme est un être vivant dont l'instinct est susceptible du développement le plus étendu et de la plus grande perfection].

99 *Ibidem*, 196: [(. . .) bornant les plaisirs de l'himen à'une seule femme, boit du vin sans scrupule,tandis que l'autre abandonnée à la poligamie la plus voluptueuse, s'abstient de cette liqueur enivrante].

100 *Ibidem*, 197: [Il n'y a pas sur la terre, une différence entre peuple et peuple; mais bien entre législateur et législateur, entre constitution et constitution].

Therefore, the causes that, for Dobruska, distinguish one people from another, are twofold: on the one hand, the "legislators" – in the aforementioned case of Christianity and Islam, they are Christ and Muhammad – and, on the other hand, their "constitutions" – the Gospels and the Koran. The different populations are thus socialized, one might say in today's sociology, according to different systems of religious beliefs, which affect the behavior and habits of people's daily lives.

We can also see in this case how Dobruska comes to the formulation of a law of cause and effect through an inductive method (from the particular to the general) and a comparison between different societies.

Auguste Comte, in the *Cours de philosohie positive*, which appeared in 1830–1842, would later theorize about how much such a method could contribute to the scientific analysis of society, to an understanding of human behavior in the social world. As I will show in the final chapter, it is possible to locate a line of development that, in this and other points, leads from Dobruska to Comte.

In Comte, we will arrive at the:

> rational comparison between the different coexisting states of human society on the different earth's surfaces, considered above all in populations fully independent of each other. Nothing is more suitable than such a procedure to characterize precisely the different essential phases of human evolution, which, consequently, can be explored simultaneously.[101]

Finally, the last methodological approach which Dobruska often uses to formulate his own "sociological" theories in the form of laws is a historical one. This is the observation of societies which have historically followed one another over time.

As an example, consider the concept of equality. According to Dobruska, equality is to be understood as equality of rights, which is the only way to guarantee the true freedom of each individual. It should not be seen as a fair distribution of economic and social resources among the citizens, which for Dobruska would be against nature.

As a demonstration of his theory, he cites a case taken from ancient Greek history, in which the equitable distribution of resources would have failed its objectives. The example concerns Sparta, under the legislator Lycurgus, to

---

101 Auguste Comte, *Physique sociale. Cours de philosophie positive (leçons 46–60) [1840–1842]* (Paris: Hermann, 1975), 146: [. . . un rapprochement rationnel des divers états coexistants de la société humaine sur les différentes portions de la surface terrestre, envisagés surtout chez des populations pleinement indépendantes les unes des autres. Rien n'est plus propre qu'un tel procédé à caractériser nettement les diverses phases essentielles de l'évolution humaine, dès lors susceptibles d'être simultanément explorées].

whom, according to tradition, we owe legislation that wanted to induce Spartans to austerity and military virtues. In order to achieve his objective, Lycurgus implemented drastic policies aimed at fairly distributing, we would say today, the socio-economic resources among citizens. Amid his interventions – recalls Dobruska – there was the abolition of the use of gold and silver and the introduction of iron coins:

> Lycurgus divided the land among his Spartans in equal parts. He destroyed the value of gold and silver, banned Lacedaemonian science and fine arts, wealth and luxury. He limited the clothing and food of the Spartans to the bare minimum.[102]

According to Dobruska, the fair redistribution of economic resources and the abolition of luxury did not produce what Lycurgus hoped for. The policies of strong redistribution of wealth would in fact have restricted the moral capacities of individual citizens linked to mutual support, bringing a consequent inertia of the material and intellectual appetite of individuals.

The historical comparison allows Dobruska both to grasp similar characteristics between past and present, as in the cited case, and to underline the differences between contemporaneity and past ages, which I will discuss below where I go deeper into the theory of the development of the stages of humanity.[103] In this regard, it is worth recalling the historical approach of Montesquieu, in *The Spirit of the Laws* of 1748:

> When I have been obliged to look back into antiquity, I have endeavoured to assume the spirit of the ancients, lest I should consider those things as alike which are really different, and lest I should miss the difference of those which appear to be like.[104]

3.7 The Revolutionary Theory

The first "revolutionary" part of the *Philosophie sociale* opens with a quote from John Locke (1632–1704): "Blind submission to the feelings of the greatest men

---

102 Dobruska, *Philosophie sociale*, 203–204: [Licurgue fit le partage des terres et les divisa entre ses Spartiates par parties égales. Il anéantit la valeur de l'or et de l'argent, il bannît les sciences et les beaux: arts de Lacédémone les richesses et le luxe. Il borna le vêtement et la nourriture des Spartiates au plus étroit nécessaire].
103 See below, 3.10.
104 Montesquieu, *Tutte le opere*, 896–899: [Quand j'ai été rappellé à l'antiquité, j'ai cherché à en prendre l'esprit, pour ne pas regarder comme semblables des cas réellement différens, et ne pas manquer les différences de ceux qui paroissent semblables], Idem, *The complete Works of M. de Montesquieu*, Volume the First, (Dublin: W. Watson, 1777), xxxviii.

has arrested the progress of knowledge more than anything else".[105] In reality, these words are not taken directly from the work of the English thinker, but from Pierre Coste's *Notice* to his own French translation of Locke's[106] *Essay on the Human Intellect*. In turn, Coste summarizes the autonomy of judgement that Locke himself repeatedly claims, detaching himself from the habit of relying on the *auctoritates* of the past.[107] The reference is not accidental, since Locke is an important source of inspiration for Dobruska. And so is, in particular, the *Essay*, published for the first time in 1690, in which Locke[108] "intended to see how human reason works, so that men can establish among themselves a form of peaceful and free coexistence, a form of coexistence that [. . .] makes it possible for everyone to seek his happiness in this world".[109]

If, for Locke, "a desire of Happiness, and an aversion to Misery [. . .] do continue constantly to operate and influence all our Actions", Dobruska's approach is similar: he examines the philosophical, moral and pragmatic foundations that allow us to build a social order in which human beings can be happy.[110]

After the fall of the absolutist and despotic monarchy of Louis XVI of Bourbon (1754–1793) and the power of the clergy, Dobruska was forced to respond to crucial and urgent philosophical, social, and political questions. On what philosophical basis and on what ethical and moral principles can the French people build a new social order? How is it possible to establish a structure that aims to achieve the happiness of the people and not their oppression? Why is a new society needed and how will it develop? What kind of political regime can guarantee the happiness of citizens? Which legislator is required?

This is precisely the aim of the *Philosophie sociale*: the construction of a new order, which provides for the establishment of a representative democratic regime. According to Dobruska, civil society within a democratic state can be achieved in three stages.

---

105 Dobruska, *Philosophie sociale*, 1: [La soumission aveugle aux sentiments des plus grands hommes, a plus arrêté le progrès des connoissances, qu'aucune autre chose].

106 John Locke, *An Essay Concerning Humane Understanding* (London: the Basset, 1690 [but 1689]). The French translation by Pierre Coste (1688–1747) was first published in Amsterdam in 1770: *Essai philosophique concernant l'entendement humain* (the passage quoted by Dobruska is on page 1).

107 See e.g. Locke, *An Essay*, I. 3. 23.

108 It has to be said that Dobruska always misspells this as "Loke".

109 *Introduzione*, in John Locke, *Saggio sull'intelletto umano*, eds., Marian and Nicola Abbagnano (Torino: Utet, 1971), 12.

110 Locke, *An Essay*, I. 3. 3 (Idem, *An Essay Concerning Human Understanding*, edited by Peter H. Nidditch, (Oxford: Oxford University Press, 1975), 67.

In the first stage, it is necessary to deconstruct and break down the old social order, which was the harbinger of so much oppression and unhappiness. Social disorganization is necessary.

In the second stage, it is a question of defining, from a theoretical point of view, the general principles of a Universal Constitution, and I will deal with this in detail later on.

In the third stage, an "explanatory framework" (*tableau*) will have to be created, i.e. a schematic summary, which will have to be displayed in the national assemblies of the legislative body[111] and of the popular sections, and will serve as a basis for the promulgation of laws and for their control.

A prerequisite for the whole process is that democracy must be representative and that there must be a clear separation between the religious and state spheres.

This philosophical reflection is revolutionary, since it is inserted in an age of radical changes of the structures and of the social order. It is divided into two interlinked moments of reflection.

The first moment concerns the process of "social disorganization" of the *Ancien Régime*, while the second refers to the "process of reconstruction of a social order", supported by a critical philosophical reflection, which defines the criteria of a good legislator and new laws for a better social order than the absolutist monarchy, or a body of rules based on a Constitution whose purpose is to make citizens happy.

3.8 Social Disorganization

In this paragraph we will dwell on the first process, that of social "disorganization", a concept that would become central in sociological discourse, from the recognized fathers of the discipline to contemporary sociologists, as we will see in the third part of this study.

Dobruska's social-philosophical thought starts from the assumption that, in order to build a new social order, aimed at the happiness of citizens, it is first necessary to destroy the old order.

Désorganisation, désorganiser, désorganisateur – these are words that come back several times under the pen of our author, with each applied to different fields. At the time when Dobruska wrote his *Philosophie sociale, désorganisation* was a new term, a neologism introduced in the eighties of the eighteenth century. It is interesting to note that the first use of the word was in the description of the

---

111 Dobruska, *Philosophie sociale*, 235–236.

techniques of mesmerism, the hypnotic-manipulative practice used by Franz Anton Mesmer (1734–1815), through which the body balance of the patient is "broken down", or "disorganized", and then reassembled.[112] The first use of *désorganiser*, in the historical-political sense, that I was able to find, recurs in a speech by Honoré Gabriel de Riqueti, Count of Mirabeau (1749–1791), printed after his death in Paris in 1791. Here it is used to describe the revolutionary storm, in which reconstruction is necessarily preceded by a process of disorganization:

> You have perceived that abuses form a system whose ramifications are intertwined and identified with public existence and that, in order to reconstruct everything, it is necessary to disorganize everything.[113]

As we can see, this is a fleeting mention, which Mirabeau does not elaborate any further. We will find this double movement, of disintegration and reconstruction, developed much more widely, in the *Philosophie sociale*.

For Dobruska, disorganization is a phenomenon attested by history, which appears in periods of transformation and revolution, thanks to outstanding personalities capable of questioning and changing the order of the past. It begins with the philosophical revolution of Socrates, passes to the revolutionary Christ of the Gospels, until arriving at Immanuel Kant, for whom Dobruska has a deep respect.[114]

The first revolution of sound reason is due to Socrates, who – writes Dobruska – was sentenced to death for having overthrown the philosophical system of the Sophists. Socrates is attributed with the affirmation of ideas not linked to experience, and not yet verified with certainty by science:

> Revolutionary Socrates, the first martyr of sound reason, of love for truth, for humanity, was condemned to death for having rejected sophistry, and demonstrated that there are

---

112 Cf., e.g., Erich J. Biester, "Magnetische Desorganisation und Sonnambulism," *Berlinische Monatschrift* 9 (1785): 126–160. See also Ralf Klausnitzer, *Poesie und Konspiration. Beziehungssinn und Zeichenökonomie von Verschwörungsszenarien in Publizistik, Literatur und Wissenschaft 1750–1850* (Berlin, New York: De Gruyter, 2007), 321–332 (*"Magnetische Organisation der Menschheit"* – *Mesmerismus*).

113 Honoré Gabriel de Riqueti Mirabeau, *Discours de monsieur Mirabeau l'aîné sur l'éducation nationale* (Paris: Lejay, 1791), 1–2: [vous avez senti que les abus formoient un système dont toutes les ramifications s'entrelaçoient et s'identifioient avec l'éxistence publique, et que, pour tout reconstruire, il falloit tout désorganiser].

114 Dobruska, *Philosophie sociale*, 47: [Socrate révolutionnaire, le premier martyr de la saine raison, de l'amour pour la vérité, pour l'humanité, fut condamné à mort pour avoir renversé la sophistique, et démontré qu'il y a des idées, que l'expérience ne nous donne point, et sur lesquelles nous n'avons point encore de science et de donnée assez certaine, pour nous mettre au-dessus de tout doute. Voilà la première révolution de la saine raison].

ideas that experience does not give us at all, and on which we do not yet have a very certain science nor data, to put us above any doubt. This is the first revolution of holy reason.[115]

The second deconstruction is that brought by the revolutionary Christ, which Dobruska defines in these terms:

> Christ is the second martyr of sound reason, crucified by Jewish priests and the Roman praetor, as a disorganizer of the astute pagan theocracy and that of Moses, and for having separated heaven from earth, affirming: I have fulfilled the prophecies of Moses, etc., by bringing morality back to good works, and by teaching that one must not only submit to the law, but also pay homage to it. Here is the second revolution of holy reason, the second degree of philosophy.[116]

For almost eighteen centuries, however, the verb of Christ has been overwhelmed by the dogmas of priests – "the scholastic hydra" (*l'hydre scolastique*) – although, writes Dobruska, philosophical and priestly revolutions have not been lacking. Just think of Luther, Zwingli, Melanchthon, Calvin, Huss, Spinoza, Leibniz, Locke and others. It is interesting to note the inclusion, in this list, of heroes of resistance to obscurantism, of promoters of the Reformation, in the company of the always revered, and very unorthodox, Spinoza. Despite the efforts of so many reformers, reason has become "ever more limping [. . .] and the night [of the spirit] ever darker".[117] It is a pessimistic vision of the early modern age, which finds its redemption only in the last "revolutionary giant". The third revolution of healthy reason is to be found in the thought of the German philosopher Immanuel Kant. The "immortal Kant", as Dobruska calls him, is the great disorganizer of all philosophical systems. But his is a revolution for insiders, understandable only to those who know how to decipher his "metaphysical-technical style". And so much innovative force of thought would have risked being lost, due to the ignorance of contemporary readers, if the revolution of the French people had not taken care of making it fully accessible:

---

115 *Ibidem*.
116 *Ibidem*, 47–48: [Le Christ révolutionnaire et second martyr de la saine raison, crucifié par les prêtres juifs, et le préteur romain, comme désorganisateur de l'astucieuse théocratie des Payens et de Moyse, et pour avoir séparé le ciel de la terre, en disant: j'ai accompli les prédictions de Moyse, etc. etc., en rappelant la morale à la bienfaisance, en apprenant qu'il ne faut pas seulement *se soumettre à la loi*, mais qu'il faut aussi lui *rendre hommage*. Voilà la seconde révolution de la saine raison, le second degré de la philosophie].
117 *Ibidem*, 48: [(. . .) malgré les diverses révolutions philosophiques et sacerdotales de Luther. Zuingle, Melanchton, Calvin, Huss, Spinosa, Hobbes, Leibnitz, Loke, et autres, la raison toujours plus chancellante, n'en devint que plus malade, les disputes, les égaremens toujours plus fréquens, et la nuit toujours plus sombre].

But finally we see appear, as a new revolutionary giant in philosophy, this destroyer of the two pillars of skepticism and dogmatism, this disorganizer of all philosophical systems, the immortal Kant. He can only be read by philosophers, having written in a metaphysical-technical style. Because of the novelty of his ideas, he was forced, so to speak, to compose a new vocabulary, which makes his works even more unintelligible to ordinary readers. But already too advanced in age, and living in Königsberg in Prussia, whose priests and the king are not so clairvoyant as intolerant, his obscure, metaphysical set serves him very well as a talisman against hemlock and the cross. Never has a man written so wisely; never has falsehood been so well unmasked; never has the truth been established in its rights with such assurance; but it has still taken the human spirit four centuries to develop, to feel his excellence, and these lessons seemed to be lost to us; it was reserved for the French nation to make us cross this space, and to make us believe that the most sublime truths, and those which, until recently, were considered the most abstract ones will now be for everyone.[118]

This praise of Kant as a disorganizer did not go unnoticed. A few months after the publication in Paris of the *Philosophie sociale*, the German philosopher Johann August Eberhard (1739–1809) took up this union between Kant's "disorganizing" philosophy and the political revolution, making it the theme of a polemical essay. As I will demonstrate in more detail in the last chapter of this essay, Dobruska's theory of disorganization was immediately echoed in the intellectual world of the time.

In the *Philosophie sociale*, disorganization identifies and critically evaluates all the social and political processes both of the society of the past, under the absolutist monarchy of Louis XVI, and of the contemporary one – the one the author is living through – that have led or may lead to great inequalities and social injustices, as well as abuses of power.

---

118 *Ibidem*, 48–49: [Mais enfin on voit paroître, comme un nouveau géant révolutionnaire en philosophie, ce destructeur des deux colonnes principales du scepticisme et de la dogmatique, ce désorganisateur de tous systèmes philosophiques, l'immortel Kant. Mais il ne peut être lu que par des philosophes, ayant écrit dans un style métaphisico-technique, pour lequel, en raison de la nouveauté de ses idées, il lui a fallu, pour ainsi dire, composer un nouveau vocabulaire, ce qui rend ses ouvrages d'autant plus inintelligibles au commun des lecteurs. Mais déjà trop avancé en âge, et vivant à Königsberg en Prusse, dont les prêtres et le roi ne sont pas si clairvoyans qu'intolérans; sa parure obscure, métaphysique lui sert très-bien de talisman contre la ciguë et la croix. Jamais homme n'écrivit avec autant de sagacité; jamais la fausseté ne fut aussi bien démasquée; jamais la vérité établie dans ses droits avec une telle assurance; mais il falloit encore à l'esprit humain un développement de quatre siècles, pour en sentir l'excellence, et ses leçons sembloient perdues pour nous; il étoit réservé à la nation françoise, de nous faire franchir cet espace, et de nous faire croire que les vérités les plus sublimes, et celles qui, n'aguères, passoient pour les plus abstraites, seront désormais à la portée de tout le monde].

Dobruska reflects critically on everything that did not work in pre-revolutionary society, developing the task that Jean-Jacques Rousseau had already undertaken in his essays on social inequalities (*Discourse on the Origin and Foundations of Inequality among Men*, 1755), and which was to be continued by subsequent social philosophers, up to the present day. Axel Honneth calls such dysfunctions "the pathologies of the social" or "social pathologies", and means "all erroneous social developments" (*soziale Fehlentwicklungen*): those processes that deviate from an acceptable ethical-social normative model, of which we will say more later.

What are the developments and processes identified by Moses Dobruska in the pre-revolutionary period, that of the absolutist monarchy, considered harmful to society and to be amended?

The first "explosive mixture" of the absolute monarchy is the division of men into different social classes. Moses Dobruska's reasoning starts from the observation that the monarchy is a form of government "against nature".

Why is it against nature? Because monarchic power is based on a false assumption: the inequality of men, who are divided into different social classes. What is more, only some of them have the right to be citizens, while others are denied that right. This is a serious error that has characterized the absolute monarchy of Louis XVI. Humanity is not divisible: it is a whole. Dobruska writes:

> Humanity is certainly an indivisible whole because only man can be found in it. Only tyrants or narrow-minded legislators have been able to divide man into different classes, by establishing various selves in the great self of society. Some (the tyrants) did not want man because they wanted to have slaves, and others (the narrow-minded legislators), not believing that it was possible for man to exercise his rights in society, molded their government on this false opinion, and by a kind of ostracism, they thus banished man from humanity.[119]

> The second explosive mixture of the absolutist monarchy is tyranny and lack of attention to the common good. This disease is due to the misallocation of legislative power and its purpose. Since not all individuals are equal before the law, only a few are allowed to reign over the rest of the population and to legislate. In a monarchic regime, it is not the legislative power based on a constitution that legislates, as in a democratic regime, but directly the executive power. The members of the executive carry out the laws exclusively

---

119 *Ibidem*, 28–29: [L'humanité est assurément un tout indivisible, car on ne peut y trouver que l'homme. Il n'y a que les tyrans ou les législateurs bornés qui en établissant divers *moi* dans le grand moi de la société, aient pu diviser l'homme en classes différentes. Les uns (les tyrans) ne vouloient pas l'homme, afin de se faire des esclaves, et les autres, (les législateurs bornés) ne croyant pas qu'il lui fût possible d'exercer *ses droits dans la société*, moulèrent leur gouvernement sur cette opinion fausse, et par une espèce d'*ostracisme*, ils bannirent ainsi l'homme de l'humanité].

to achieve their own personal ends, essentially following their own whims instead of the common good of society. Dobruska writes: "[. . .] the monarchy, this regime against nature, where force, the executive power, made the law for the execution of its whims, of its licenses".[120]

Finally, this leads to great abuses of power and privileges by an oppressive majority that often imposes its will through the law of the strongest, and, in the final analysis, this means a lack of freedom for those who are oppressed by it. This is the third big mistake, which he calls the great "political crime".[121]

Moses Dobruska's social philosophy, however, not only highlights the errors and criticisms of the social order of the absolutist monarchy, but also the social risks of proposals for democratic change which are not based on the Universal Constitution envisaged by him.

Unlike Jean-Jacques Rousseau, Moses Dobruska is convinced that a democracy whose right is not anchored in the Constitution, and which is not rooted in the laws of nature but in the general will of the majority in power, is a serious risk to future society. He wisely states:

> We just changed the mode of despotism. After destroying the monarchy [. . .] we put on the throne, in its place, the whims and licenses of the will, of the legislative power: anequally oppressive regime, and one against nature, since it does not reduce the physical [dimension], that is, the force, the execution to slavery, does not reduce the possibility of being able to surrender to license or tyranny.[122]

The *Philosophie sociale* outlines the social issues (*les questions sociales*) of both a monarchic regime and a democratic system that is not anchored in the Universal Constitution, which he considers essential.

---

120 *Ibidem*, 13: [la monarchie, ce régime contre nature, où la force, la puissance exécutive faisoit la loi pour l'exécution de ses caprices, de ses licences].

121 For a sociological and diachronic evaluation of power processes and institutions see Karl-Siegbert Rehberg, "Institutionelle Machtprozesse im historischen Vergleich. Einleitende Bemerkungen", in *Dimensionen institutioneller Macht. Fallstudien von der Antike bis zur Gegenwart*, eds., Gert Melville and Karl-Siegbert Rehberg (Köln, Weimar, Wien: Böhlau, 2012), 1–16; Karl-Siegbert Rehberg, "Institutionelle Analyse und Historische Komparatistik," *ibidem*, 417–443; *Symbolische Ordnungen. Beiträge zu einer soziologischen Theorie der Institutionen*, eds. Karl-Siegbert Rehberg and Hans Vorländer (Baden-Baden: Nomos, 2014).

122 *Ibidem*: [Nous n'avons donc changé que le mode du despotisme, et en détruisant la monarchie, ce régime contre nature, où la force, la puissance exécutive faisoit la loi pour l'exécution de ses caprices, de ses licences, nous plaçâmes donc sur le trône les caprices et les licences de la volonté, de la puissance législative: régime également oppressif, et contre nature, puisqu'il ne réduit le physique, c'est-à-dire, la force, l'exécution à l'esclavage, qu'afin de pouvoir s'abandonner plus aisément lui-même à la licence ou à la tyrannie].

As we have seen in the previous paragraph, Dobruska, in addition to pointing out everything that is wrong with social reality, also outlines a political criticism. It is a criticism that addresses a specific regime, the monarchist regime, and its protagonists, but it is also a criticism that invites the recipients of his *Philosophie* to transform social reality.[123]

Like the natural scientists, after the "diagnosis" he also tries to identify the "causes" of the serious errors of the previous political regime, which led to the rebellion of the population and what he calls the "social disorganization".

As we have already mentioned, there are many causes. These reside primarily in the distinction between men and citizens and all those who, by definition, do not enjoy the rights of citizenship. Other causes of disorganization are to be identified in the stratification into social classes and in the possibility, on the part of the executive power, of legislature taking into account only personal interests, or "whims", as Dobruska calls them.

Dobruska praises Jean-Jacques Rousseau as one of the first to encourage men to free themselves from the yoke of submission. Rousseau is, in the *Philosophie sociale*, the father of the French Revolution and the benefactor of humanity.[124] The dissemination of his writings had the merit of inspiring the French people and thus initiating the revolutionary process in France. It is primarily thanks to him that the French have become aware of the lack of freedom and the oppressive daily life imposed on them by the absolutist monarchy, and have been able to free themselves from the yoke of tyranny.

Suffice it to recall, in this regard, the famous opening of the first chapter of *The Social Contract* (1762):

> Man is born free; and everywhere he is in chains. One thinks himself the master of others, and still remains a greater slave than they. How did this change come about? I do not know. What can make it legitimate? That question I think I can answer.

> If I took into account only force, and the effects derived from it, I should say: "As long as a people is compelled to obey, and obeys, it does well; as soon as it can shake off the yoke, and shakes it off, it does still better" [. . .] To renounce liberty is to renounce being a man, to surrender the rights of humanity and even its duties. For him who renounces everything no indemnity is possible. Such a renunciation is incompatible with man's nature; to remove all liberty from his will is to remove all morality from his acts.[125]

---

123 Fischbach, *Manifeste pour une philosophie sociale*, 38.

124 Dobruska, *Philosophie sociale*, 19.

125 Jean-Jacques Rousseau, *Du contrat social. Ou, Principes du droit politique* (Amsterdam: Chez Marc-Michel Rey, 1762), I. 1. 3, I. 4. 16: [L'homme est né libre, et par-tout il est dans les fers. Tel se croit le maître des autres, qui ne laisse pas d'être plus esclave qu'eux. Comment ce changement s'est-il fait ? Je l'ignore. Qu'est-ce qui peut le rendre légitime ? Je crois pouvoir

Dobruska completely agrees with Rousseau. Lack of freedom must be combated, independence must be regained at all costs, oppression must be resisted, and tyranny must be broken down.[126] Lack of freedom and oppression are the negative traits that have marked the social order of the absolutist monarchy and that must be banned from the new society.

3.9 Critical Diagnosis and Conditions for Overcoming Social Disorganization

If Dobruska's social philosophy is against the pre-revolutionary regime, it also presupposes some hypotheses on how it is possible to create a society that makes citizens happy.

A first hypothesis refers to the elimination of the distinction between citizens and non-citizens, between politicians and civilians, which were introduced by the monarchy.[127] For Moses Dobruska all men are social beings who live in close association, are equal before the law, and must be able to participate as citizens in democratic society.

A second hypothesis refers to what is to be understood by man, that is, in the language of the *Philosophie sociale*, by the *être-homme*. For Dobruska, man "is a living being whose instinct is susceptible to the greatest development and perfection".[128]

The condition in which human being can develop his own power and reach the highest level of perfection is freedom. As we know, for Dobruska, freedom means equal rights. This is the third condition for the realization of a just and happy society.

---

résoudre cette question [. . .] Si je ne considérois que la force, et l'effet qui en dérive, je dirois ; tant qu'un Peuple est contraint d'obéir et qu'il obéit, il fait bien ; sitôt qu'il peut secouer le joug et qu'il le secoüe, il fait encore mieux [. . .] Renoncer à sa liberté c'est renoncer à sa qualité d'homme, aux droits de l'humanité, même à ses devoirs. Il n'y a nul dédommagement possible pour quiconque renonce à tout. Une telle renonciation est incompatible avec la nature de l'homme, et c'est ôter toute moralité à ses actions que d'ôter toute liberté à sa volonté], Idem, *The Social Contract, and Discourses,* introduction by G. D. H. Cole, (London: J.M. Dent & Sons, Ltd, 1910), 10.

126 *Philosophie sociale*, 1.
127 *Ibidem*, 82: [L'être-homme est-un être vivant dont l'instinct est suscetible du développement le plus étenduet de la plus grande perfection].
128 *Loc. cit.*

It follows – and this is the fourth condition – that freedom is guaranteed only by the application of the Universal Constitution. As we shall see later, the Universal Constitution drawn up by our author contains all of the ethical and social principles or rules, the purpose of which is to reorganize society in a democratic way, while guaranteeing the happiness of citizens.

Finally, one last important condition, which prevents the occurrence of what Moses Dobruska calls the "monstrous mixtures" (*mélanges monstrueux*), is the separation between religious power and political power – a separation that was not practised in the regime of the absolute monarchy of Louis XVI.

The justification for monarchic power from antiquity to the French Revolution has always been based on the divine descent of the monarchs themselves. In this regard, Dobruska notes in the first part of his work:

> In ancient times, the whole land was subject to the sovereignty of the gods. The sovereigns were their representatives. All forms of government were theocratic. Kings, heroes and all those who commanded a people – whatever their name – were so identified with the divinity of their nation that attacking one meant attacking the other. History and the Bible provide us with constant proof of this truth. I could never conceive how men, even the most enlightened of our century, could consider such a monstrous mixture, this disastrous identification, as a necessary fact of the organization of primitive nations, as an advantage and a perfection of the same. I have always thought, however, that legislators who did not have a primitive people to establish, but who had to regulate a government of a people already dominated by superstition, saw this vicious union as a tool for them and as a necessary evil.[129]

It can be seen from all of this that the *Philosophie sociale* has a strongly evaluative and normative dimension. This is a characteristic of normativity, which will shape all future social philosophy.[130]

---

129 *Ibidem*, 40: [Toute la terre étoit anciennement soumise à la souveraineté des Dieux. Les rois étoient leurs représentans. Toutes les formes du gouvernement étoient théocratiques. Les rois, les héros, et tous ceux qui commandoient à un peuple; quelle qu'ait été leur dénomination étoient tellement identifiés avec la divinité de cette nation, qu'attaquer l'une, c'étoit aussi attaquer l'autre. L'histoire et la bible nous offrent la preuve continuelle de cette vérité. Je n'ai jamais pu concevoir comment les hommes, même les plus éclairés de notre siècle, avoient pu considérer ce mélange monstreux, cette identification funeste, comme un effet nécessaire de l'organisation des nations primitives; et par suite, comme un avantage et une perfection de cette constitution; mais j'ai toujours pensé, que les législateurs qui n'avoient point eu un peuple primitif à instituer, mais à réguler le gouvernement d'un peuple déjà dominé par la superstition, j'ai toujours pensé, dis-je, que ces législateurs avoient regardé cette réunion vicieuse, comme un moyen pour eux, et comme un mal nécessaire]. See also below, 7. 3. 3.
130 See Jaeggi, Celikates, *Sozialphilosophie*, 8; Fischbach, *Manifeste pour une philosophie sociale, passim.*

3.10 Theory of the Historical Development of Social Organizations

As we shall see in more detail in the final chapter, Dobruska is a forerunner of the law of the three stages of humanity, elaborated later, in the nineteenth century, by Auguste Comte.

According to the thesis developed in the first part of the *Philosophie sociale*, humanity has built different social organizations, each one of them belonging to a specific epoch, and characterized by peculiar sources of legitimacy of power.

In the first phase of the development of humanity, what we might call the "theocratic" phase, the source of legitimacy of societies was the gods. The first source of legitimacy for political regimes, from antiquity to the absolute monarchy of the pre-revolutionary era, was therefore of a religious nature. The leaders of the ruling classes identified with the gods. This correlation, which turned into a disastrous identification of temporal power and religious power, is, according to Dobruska, a "monstrous mixture" (*mélange monstreux*), "[. . .] a necessary effect of the social organization of primitive nations".[131] In primitive social organizations, the legislator couldn't educate the people, subject as they were to superstition, so this vicious union between secular and religious power was a necessary evil.

This first phase of social organizations was followed by a second phase, although Dobruska does not provide historical details. In this phase, social organizations were justified and sustained on the basis of a constitution and legislation, which had their roots in a metaphysical system of thought, that is, one that looks beyond the sensible world, in search of the ultimate goals of man's existence, and the deeper meaning of his life.

In the second part of the *Philosophie sociale*, we learn how a social organization, whose normative system is based on a metaphysical system that transcends empirical reality, can only cause "trouble". It won't be able to make its members happy.

Dobruska emphatically states:

Woe to them [the people] if they seek another basis for his own judgment! Because then they throw themselves into the circle from which they have struggled to escape [the theocratic one] [. . .] It is in this way that trouble persecutes the metaphysicist at every step, who dives into the syllogisms and their painful consequences, copies and forms his

---

131 Dobruska, *Philosophie sociale*, 40: [ce mélange monstreux [. . .] un effet nécessaire de l'organisation des nations primitives].

system, following everything but nature. It is for this reason that in legislation the in-depth debate became painful and dictated by the word metaphysics.[132]

In order to achieve the happiness of citizens, the new social organization will have to distinguish itself from theocratic and metaphysical social organizations.

We have thus reached the third and final historical phase, in which another ideal type of social organization is realized. The source of legitimacy of power is no longer based on theology, nor on metaphysics, but on the "laws of nature".

This social organization, which was born in the aftermath of the French Revolution, is the one that Dobruska intends to achieve with his work. It is a democratic society, whose order is based on the Constitution. The inspiring principle is no longer metaphysics but *physis*, nature, with its laws.

Dobruska writes:

> It is true that when the legislation will have found the solid foundations of nature, and will apply physics in a perfect way, we will no longer need metaphysics, in this sense we can say with Bacon *post veram inventam physicam nulla metaphysica erit*. That is to say that once we have known nature, we should no longer seek beyond it.[133]

As we shall see below, with regard to the essence and form of the Universal Constitution, Dobruska is convinced that constitutional principles must be sought in the laws of nature and no longer in metaphysics or even in religion.

Once the Constitution has been drawn up, with the principles for achieving a democratic society in which citizens are happy, it will be sufficient for legislative assemblies to meticulously apply the principles set out in it.

The similarity with the thought of Auguste Comte is immediately apparent. As sociologist Lewis Coser recalls in his book on the *Masters of Sociological Thought*, Comte argues that:

---

132 *Ibidem*, 54–55: [Malheur à lui, s'il [le peuple] cherche une autre bâse à son jugement! car alors il se jette dans le cercle dont il avait eu tant de peine de à sortir [celui théocratique] [. . .]. C'est ainsi que le malheur poursuit à chaque pas le métaphysicien qui, plongé dans des sillogismes et des conséquences pénibles, copie et forme son systême, suivant tout, excepté suivant la nature. C'est par cette raison que dans les législations toute discussion approfondie devenoit odieuse et proscrite par le mot métaphysique].

133 *Ibidem*, 55: [Il est vrai que lorsque la législation aura trouvé les bases solides de la nature, en fait l'application parfaite de la physique, nous n'aurons plus besoin de la métaphysique, dans ce sens, nous pourrions dire avec Bacon, *post veram inventam physicam nulla metaphysica erit*. C'est-à-dire, quand nous connoîtrons une fois la nature, nous n'aurons plus à chercher au-delà d'elle]. See also below, 7. 3. 3.

In order for man to be able to transform his nonhuman environment to his advantage, he must know the laws that govern the natural world, "For it is only by knowing the laws of phenomena, and thus being able to foresee them, that we can . . . set them to modify one another for our advantage . . . Whenever we effect anything great it is through a knowledge of natural laws . . . From science comes Prevision; from Prevision comes Action (*Savoir pour prévoir et prévoir pour pouvoir*). In a like manner, social action beneficial to mankind will become possible once the laws of motion of human evolution are established, and the basis for social order and civic concord is identified".[134]

Comte also affirms the need to know the world of nature in order to understand the laws that govern social life. It is only through this knowledge that people can transform the environment in which they live.

The analogy between Dobruska's anticipatory thought and Comte's later one certainly doesn't stop here. As we have already mentioned, and we will illustrate later, Comte elaborates a theory of the development of humanity that goes from a theological stage, to a metaphysical one, up to the positive one, of science. The roots of these stages are to be found in the theory of social organizations, formulated in the *Philosophie sociale*.

3.11 Criticism of Rousseau

Rousseau, tutelary deity of the French Revolution, is exalted in the *Philosophie sociale* in truly flattering terms: "sacred flame, torch of truth that has enlightened the people and that has burned a multitude of ancient and vexatious laws".[135]

However, these are praises that must not be overestimated. Beyond the appreciation for the figure of the thinker and innovator, Dobruska expresses himself very sharply against the *Social Contract* of Rousseau, considering it unsuitable to sustain the construction of the future French democratic society. On the contrary, Rousseau's thought would actually only lead to social disorganization and perpetual revolution.

According to Dobruska, it is essential that the French people have a solid body of law, based on a constitution. This body of work is necessary if a new democratic society is to be built. According to our author, a good constitution

---

134 Lewis A. Coser, *Masters of Sociological Thought. Ideas in historical and social context*, 2nd ed. (San Diego: Hartcourt Publishers, 1977) (I ed. 1971), 4.
135 Dobruska, *Philosophie sociale*, 1: [Rousseau fut cette flamme sacrée, ce flambeau de la vérité, qui, en éclairant le peuple, consuma le recueil de ses loix antiques et vexatoires].

supports the most rigorous equality, just as we find it in nature, no privileges, no preferences. Equal freedom for all; because it is the natural property, and an indispensable need for happiness for everyone.[136]

In the very first page of his *Philosophie sociale*, Dobruska therefore states with emphasis: "We must make new [laws]. We have overthrown, dismissed: let us build, constitute! This is the cry of all the French people and of the whole world, who await us."[137]

Dobruska has five basic critical arguments against Rousseau: the choice of political regimes based on the size of a State and the number of its inhabitants; the lack of a hierarchy of sources of law; the conception of legislative and executive power of a representative democracy; the concept of morality as a will; the lack of a separation between Church and State.

The first criticism of Rousseau refers to the choice of different political regimes, based on the size of a State and the number of its inhabitants. Dobruska criticizes Rousseau's thesis that not all types of political regimes are suitable for different populations and different States. It follows from this thesis that, for larger countries with a higher population density, monarchic regimes are more suitable, for the medium-sized ones aristocracy is more suitable, while the smaller countries with a lower population density are more suitable for democratic regimes. In the eighth chapter of the third book of the *Social Contract*, entitled *Every form of government is not suitable for every country*, Rousseau observes:

> It follows that, the more the distance between people and government increases, the more burdensome tribute becomes: thus, in a democracy, the people bears the least charge; in an aristocracy, a greater charge; and, in monarchy, the weight becomes heaviest. Monarchy therefore suits only wealthy nations; aristocracy, States of middling size and wealth; and democracy, States that are small and poor.[138]

---

136 *Ibidem*, 43: [En partant de là, (d'une bonne constitution,) nous trouverons généralement et en somme la plus rigoureuse égalité, telle qu'elle est dans la nature, nul privilège, nulle préférence. Liberté égale pour tous; parce qu'elle est la propriété naturelle, et un besoin indispensable au bonheur d'un chacun].

137 *Ibidem*, 1: [Mais il faut en faire de nouvelles. [. . .] Nous avons renversé, destitué; édifions, constituons: voilà le cri du Peuple François et du monde entier, qui nous attend].

138 Rousseau, *Du contrat social* III. 8: [. . . the further the distance from the people to the Government increases, the more expensive the tributes become; thus in Democracy the people are the least charged, in the Aristocracy they are more so, in the Monarchy they carry the greatest weight. The Monarchy is therefore only suitable for wealthy nations, the Aristocracy for states that are mediocre in wealth and size, Democracy for small and poor states] (Idem, *The Social Contract*, 69).

To this thesis, Dobruska responds with emphasis:

> Unhappy humanity! The largest part of humanity is condemned to endless slavery. After the most vigorous struggles against tyranny, does it only have the sad prospect of a new slavery? And you, above all, the French people! What about your great efforts, your great sacrifices that you have made to eradicate tyranny? And your neighbors, who were waiting for your liberating weapons, will have to lower their heads more than ever, since you yourself, after your countless triumphs, will see the sun darken again because of the corrupt spirit of despotism. No, it will be otherwise. The revolutionary genius, your benefactor J.-J. [Rousseau] was wrong. And to convince you, let us examine and ask ourselves: What is a small-, great-, and medium-sized people?[139]

Against Rousseau's thesis that the political regime best suited to a people is related to the size of the territory and the size of the population, Dobruska writes:

> A small State is a society made up of a small number of inhabitants. A large people is a grouping of many individuals and an average people is a society made up of more people than a small society but fewer than a large society. We will discuss in the following the influence of different climates and the nuances that customs can provoke on the wide range of humanity. Here we limit ourselves to emphasizing that man always remains a man, regardless of whether he is united with a few, many, or an intermediate number of individuals. The tree does not change its essence whether it is planted in a large forest, in a smaller forest or almost isolated from other trees. Let's add another truth: a large forest is more resistant to the shock of the winds than a tree that is found only in the plain or in a not very dense forest. Likewise, a large population has more resources for the preservation of its own self (*son moi*) than a weaker population, as it can multiply and renew its efforts without losing its energy. The one who claims to see the whole of humanity in a different way from the collection of equal human beings multiplied equally and not differently increased, is similar to the one who, in observing a forest, sees everything but the tree.[140]

---

139 Dobruska, *Philosophie sociale*, 25: [Malheureuse humanité! ainsi donc tes portions les plus grandes sont condamnées à un esclavage sans fin, où après les luttes les plus vigoureuses contre la tyrannie, elles n'auront donc que la triste perspective d'un nouvel esclavage? et toi sur-tout Peuple françois! ils auront donc été vains tes efforts généreux, ils seront donc perdus tous les sacrifices que tu as faits pour l'extirpation de la tyrannie? Tes voisins qui attendoient tes armes libératrices, n'auront donc qu'à courber plus que jamais leur tête, puisque toi-même après des triomphes sans nombre, tu dois voir ton sol flétri de nouveau, par l'haleine impure du despotisme. Non: il en sera autrement. Ton génie révolutionnaire, ton bienfaiteur J.-J. s'est trompé en en parlant ainsi, et pour nous en convaincre, examinons et demandons: Qu'est-ce qu'un peuple petit, un grand peuple, et un peuple médiocre?].
140 *Ibidem*, 25–26: [Un petit Etat est une société composée d'un petit nombre d'hommes; un grand peuple est le rassemblement de beaucoup d'hommes; et un peuple médiocre, est une société plus nombreuse que la première, et moindre que la seconde. Nous parlerons dans la suite de la diversité des climats, des nuances que les mœurs ou d'autres accidens peuvent jetter sur le grand tableau, l'*humanité*. Nous nous bornerons ici à dire, que l'homme est toujours homme, soit qu'il se trouve rassemblé en petite, en grande, ou en moyenne quantité. L'arbre

It is clear that Dobruska understands very well how men act and behave in their daily practices in very different ways, depending on the social and cultural context in which they are "socialized". However, it is also clear to him how, while belonging to different societies, all men share the same essence. As a result, a democratic regime is suitable for any nation, whether large or small, poor or rich. As such, monarchic and aristocratic regimes must be rejected because they are "too contrary to freedom and equality".[141]

The second criticism of the political philosophy of the *Social Contract* of J.-J. Rousseau focuses on the lack, in the thought of the Genevan, of a hierarchy of the sources of law, which hinders the promulgation of laws. As we shall see below, Dobruska's social philosophy very clearly indicates the need for a hierarchy of regulatory sources.

While it is true that Rousseau outlines the principles for the achievement of a good state and good governance which, as we know, must support the preservation and prosperity of its members,[142] he does not make them binding. Although these principles are the foundation of the laws, they are not anchored by a Constitution. They risk being baseless. In this regard Dobruska cites a significant passage from the twelfth chapter of the second book of the *Social Contract* of Rousseau:

> The laws which regulate this relation bear the name of political laws, and are also called fundamental laws, not without reason if they are wise. For, if there is, in each State, only one good system, the people that is in possession of it should hold fast to this; but if the established order is bad, why should laws that prevent men from good be regarded as fundamental? Besides, in any case, a people is always in a position to change its laws, how ever good; for, if it chooses to do itself harm, who can have a right to stop it?[143]

---

ne change point dans son essence, soit qu'il se trouve dans une vaste forêt, qu'il soit planté dans un bois moins étendu, ou presque isolément. Mais nous dirons avec vérité, qu'une grande forêt présente au choc des vents, une résistance plus forte que l'arbre qui se trouve seul dans la plaine, où dans un bois clair semé. De même, un grand peuple a-t-il plus de ressources pour la conservation de son *moi*, qu'un peuple foible, en ce qu'il peut multiplier à la fois et renouvelle ses efforts, sans qu'ils perdent pour cela de leur énergie; et celui qui voudrait regarder le grand tout de l'humanité autrement, que comme le rassemblement du même être multiplié d'une manière égale, et non pas différemment augmenté, ressembleroit à celui qui, observant une forêt, verrait tout excepté l'arbre].

141 *Ibidem*, 22.

142 Rousseau, *Du contrat social*, III. IX (Idem, *The Social Contract*, 73).

143 *Ibidem*, II. XII: [Les loix qui règlent ce rapport partent le nom de loix politiques, et s'appellent aussi loix fondamentales, non sans quelque raison si ces loix sont sages. Car s'il n'y a dans chaque Etat qu'une bonne manière de l'ordonner, le peuple qui l'a trouvée doit s'y tenir: mais si l'ordre établi est mauvais, pourquoi prendroit-on pour fondamentales des loix qui l'empêchent d'être bon? D'ailleurs, en tout état de cause, un peuple est toujours le maître de

For Dobruska, it is in no way acceptable for a nation to be able to change its laws and replace them with a body of legislation that aims at the evil and destruction of the people themselves. It is for this reason that he intends to draw up a Universal Constitution, containing, as its first principle, the preservation and happiness of citizens. The remaining laws must descend hierarchically from this fundamental principle. If this binding hierarchy, which protects the people from self-destruction, is lacking, a philosophical system cannot serve as a model for building a new social order. In fact, it would be an unstable philosophical system, a harbinger of social disorganization instead of organization. Dobruska says:

> But of course, I will demonstrate more widely in the following that his system [i.e. Rousseau's], being disorganizing and perpetually revolutionary, cannot serve as a basis for the Constitution, from which must result the laws that guarantee the duration of freedom. Without freedom there can be no public happiness.[144]

The third criticism of Rousseau's philosophical and political thought is closely linked to the second one. It focuses on the conception of legislative and executive power in a representative democracy.

Rousseau speaks of these two powers in the third book of his *The Social Contract*, dedicated to the different forms of government (democracy, aristocracy and monarchy):

> Every free action is produced by the concurrence of two causes; one moral, *i.e.* the will which determines the act; the other physical, *i.e.* the power which executes it. When I walk towards an object, it is necessary first that I should will to go there, and, in the second place, that my feet should carry me. If a paralytic wills to run and an active man wills not to, they will both stay where they are. The body politic has the same motive powers; here too force and will are distinguished, will under the name of legislative power and force under that of executive power.[145]

---

changer ses loix, mêmes les meilleures; car s'il lui plait de se faire mal à lui-même, qui est-ce qui a droit de l'en empêcher?]. (Rousseau, *The Social Contract*, 47).

144 Dobruska, *Philosophie sociale*, 1–2: [Mais certes, et je le démontrerai plus amplement dans la suite, son système n'étant que désorganisateur et perpétuellement révolutionnaire, ne peut plus servir de base à une constitution, d'où doivent découler des loix, qui nous garantissent la durée de la liberté, sans laquelle il ne saurait y avoir de bonheur public].

145 Rousseau, *Du contrat social*, III. 1. 122–123: [Toute action libre a deux causes qui concourent à la produire, l'une morale, savoir la volonté qui détermine l'acte, l'autre physique, savoir la puissance qui l'exécute. Quand je marche vers un objet, il faut premièrement que j'y veuille aller ; en second lieu, que mes pieds m'y portent. Qu'un paralytique veuille courir, qu'un homme agile ne le veuille pas, tous deux resteront en place. Le corps politique a les mêmes mobiles ; on y distingue de même la force et la volonté ; Celle-ci sous le nom de *puissance*

In other words, for Rousseau, the political body must be understood as a physical body. Legislative power corresponds to will, understood as morality, while executive power is force.

For Dobruska, the legislative power has the task of enacting laws, which are expressions of the moral faculties of the legislator. However, these laws – and this is a central point of his entire social philosophy – must be based on law, which in turn is based on the ultimate principle and on the seventy constitutional principles. Or rather, laws must be subject to constitutional principles, which are based on reason and observation of nature.

The executive power, completely subordinate to the legislative one, must merely obey and execute. It has no deliberative power, no force of its own, as Rousseau suggests.

Legislative power should therefore be understood as a *moral legislative power*.

Dobruska says:

> . . . about the comparison, which J.J. Rousseau proposes to us, I will say: that it is basically true. But I will also say that, although Rousseau did not confuse the mechanic with the machine, he seems to assume that the mechanic is a dual being. According to his system, it is mistakenly divided into an author of larger and important wheels and another of smaller and less important wheels. Actually, it's still the same being. He is always the artist who made the same machine whether it has big wheels or small ones.[146]

The fourth criticism of the *Social Contract* is directed against the way of conceiving the moral faculty of the legislative power. If for Rousseau the will represents the only moral instance attributed to the legislative power, for Dobruska the moral instances, of which we will say more later, are always two: sentiment and reason.[147]

The fifth and final criticism concerns the lack of separation between religion and politics.

Dobruska criticizes the thesis of the seventh chapter of the second book of the *Social Contract*, in which Rousseau states that, since nations existed, there

---

législative, l'autre sous le nom de *puissance exécutive*] (Idem, *The Social Contract*, 49). This passage is quoted in *Philosophie sociale*, 5–6.

146 Dobruska, *Philosophie sociale*, 7: [. . . de la comparaison, que J.J. Rousseau nous propose, je dirai: qu'au fond elle est véritable; mais je dirai aussi que si Rousseau n'a pas tout-à-fait confondu le mécanicien avec la machine, il semble pourtant qu'il regard le mécanicien comme un être double, qui, d'après son système, est faussement divisé en auteur des roues plus grandes et plus importantes de la machine, et en auteur des roues plus petites et moins importantes, mais qui en effet est toujours un seul et même être, c'est-à-dire, toujours l'artiste qui a fabriqué la machine elle-même, soit qu'il en fasse les grandes ou petites roues].

147 *Ibidem*, 19.

has always been an instrumental link between politics and religion. This is the text by Rousseau:

> The Judaic law, which still subsists, and that of the child of Ishmael, which, for ten centuries, has ruled half the world, still proclaim the great men who laid them down; and, while the pride of philosophy or the blind spirit of faction sees in them no more than lucky impostures, the true political theorist admires, in the institutions they set up, the great and powerful genius which presides over things made to endure.[148]

From all this, Rousseau stresses, we must not conclude with the English theologian William Warburton (1698–1779) that politics and religion have a common object. In the origin of nations, one serves as an instrument to the other.[149]

According to Dobruska, for the construction of a democratic society, there must be a separation between Church (conceived as different from the religious thought of Christ) and politics. In fact, in the hands of impostors, religion can only be used for personal purposes and can be harmful to young people.[150]

Dobruska is convinced that, despite its merits, the *Social Contract* does not offer a convincing guide to a solid foundation on which to reconstruct a democratic society. For this reason, after having offered the criticism that we have summarized, the *Philosophie sociale* discusses what legal, political and philosophical basess can be used to build a new social order, a new society able to overcome the "social pathologies" of the *Ancien Régime* – from tyranny to lack of freedom and equality. According to Dobruska, there are three cornerstones of a new democratic order. The first basis is legal, and this provides for a good Constitution, which justifies the established order. In the first part of the *Philosophie sociale*, which has moreof a philosophical and revolutionary intonation, we read:

> Let's start from there (from a good constitution). We will generally and briefly find the most rigorous equality, as in nature. No privileges, no preferences. The same freedom for everyone, since this is the natural property and an indispensable need for the happiness of each individual.[151]

---

148 Rousseau, *Du contrat social*, II. 7. 91: [La loi judaïque, toujours subsistante, celle de l'enfant d'Ismaël, qui depuis dix siècles régit la moitié du monde, annoncent encore aujourd'hui les grands hommes qui les ont dictées; et tandis que l'orgueilleuse philosophie ou l'aveugle esprit de parti ne voit en eux que d'heureux imposteurs, le vrai politique admire dans leurs institutions ce grand et puissant génie qui préside aux établissements durable] (Idem, *The Social Contract*, 38*)*.
149 *Loc. cit.*
150 Dobruska, *Philosophie sociale*, 39.
151 *Ibidem*, 43: [En partant de là, (d'une bonne constitution) nous trouverons généralement et en somme la plus rigoureuse égalité, telle qu'elle est dans la nature, nul privilège, nulle préférence. Liberté égale pour tous; parce qu'elle est la propriété naturelle, et un besoin indispensable au bonheur d'un chacun].

From this first strand follows logically the second one. If a new democratic society is to be achieved, one that is rooted in the Universal Constitution, the principle that justified previous social orders, namely the pernicious identification of the gods and sovereigns, who represented the divinity, must be abolished.[152]

Therefore, Dobruska invites both the wise men of every nation (*les sages de la terre*), who desire the happiness of mankind, and the French people, to move from a traditional legitimacy of the social order, as Max Weber would express it, based on divinity, to a principle of legal-rational legitimacy, based on his Universal Constitution, of which we will go into more detail shortly.

The last cornerstone of Dobruska's social philosophy refers to the ultimate source of the principles of the Universal Constitution. Such a source is to be found in thinkers and in philosophical and religious traditions in which love for the truth is expressed. For our author, there are three emblematic figures: revolutionaries who have marked the development of "healthy reason".

He begins with Socrates, and then passes to the revolutionary Christ of the Gospels, until he reaches Immanuel Kant.[153]

The first revolution of sound reason was brought about by Socrates' philosophy, to which goes the merit of having overthrown the philosophical system of the Sophists. Socrates encourages us to search for the truth, to reach the knowledge that springs from the theoretical reflection of thought, rather than from that of the senses.

The second revolution is that of Christ, whom Dobruska considers the second martyr of sound reason, crucified by Jewish priests and Roman praetors.[154] He is the great disorganizer of the astute pagan theocracy and of the theocracy of Moses, and has had the merit of separating heaven from earth – the transcendent questions, linked to faith and spirit, from the worldly ones. He urged the believer to submit to his law and pay respect to it. The verb of Christ, however, has been sunk by the dogmas of priests for almost eighteen centuries – as we read in the *Philosophie sociale* – although there have been several revolutions in the ecclesiastical sphere. Just think of Luther, Zwingli, Melanchthon,

---

152 *Ibidem*, 42.

153 *Ibidem*, 47.

154 *Ibidem*, 48: [Le Christ révolutionnaire et second martyr de la saine raison, crucifié par les prêtres juifs, et le préteur romain, comme désorganisateur de l'astucieuse théocratie des Payens et de Moyse, et pour avoir séparé le ciel de la terre, en disant: j'ai accompli les prédictions de Moyse, etc. etc., en rappelant la morale à la bienfaisance, en apprenant qu'il ne faut pas seulement se soumettre à la loi, mais qu'il faut aussi lui rendre hommage. Voilà la seconde révolution de la saine raison, le second degré de la philosophie].

Calvin, Huss, Spinoza, Leibniz, Locke and others. During all these centuries, reason has begun more and more to stagger, its losses become more and more frequent, and the night more and more deep.[155]

The third revolution of healthy reason is to be found in the thought of the German philosopher Immanuel Kant. Kant was the great disorganizer of all philosophical systems. It is due to the immortal Kant, as Dobruska calls him, if humanity has overcame the second stage and has been able to embrace the third stage of its development. We will see later how this definition of Kant as a revolutionary and "disorganizer" of philosophical thought had immediate echos in the German intellectual world, through the writing of Johann August Eberhard. After having placed himself under the strong and authoritative sign of Kantian work, Dobruska makes a forecast of the future full of pathos:

> Religion of the Truth of Principles! I already see the nameless sages preparing their hearts to receive your worship. Come, come, after so many idolatries and idols, so that finally humanity can rejoice in your divinity![156]

3.12 Essence and Form of the Universal Constitution

In the second section of the *Philosophie sociale* the Universal Constitution is outlined, divided into two fundamental parts (Fig. 2).

The first part of the Constitution contains the exposition of the ultimate principle (the principle of self-preservation) and of the seventy principles that follow from it and that govern society. This part is mandatory and cannot in any way be called into question by members of society. The second part of the Constitution, which is subordinate to the first, represents the application of the principles themselves. The latter, in fact, when put into practice, give rise to

---

155 *Loc. cit.*: [Mais l'hydre scolastique dont toutes les têtes n'avoient pu être abattues, reparaissant bientôt, infecta la saine et naturelle doctrine du Christ, en la couvrant d'un amas confus et informe de dogmes sacerdotaux, de commentaires et de nouveaux systêmes philosophiques; fléau du genre humain, pendant presque dix-huit siècles, malgré les diverses révolutions philosophiques et sacerdotales de Luther, Zuingle, Melanchton, Calvin, Huss, Spinoza, Hobbes, Leibnitz, Loke, et autres,la raison toujours plus chancellante, n'en devint que plus malade, les disputes, les égaremens toujours plus fréquens, et la nuit toujours plus sombre].

156 *Ibidem*, 50: [Religion de la vérité des principes! je vois déjà des savans sans nombre préparer tous les cœurs à recevoir ton culte. Viens, ô viens, et qu'après tant d'idolâtries et d'idoles, qui t'ont occupée, l'humanité jouisse une fois de ta *divinité*!].

the political institutions and the entire body of legislation of a democratic state.[157] The implementation of the second part of the Constitution is the responsibility of the general assemblies and is not dealt with by Dobruska in his work.

The basic thesis, expressed in the first part of the Constitution, is that the principles that inspire the latter must be sought "in the general order of nature, in the immense system of created beings".[158]

It is thanks to nature that everything lives and moves.[159] If you want to judge a Constitution and its principles, you will have to consider whether these principles reflect the laws of physical nature.[160]

Why is the first part of the Constitution mandatory, while the second part must be subordinate and "obey" the first? There are two reasons. The first reason is that, thanks to the application of the first part of the Universal Constitution, society acquires important prerogatives: rights, freedom, independence and sovereignty.[161] The second reason is that only the strict application of the principles can guarantee the stability of the established social order and avoid revolutionary crises, which are intended to break it down. Dobruska thus comes to an important conclusion:

> We can then affirm that a people that does not want to expose itself to revolutionary crises, or submit to the sword of despots, must hurry to establish and recognize the inviolable authority of the first part of a veritable Constitution; if the people will submit to such a point [i.e. to the first part of the Constitution], thus subordinating the second part in such a way that it [i.e. the second part] will be nothing more than the enactment [of the first] and its guarantee; once such a regime is assured, the people will no longer have to fear revolutions, nor foil conspiracies, nor break down tyrants, because one part of the Constitution will be the guarantee of the other.[162]

---

157 *Ibidem*, 53.
158 *Loc. cit.* [C'est dans l'ordre général de la nature, dans l'immense système des êtres créés, qu'il faut chercher la première partie].
159 *Loc. cit.*
160 *Ibidem*, 54.
161 *Ibidem*, 58.
162 *Ibidem*, 58: [Nous pouvons donc affirmer, qu'un peuple qui ne veut point s'exposer aux crises révolutionnaires, ou se livrer au glaive des despotes, se hâtera d'instituer et de reconnoître l'inviolable autorité de cette première partie de toute véritable Constitution; et qu'il lui subordonnera tellement la seconde, qu'elle n'en sera jamais que l'émanation et la garantie; bien assuré qu'avec un tel régime, il n'aura ni révolutions à craindre, ni complots à déjouer, ni tyrans à détruire, puisque toujours une partie de sa Constitution sera la garantie de l'autre].

Our author also reminds us that the first part of the Constitution is nothing more than an elementary code, in which the legislator finds his frame of reference for legislating, while the people draw from it indications for sanctioning the laws, drawn up by the legislator himself.

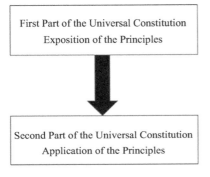

First Part of the Universal Constitution
Exposition of the Principles

Second Part of the Universal Constitution
Application of the Principles

Fig. 2: Essence and Form of the Universal Constitution.
Source: author.

According to Dobruska, the promulgation of laws by the legislator must respect the hierarchy of regulatory sources. It starts from the basic principle of the Constitution, which is the principle of self-conservation and the happiness of individuals (*le Principe*). From this principle arise the other principles, which concern the different thematic areas addressed in the Constitution (freedom, equality, education, sovereignty, the legislative and executive body, etc.). The law must be based on the ultimate principle (Fig. 3).

According to Dobruska, "laws are not, and must not be, but the guarantee of freedom and equality, or the right to exercise all efforts aimed at achieving supreme happiness in society".[163]

In a democratic society, the people are given the right and the power to control the content of laws, which may be passed or rejected by them. The right of the people lies in verifying that the laws are in conformity with the ultimate principle, i.e. self-conservation, with all the principles elaborated in the Universal Constitution, and with the rights that derive from these same principles. Only through this process of continuous monitoring and verification of legislation is it possible to achieve the ultimate goal of society: the happiness and prosperity of citizens.

---

163 *Ibidem*, 89: [Les loix ne sont donc et ne doivent être que la garantie de la liberté et de l'égalité, ou du droit de l'exercice de tous ses efforts, pour atteindre le suprême bonheur dans la société].

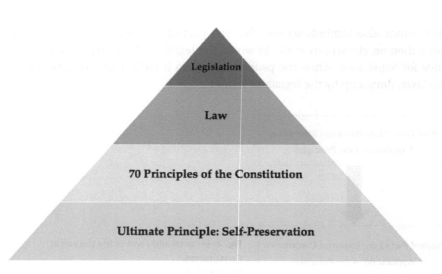

Fig. 3: Hierarchy of the Sources of Law according to the Universal Constitution of Dobruska. *Source*: author.

But how does the people verify that the ultimate principle and the principles of the Universal Constitution are respected by the laws? How does the people know these principles? Dobruska proposes a solution:

> Now, the process of bringing the people to this knowledge is very simple. The different definitions of the principle and of the law that can result from it, will be written on a tablet, in the form of commandments. This tablet will be displayed both before the eyes of the people, in the popular sections, and before the eyes of the legislators, in the national assembly. Each law will be preceded by an explanatory notation of the right on which it is based. Looking at the table, the people judge the truth or falsehood of the explanatory notation, and the consequence of it. The people then grant or refuse to grant that law, with their decision preceded by an explanatory notation, as the legislator has done, of whether they accept or reject what has been proposed.[164]

---

164 *Ibidem*, 59–60: [Or, pour amener le peuple à cette connoissance, le procédé est bien simple. Sur un tableau toujours exposé aux yeux du peuple dans les sections populaires, comme aux yeux des législateurs dans l'assemblée nationale, seront écrites en forme de commandement les diverses définitions du principe et du droit qui peut en résulter. Chaque loi étant précédée d'un considérant explicatif du droit, sur lequel elle se fonde. Le peuple en jettant les yeux sur le tableau, juge de la vérité ou de la fausseté du considérant, et de la conséquence qu'on en a tirée ; dès-lors il accorde ou refuse sa sanction, en faisant, ainsi que le législateur, précéder sa décision d'un considérant, soit qu'il accepte ou qu'il refuse].

As we can see, the ultimate principle (self-preservation) and the seventy principles of the Universal Constitution that derive from the analysis of the various thematic nuclei of the Constitution (freedom, equality, etc.) are to be considered as real "commandments written on a table, exposed to the people in the popular sections and to the legislator in the national assembly".

One cannot but notice the similarity with the commandments dictated, according to the biblical account, by God to Moses on the tablets of the law. Now it is no longer God who dictates the commandments to the legislator but nature, through acute observation, which aims to be scientific and truthful, based as it is on the reason that regulates physical reality. The principles, contained in the first part of the Constitution, are equivalent to truths, which cannot be called into question.

That these principles should not be questioned is very well understood by the generation that lived (and often suffered) under the *Ancien Régime*. This generation subsequently fought for the French Revolution and identified itself with it,[165] even women[166] and children.

But what will happen when the revolutionary crisis is over? How will it be possible to guarantee that the following generations can still believe with conviction and passion in the principles of the Universal Constitution, without letting themselves be distracted or enchanted by some "meddlesome person of their time, possessor of the mystery" and believing in him instead? This kind of case presents a risk of returning to the pre-revolutionary starting point. Dobruska wonders about the prospects of the order that came out of the revolution.

In order to avoid a return to the past, future generations will have to be taught the first part of the Constitution, which contains "stable and precise definitions, clear and well-argued ideas on freedom, equality, the sovereignty of the people, powers, principles, and rights".[167]

---

165 *Ibidem*, 65.

166 *Ibidem*, 64. This is unfortunately the only time that Moses Dobruska mentions women and puts them on the same level as children. Historical literature shows that women – starting with Olympe de Gouges (1748–1793), who drew up the famous *Declaration of the Rights of Woman and the Female Citizen* in 1791 – played an important role in the French Revolution. See, for example, Erica Joy. Mannucci, *Baionette nel focolare. La Rivoluzione francese e la ragione delle donne*, (Milano: Franco Angeli, 2016).

167 *Ibidem*, 66: [Il nous faut donc dans cette première partie de la constitution, des définissions stables et pré-cises, des idées claires et bien développées, sur la liberté, sur l'égalité, sur la souveraineté du peuple, sur les pouvoirs, sur les principes et sur le droit; idées sans le secours desquelles on ne pourra jamais décider justement ce que sont et ce que doivent être les loix].

These ideas and principles form the basis of the laws to be enacted by the legislator. So future generations will not only *feel* these principles with emotion but will also *know*[168] them. In fact, the healthy truth "penetrates into the heart and spirit. It warms the sensitivity of one [heart] and the understanding of the other [spirit]. It lives with both of them in an eternal bond of love and trust. This is the prerogative of the healthy truth".[169]

It is still not enough for the first part of the Constitution to be taught to the next generation with passion and intellectual rigor. Dobruska recommends that ideas and arguments be written simply and in precise language: clear, and not as obscure as the language used by philosophers. It must be written in a convincing way: only in this way can the Constitution serve the young, the next generation, as an elementary and catechetical book. Only in this way will the youth be educated and socialized – we would say today – according to this "religion of principles". According to Dobruska, "light will be drawn from it instead of the formulas of a creed, conviction instead of mysteries, duties instead of sacraments".[170]

According to our author, an example of an unclear and confusing argument is a famous sentence from the *Social Contract* of Jean-Jacques Rousseau. As is well known, the Geneva philosopher writes in his work: "Man is born free; and everywhere he is in chains".[171] According to Dobruska this sentence is unclear. Which man is Rousseau talking about? The one in the natural state or the social man? He cannot have in mind the man in the state of nature, who we know to be free. Does he mean the man who lives in society? If this were the case, however, the statement would be likewise obscure because in the state of culture man was certainly not born free, but strongly dependent on others.[172] Criticism

---

168 *Ibidem*, 67.

169 *Ibidem*, 68: [La saine vérité pénètre à la fois dans le cœur et dans l'esprit; elle échauffe la sensibilité de l'un en frapant l'entendement de l'autre, et vit avec tous deux dans une liaison éternelle d'amour et de confiance; tel est l'apanage de la saine vérité].

170 *Ibidem*, 72: [Elle y puiseroit la lumière au lieu de formules de croyance, la conviction au lieu de mystères, et les devoirs au lieu de sacremens].

171 Rousseau, *Du contrat social*, I. 1. 3 (Idem, *The Social Contract*, 5).

172 Dobruska, *Philosophie sociale*, 70–71: [De quel homme parle-t-il? de l'homme dans l'état de nature, ou de l'homme social? Il ne peut avoir en vue l'homme de la nature, celui-là n'est point dans les fers. Il parcourt aujourd'hui librement comme autrefois les forêts. Il cherche sans contrainte sa boisson et sa nourriture. Est-ce de l'homme social que veut parler l'immortel philosophe? alors comment concevoir que celui-ci peut être considéré comme né libre? Il est né dépendant et très – dépendant. Quelle serait son existence future dans la société s'il demeuroit sans éducation, et ses facultés sans développement; enfin, si absolument informe, il

is not so much directed at the principle theorized by Rousseau, which Dobruska has understood perfectly and with which he agrees, but at the lack of clarity and precision of the sentence.

According to Dobruska, Rousseau should have formulated his principle in this way:

> Man in the state of nature is free and independent like all other animals. Nature has pro-vided him with an instinct, which is sufficient for him in an independent regime; he has then joined in society, and in the whole known world, we find the man who lives with his fellow men. In this more or less developed union, needs have increased proportionally. Almost everywhere, the more the culture of instinct was perfected, the more advantage was taken of it to oppress man and tighten the limits of his dependence; and *he is every-where in chains*.[173]

As we shall see later, individuals in society are no longer autonomous, as was the case in the natural state, but increasingly dependent on each other. How-ever, as Rousseau thought, this does not mean that they should not be free, al-ways in chains or unhappy. In order to achieve happiness in society, it is necessary that laws based on constitutional principles are correctly applied and that the people are vigilant and control the work of the legislative body. This is the main task of the people: to watch over, "in a scrupulous way and with sin-cerity, the preservation of the first part of the Constitution".[174]

The constitutional principles elaborated by Dobruska are based, as it emerges more clearly in the following, on the knowledge and the acute observa-tion of the human soul and behavior, but also on observations of nature and the natural order from which they draw inspiration. For this reason, constitu-tional principles are, first and foremost, statements of truth,[175] from which we can derive the rules governing social life. They therefore represent, for the

---

devoit être élevé dans l'état de pure nature, et destiné, à jouir de l'indépendance animale, cette destination même dépend tout-à-fait du vœu de ses parens ou de ses tuteurs].

173 *Ibidem*, 71–72: [L'homme dans l'état de nature est libre et indépendant comme tous les autres animaux. La nature l'a pourvu d'un instinct, qui lui suffisent dans un régime indépend-ant; il se réunit après en société, et dans tout le monde connu, nous trouvons l'homme vivant en société avec ses semblables. Dans cette réunion plus ou moins développée, les besoins aug-mentèrent proportionnellement. Presque partout, plus la culture de l'instinct se perfectionnoit, plus on en tiroit avantage pour opprimer l'homme et-serrer les liens de *sa dépendance*; et *il est partout dans les fers*].

174 *Ibidem*, 60: [un peuple qui veille avec scrupule et sincérité à la conservation rigoureuse de la première partie de sa Constitution].

175 *Loc. cit.*: [nous devons nous hâter de prévenir les idées, que pourraient faire naître ce tableau uniquement destiné à contenir l'énonciation des vérités, qui sont la base de la Constitution].

legislator, guides for the promulgation of laws. Dobruska wonders: "Are the principles the only infallible guides, then? Of course!"[176]

In the first part of the Constitution, Dobruska proposes an in-depth analysis of individuals and society, through the lenses of the social philosopher and sociologist. Seventeen chapters analyze a number of key issues in order to reach, at the end of each chapter, the relative "principles", that is to say the rules or norms of action that the legislator will have to apply, through the promulgation of laws, in order to achieve the ultimate goal of the Universal Constitution: the happiness and prosperity of citizens and of the whole of society.

Our author bases his analysis both on philosophical literature by ancient and pre-modernthinkers, as well as his contemporaries, and on the direct observation of nature and men.

3.12.1 The Seventy Principles of the Universal Constitution

The seventy principles that Dobruska distills from popular philosophical-social and sociological analysis are set out in seventeen chapters, dedicated to the following themes:
- man
- social contract
- principle, rights and selfishness
- morality of the individual
- morality and immorality of society
- the right of the strongest and the right to deception
- law, power, and body of law
- sovereignty
- public contributions
- administration
- liberty
- equality
- education
- penalties and offences
- the unity of interest
- democracy, aristocracy, monarchy, representative democracy
- conclusion

---

176 *Loc. cit.*: [Les principes sont donc les seuls guides infaillibles? Sans doute].

For the sake of clarity, we have listed all seventy principles in the second appendix, while in the following they will be presented in a discursive and concise manner.

3.12.2 Social Functions of the Universal Constitution

Before examining the new themes and their principles in more detail, it is worth summarizing what has been said so far. The functions of Dobruska's Universal Construction are essentially threefold.

The first function is that of a primary vehicle for social education, which teaches citizens how to live and interact in society, with their peers and with political institutions. Today we would call this civic education. The first part of the Constitution nourishes and improves people, because it educates them and gives them a profound knowledge of how to live together, so that there will be no abuse of power and freedom will dominate.

The nourishment that the Universal Constitution can offer is not only that its study touches feelings and transmits knowledge. It also indicates a clear orientation for life in society, which brings well-being to all individuals.

These are real benefits which individuals have in a democratic society. And these real advantages derive from the fact that the Universal Constitution affords to men the possessionof rights, such as, for example, the right to freedom, equality, freedom of religion, and private property.

This brings us to the second fundamental function of the Universal Constitution, that of conferring citizenship. All individuals living in a democratic society based on the Constitution are always citizens, i.e. people with citizenship rights.

It is unthinkable that in a democratic society there is a division between being men and being citizens, as was the case during the absolutist monarchy of the *Ancien Régime*. Human beings interact with each other. Throughout their lives, some people progress more than others in different areas of social action – in their spiritual and intellectual lives and in economic prosperity. Nevertheless, they still belong to the same category, the human race. We read in the *Philosophie sociale*:

> It is therefore clear that the first part of the Constitution is nothing more than a social education, which provides an instrument, based on law, according to which man must live with his fellow human beings in society, without being changed in his essence by this association, that is, remaining the same, without becoming a being of another kind.

> This false and counter-natural distinction characterizes instead the monarchic and tyrannical system, which has established the division between man and citizen.[177]

The fact that the status of citizens always belongs to the human being is one of the cornerstones of the Universal Constitution of Dobruska:

> Does man cease to be such just because he lives in society? Living in society is only a state of improvement and refinement. Is it possible to assume that man loses the enjoyment of his rights because he finds himself living with his fellow men, in order to develop and perfect the natural advantages of each other? The purpose of his association is nothing more than to enjoy human rights, together with those of a citizen, that is to say, of a cultured man.[178]

It must be stressed that, for Dobruska, every individual in a democratic state must always be a citizen, that is to say, a holder of rights. Furthermore, all citizens must enjoy the same rights.

Dobruska's harsh criticism of the absolutist monarchy of Louis XVI of Bourbon, guillotined on January 21, 1793, is clear. Under the monarchy of Louis XVI, French society, which in 1780 included about 28 million people, was mainly agrarian and strongly stratified, with little upward social mobility. The upper social classes and the centers of political and spiritual power revolved around the monarchy and its court, and included the nobility and the clergy. At a lower level of social stratification was the so-called "third estate", which contained peasants and members of the upper middle class alike. The final step of the social stratification was occupied by the peasant serfs. In the eighties of the eighteenth century, there were still about half a million serfs in France, mainly in France-Comté and Nivernais.[179] In the countryside, there was a subsistence agricultural economy for farmers' families, not a rural market economy.

---

177 *Ibidem*, 74: [Il est donc évident que la première partie d'une Constitution n'étant purement qu'une éducation sociale, laquelle ne donne que le moyen fondé en droit d'après lequel l'homme doit vivre en société avec ses semblables, sans être changé dans son essence par cette association, sans qu'il soit possible qu'il ne reste pas le même être, ni qu'il puisse devenir un être d'un autre genre, cette distinction fausse et contre nature ne peut être que le système du monarchisme et de la tyrannie, qui ont établi ce système de distinction et de division entre l'homme et le citoyen].

178 *Ibidem*, 74–75: [Car pour vivre en société, l'homme cesse-t-il d'être homme ? L'état social n'étant pour lui qu'un état d'amélioration et de perfection, peut-il perdre la jouissance de ses droits d'homme, parce qu'il s'est réuni avec ses semblables pour développer et perfectionner mutuellement ses avantages naturels? tandis que son association n'a pour but que de jouir de ses droits d'homme réunis avec ceux de citoyen, c'est-à-dire, d'homme cultivé].

179 Peter McPhee, *A Social History of France 1780–1914* (New York: Palgrave, 2004), 10 (I ed. 1992).

Membership of a social class was not usually acquired on merit, since only in exceptional cases could a person be ennobled. Almost always, it was a status ascribed by birth. The rights and privileges of a legal and fiscal nature, or linked to a specific French territory, depended on social hierarchy and wealth, but also on personal identity.[180] In eighteenth century France, the majority of the population was Catholic: those belonging to other faiths were discriminated against. Think, for example, of the strong restrictions on the civil rights of Protestants (who could marry only after obtaining a license from the sovereign), or the poll tax for Jews.[181] Consequently, depending on the position they occupied in the social stratification in the *Ancien Régime*, some enjoyed many fiscal and legal rights and privileges compared with others who had none at all, such as peasant serfs.

In a monarchic or tyrannical regime, human beings are treated as unequal, and a distinction is made between man and citizen:

> [. . .] this distinction, false and against nature, can only belong to a monarchic or dictatorial regime, which has established this system of separation between man and citizen. But the reason is well understood: wanting to get rid of human rights, the despots hurry to banish man from society. On the one hand, human rights, on the other hand, those of the citizen. It is understandable that tyrants are more comfortable separating something that cannot be separated.[182]

The Universal Constitution of Dobruska aims to abolish the possibility of great privileges and enormous inequalities in rights between individuals, thanks to its guarantee of freedom, understood – and we will see later – as equality of rights. To this end, the duty of reciprocity between human beings and popular sovereignty must be affirmed.

Democratic society, to which the social philosophy of Dobruska aspires, is based on constitutional principles and laws, which guarantee equal rights for all citizens. In such a society, everyone must contribute as much as they can to the common good. No one can be excluded any more.

---

180 McPhee, *A Social History of France 1780–1914*, 38.

181 *Ibidem*, 43.

182 Dobruska, *Philosophie sociale*, 74: [. . .] cette distinction fausse et contre nature ne peut être que le système du monarchisme et le la tyrannie, qui ont établi ce système de distinction et de division entre l'homme et le citoyen. Mais on en conçoit bien la raison; c'est qu'étant gênés par les droits de l'homme, les despotes se hâtèrent de bannir l'homme de la société. De-là les droits de l'homme et ceux du citoyen. On conçoit que les despotes étoient bien plus à leur aise, séparant ainsi une chose qui ne pouroît eus séparée].

Finally, the last function of the Universal Constitution is to avoid social disorganization and the re-emergence of tyrants or the reaffirmation of a monarchic regime. As we have seen, if the legislator, under the strict control of the people, meticulously applies the principles of the first part of the Constitution, abuse of power and rebellion can be avoided. In this way, the stability of the social order is not endangered.

3.12.3 The Purpose of the Universal Constitution

As we shall see in more detail below, the ultimate aim of the Universal Constitution is the happiness of citizens and society as a whole. It is now necessary to focus on the principles that follow from this. The starting point in such a discussion can only be a definition of the human being.

Dobruska questions the nature, the aspirations, the desires, the needs of the human being, whom he calls the "new sovereign", the *nouveau souverain*, both in the state of nature and in that state of culture, that is, in society.

The first general definition, from which the *Philosophie sociale* starts, is that of *être-homme*,[183] that is to say of a human being. This is a dynamic living being in transformation, capable of evolving and reaching the highest material, cultural, and spiritual peaks. In fact, the human being must be understood as "a living being, whose instinct is susceptible to the widest development and the greatest perfection".[184]

Dobruska goes on to say that "this definition presents us with man in all his scope, from the cradle of brute instinct, so to speak, to the highest degree of his culture and his virility".

It is an anthropological vision, which "endows man with knowledge, virtue and happiness in the same way as error, vice and unhappiness". In addition to having the greatest faculties to evolve, improve, and reach the highest degree of perfection in the most diverse areas of intellectual, moral, and material life, man is also capable of harmful and destructive actions.

This philosophical reflection on man's possibility of perfecting himself is certainly not new. It is part of a theoretical perspective widespread among the

---

183 *Ibidem*, 82.
184 *Loc. cit.* [Nous définirons généralement l'être-homme. L'être-homme est un être vivant dont l'instinct est susceptible du développement le plus étendu et de la plus grande perfection. Cette définition nous présente l'homme dans toute son étendue, depuis le berceau de l'instinct brut pour ainsi parler, jusqu'au plus haut degré de sa culture et de sa virilité].

Enlightenment thinkers of the time, which emphasised the concept of man's "perfectibility".

Although there is not complete unanimity among scholars,[185] the term "perfectibility" is generally attributed to Jean-Jacques Rousseau, whose writings were well known to our Dobruska. It is in his second speech to the Academy of Dijon, on the origin and foundations of inequalities, written in 1754, that Rousseau sets out his idea of the perfectibility of man in the civil state, compared to man in the natural or primitive state. Rousseau reminds us that the difference between man and animal lies in a specific faculty of the former, that of "perfecting oneself". More precisely, the Genevan philosopher states:

> However, even if the difficulties attending all these questions should still leave room for difference in this respect between men and brutes, there is another, very specific, quality which distinguishes them and which will admit of no dispute. This is the faculty of self-improvement, which, by the help of circumstances, gradually develops all the rest of our faculties, and is inherent in the species as in the individual: whereas a brute is, at the end of a few months, all he will ever be during his whole life, and his species, at the end of a thousand years, exactly what it was the first year of that thousand. Why is man alone liable to grow into a dotard? Is it not because he returns, in this, to his primitive state; and that, while the brute, which has acquired nothing and has therefore nothing to lose, still retains the force of instinct, man, who loses, by age or accident, all that his *perfectibility* had enabled him to gain, falls by this means lower than the brutes themselves?[186]

Dobruska assumes that man can improve and perfect his human nature, that he retains the potential for change in himself, even though his soul is very complex, made up of lights and shadows.

---

185 Gianluca Dioni, "Perfectibilité e perfectio. Rousseau e Wolff, armonie e dissonanze," in *La filosofia politica di Rousseau*, eds. Giulio Maria Chiodi and Roberto Gatti (Milano: Franco Angeli, 2012), 151.

186 Jean-Jacques Rousseau, *Discours sur l'origine et les fondements de l'inégalité parmi les hommes* (Amsterdam: Chez Marc-Michel Rey, 1755), 31: [Mais, quand les difficultés qui environnent toutes ces questions laisseraient quelque lieu de disputer sur cette différence de l'homme et de l'animal, il y a une autre qualité très spécifique qui les distingue, et sur laquelle il ne peut y avoir de contestation, c'est la faculté de se perfectionner; faculté qui, à l'aide des circonstances, développe successivement toutes les autres, et réside parmi nous tant dans l'espèce que dans l'individu, au lieu qu'un animal est, au bout de quelques mois, ce qu'il sera toute sa vie, et son espèce, au bout de mille ans, ce qu'elle était la première année de ces mille ans. Pourquoi l'homme seul est-il sujet à devenir imbécile? N'est-ce point qu'il retourne ainsi dans son état primitif, et que, tandis que la bête, qui n'a rien acquis et qui n'a rien non plus à perdre, reste toujours avec son instinct, l'homme reperdant par la vieillesse ou d'autres accidents tout ce que sa perfectibilité lui avait fait acquérir, retombe ainsi plus bas que la bête même?] (Idem, *A Discourse on a Subject proposed by the Academy of Dijon*, in *The Social Contract*, 184–185).

He mentions in this regard already on the cover of his work the second verse of *An Essay on Man*, by the English poet Alexander Pope (1688–1744), published in 1733–34.[187] In the second epistle of the poem, Pope writes:

> Know then thyself, presume not God to scan;
> The proper study of mankind is man.
> Plac'd on this isthmus of a middle state,
> A being darkly wise, and rudely great
> With too much knowledge for the Sceptic side,
> With too much weakness for the Stoic's pride,
> He hangs between; in doubt to act, or rest;
> In doubt to deem himself a God, or Beast

Although it is written in verse, in reality it is a philosophical essay, which gave Alexander Pope a great reputation and influenced many thinkers of the seventeenth century, including René Descartes (1596–1650), Blaise Pascal (1623–1662) and Samuel von Pufendorf (1632–1694). The 18th-century Enlightenment also drew inspiration from it, and traces of Pope's text can be found, among others, in Georges-Louis de Buffon (1707–1788), Denis Diderot (1713–1784), Rousseau, and Anne Robert Jacques Turgot (1727–1781).

In fact, it's no accident that Dobruska quotes Pope on the cover of the *Philosophie sociale*. He is joined to the English poet by a common cognitive project, that of investigating, in an impartial manner, the human soul, to understand all its facets. A search that also extends to the contradictions, the sublime, and the most miserable aspects of man, in the desire to discover what can bring him happiness. In a nutshell, this attention to the complexity of human nature and its dual character, which extends from the highest good to the lowest evil, are to be found in fifteenth-century humanism and, in particular, in the *Oratio de hominis dignitate* of Count Giovanni Pico della Miarandola (1463–1494).[188]

In his *Oration on the Dignity of Man*, Giovanni Pico affirms:

> Neither a fixed abode nor a form that is thine alone nor any function peculiar to thyself have we given thee, Adam, to the end that according to thy longing and according to thy judgment thou mayest have and possess what abode, what form, and what functions thou thyself shalt desire. The nature of all other beings is limited and constrained

> within the bounds of laws prescribed by Us. Thou, constrained by no limits, in accordance with thine own free will, in whose hand We have placed thee, shalt ordain for

---

187 Alexander Pope, *An Essay on Man. Epistle I–IV* (London: J. Wilford, 1733–1734).
188 Silvana Greco, "Heresy, Apostasy, and the Beginnings of Social Philosophy. Moses Dobruska reconsidered," *Materia giudaica* 20–21 (2015–2016), 458.

thyself the limits of thy nature. We have set thee at the world's center that thou mayest from thence more easily observe whatever is in the world. We have made thee neither of heaven nor of earth, neither mortal nor immortal, so that with freedom of choice and with honor, as though the maker and molder of thyself, thou mayest fashion thyself in whatever shape thou shalt prefer. Thou shalt have the power to degenerate into the lower forms of life, which are brutish. Thou shalt have the power, out of thy Soul's judgment, to be reborn into the higher forms, which are divine.[189]

Instead of the mystical ascent suggested by Pico, Dobruska, who is influenced by the *esprit* of the time, conceived the perfection of man as the development of intellectual and material desires (*Begehrungsvermögen,* in his original German draft), which can only be achieved in society, thanks to social interactions with others. His theory combines the concept of Rousseau and partly that of Wolff. Rousseau, in fact, had already pointed out in his *Discourse on the Origin of Inequality* how the improvement of the human intellect is supported and spurred on by passions, which lead to new knowledge. Behind passions, man's deep needs are often hidden beyond the primary ones, which for Rousseau are nourishment, sexuality, and rest:

> The passions, again, originate in our wants, and their progress depends on that of our knowledge; for we cannot desire or fear anything, except from the idea we have of it, or from the simple impulse of nature.[190]

For Dobruska, both intellectual and material desires encourage man to seek perfection.

In order to achieve the highest perfection in society, however, a fundamental condition must be met: the enjoyment by every person of full citizenship.[191] Only where class and rank privileges are abolished and freedom, understood as "equality of rights", is guaranteed, can man reach the highest level of culture and virility.

The term "virility" should not be understood in opposition to that of "femininity", as the stereotyped traits associated with the social construction of mas-

---

189 Giovanni Pico della Mirandola, *Discorso sulla dignità dell'uomo,* ed., Francesco Bausi (Parma: Gianda, 2003), 11 (*The Renaissance Philosophy of Man,* edited by Ernst Cassirer, Paul Oskar Kristeller and John Herman Randall Jr. (Chicago: University of Chicago Press, 1948): 224–225).

190 Rousseau, *Discours sur l'origine et les fondements de l'inégalité,* 36: [Les passions, à leur tour, tirent leur origine de nos besoins, et leur progrès de nos connaissances; car on ne peut désirer ou craindre les choses que sur les idées qu'on en peut avoir, ou par la simple impulsion de la nature] (Idem, *A Discourse on a Subject,* 186).

191 Greco, *Heresy,* "Apostasy, and the Beginnings of Social Philosophy," 459.

culinity might suggest. It is not a "gender issue",[192] but a call to "virtue", in the sense of the strength and courage to oppose the aristocrats, seen as inept and immoral.

As Antoine de Baecque reminds us, the whole political discourse in the revolutionary era hinges on two antagonistic poles: the aristocrat and the patriot. The revolutionary ideology, as often happens with any populist ideology, was also supported by a bodily policy and bodily practices.[193] According to Agnès Steuckardt-Moreau, the attributes of the aristocrat were essentially three: "degeneration, the grotesque, and the mask", while the patriot was characterized "by hygiene, virility, and luminosity".[194] It is well known that the aristocrats paid particular attention to the care of their bodies, making considerable use of makeup, wigs and perfumes.[195] In addition, they paid a lot of attention to their clothes, with their bright colors and precious fabrics.

The fighter for the French Revolution and for the ideals of freedom, equality and brotherhood, on the other hand, was a completely different person, and far from the aristocrat, who lived in a degenerate and embellished way. A new masculinity emerged, based on courage, strength, work and the elimination of male coquetry. This is the man whose intrinsic perfectibility will be promoted by the Universal Constitution, in Dobruska's intentions, in a democratic, free and virile way.

---

192 Although women played a non-marginal role at the time of the French Revolution, Moses Dobruska, unlike other thinkers such as Condorcet, does not devote any specific reflection to women, let alone to their often deplorable condition.

193 A. de Baecque, *Le corps de l'histoire. Métaphores et politique, 1770–1800* (Paris: Calmann-Levy, 1993).

194 Agnès Steuckardt-Moreau, *Endormeur chez Marat (1790–1792)*, in INALF, *Dictionnaire des usages socio-politiques (1770–1815)* (Paris: Klincksieck, 1989) 87–110, esp. 89: [On repère dans la figure de l'aristocrate trois attributs: 'la dégénérescence, le grotesque et le masque' tandis que l'idéal corporel que représente le patriote se caractérise par 'l'hygiène, la virilité, et par la luminosité].

195 Audrey Robin, *Une sociologie du beau sexe. L'homme et les soins de beauté de hier à aujourd'hui* (Paris: L'Harmattan, 2005).

4 Man and Society

4.1 Ethical and Social Principles That Govern Life in Society

The structure of the Universal Constitution, outlined by Dobruska, has its roots in natural law, which serves as a model for the various positive rights. In the following we will seehow our author takes up some theories of the leading exponents of natural law of the seventeenth and eighteenth centuries, while at the same time elaborating new conceptual schemes.

Among the naturalists active in the seventeenth century were Johannes Althusius (1563–1638) and Ugo Grotius (1583–1645),[196] followed by Thomas Hobbes (1588–1679),[197] Baruch Spinoza (1632–1677), Samuel von Pufendorf (1632–1694), and Christian Thomasius (1655–1728). Montesquieu, Locke, Rousseau, and Kant belong to the Enlightenment phase.

Although there are multiple currents of thought within natural law, which even stand in contrast to each other, they are all based on two main theses.

The first thesis is that, in addition to the "positive" law conceived and implemented by men, there is also a non-positive law implicit in "nature".

The second thesis sees natural law as axiologically superior to positive law, so much so that positive law deserves obedience only if it adheres to natural law.[198] The concept of natural law presupposes that there are "norms, which do not depend on the will, but simply on knowledge: norms that can be derived from knowledge of "nature" (the nature of man or the nature of things, as the case may be)".[199]

Starting from these two theses, many exponents of seventeenth- and eighteenth-century natural law share a "model" for the construction of a State and its necessary regulatory framework, characterized by the following three elements.

The first element deals with the idea of a state of nature, a state that precedes the *polis*, i.e. which is pre-political. Individuals in the state of nature are autonomous and, for some thinkers, among them Rousseau, are also free. Almost no natural lawmaker conceives this state of nature as historically located.

---

196 See for example, Guido Fassò, *Storia della filosofia del diritto. II. L'età moderna* (Bari-Roma: Laterza 2001, I. ed. 1968), 81; Antonella Barberini, "La proprietà della Costituzione," *Proprietà e diritti reali*, Vol. 1 (2011): 47.

197 Norberto Bobbio, "Hobbes e il Giusnaturalismo," *Rivista critica di storia della filosofia* 17 (1962), 470.

198 *Ibidem*, 475.

199 Riccardo Guastini, "Sulla validità della costituzione dal punto di vista del positivismo giuridico," *Rivista internazionale di filosofia del diritto* 66 (1989): 426.

The second constituent element is the *pact*, or *social contract*. This is the instrument with which the State is founded, through which civil laws replace natural laws. It must be said that each author fleshes out this model in a different way, according to his own anthropological and political conception. Finally, this social pact gives rise to the last element, namely *the State*.

Dobruska clearly fits into this current of thought and has four main points of interest: (1) the state of nature, (2) the social contract, (3) the state of culture or society, (4) the democratic State. As we can see, with respect to the tripartite scheme of natural law, our author also devotes particular attention to a further step, namely the clarification of the state of society.

4.2 The State of Nature

Like most jusnaturalists, Dobruska conceives the state of nature as a pre-social condition, not historically and geographically determined.

In the state of nature (*Naturzustand*), man (*Naturmensch*), like other living beings, is free and has an instinct for self-preservation and propagation of his own species. He moves freely in the forests, is able to get food, lives in caves,[200] and is able to defend himself from aggression. He hasn't developed a language yet, because he doesn't need it to communicate with other human beings. He is in fact completely autonomous, independent, perfect and sovereign.[201]

Precisely because of this autonomy, man is not forced, in the state of nature, to relate to other human beings, in respect of whom he has not developed his own morals. He's selfish, because he doesn't have to give anything to his fellow men.[202]

The only duty that nature imposes on him is towards himself, towards his own physical body. Towards himself he has a "duty of relationship", a duty of reciprocity, aimed at achieving his own goal: self-preservation or individual conservation.[203]

In the state of nature, all men enjoy the most perfect equality. That is to say, they have the same natural rights and equal access to resources; no one has special private rights and no one is treated preferentially.

---

200 Dobruska, *Philosophie sociale*, 83.
201 *Ibidem*, 144.
202 *Ibidem*, 70 also 83.
203 *Ibidem*, 105, 116.

Unlike the English natural law philosopher Thomas Hobbes, Dobruska believes that men, in their natural state, are not equal to each other in terms of skills and competences.

In the thirteenth chapter of *Leviathan*, Hobbes reminds us that men are equal in both their bodily and spiritual faculties:

> Nature hath made men so equall, in the faculties of nature body, and mind; as that though there bee found one man sometimes manifestly stronger in body, or of quicker mind then another; yet when all us reckoned together, the difference between man, and man, is not so considerable, as that one man can thereupon claim to himselfe any benefit, to which another may not pretend, as well as he. For as to the strength of body, the weakest has strength enough to kill the strongest, either by secret machination, or by confederacy with others, that are in the same danger with himselfe. And as to the faculties of the mind, (setting aside the arts grounded upon words, and especially that skill of proceeding upon generall, and infallible rules, called Science; which very few have, and but in few things; as being not a native faculty, born with us; nor attained, (as Prudence,) while we look after somewhat els,) I find yet a greater equality amongst men, than that of strength. For Prudence, is but Experience; which equall time, equally bestowes on all men, in those things they equally apply themselves unto.[204]

Dobruska, on the other hand, believes that men, although belonging to the same species, differ in their body, intellectual abilities and customs. Equality in physical strength and ability would be for Dobruska "against nature":[205]

> Has nature ever created two beings of the same species, in a perfectly identical form? In the inequality of nuances, [nature] varies itself infinitely and struggles at every moment to create new inventions, so much so that it seems to hate mechanical and laborious equality.[206]

For Hobbes, equality also means having the same ends; that is why men are in bitter competition with each other:

> From this equality of ability, ariseth equality of hope in the attaining of our Ends. And therefore if any two men desire the same thing, which neverthelesse they cannot both enjoy, they become enemaes; and in the way to their End, (which Is princlpally their owne conservation, and sometimes thetr delectation only,) endeavor to destroy, or subdue one an other.[207]

---

204 Thomas Hobbes, *Leviathan*, I. 13 (London: Crooke, 1651, 60–61).
205 Dobruska, *Philosophie sociale*, 189.
206 *Ibidem*, 208: [Créa-t-elle jamais deux êtres de là même espèce, d'une forme parfaitement égale? elle qui, dans l'inégalité de ses nuances, se varie jusqu'à l'infini, et qui se fatigue pour ainsi dire à chaque instant pour des inventions nouvelles, tant elle paroît haïr l'égalité méchanique et fatiguante].
207 Hobbes, *Leviathan*, 61.

Dobruska agrees instead with the diversity postulated by Montesquieu,[208] and with the physical inequality of Rousseau. Precisely because they are not equal in their abilities, even though they are able, in their natural state, to preserve themselves without the help of other human beings,[209] men are not in perpetual conflict with each other. So don't say, with Hobbes, *homo homini lupus*.

At the same time, Dobruska does not share the philosopher's vision of a lost paradise, as Rousseau did. For the latter, in the state of nature, man is not evil, but capable of mercy and compassion, carrying an innate instinct not to make his fellow man suffer. Rousseau observes, in his *Discourse on the Origins of Inequality*:

> Let us conclude then that man in a state of nature, wandering up and down the forests, without industry, without speech, and without home, an equal stranger to war and to all ties, neither standing in need of his fellow-creatures nor having any desire to hurt them, and perhaps even not distinguishing them one from another; let us conclude that, being self-sufficient and subject to so few passions, he could have no feelings or knowledge but such as befitted his situation; that he felt only his actual necessities, and disregarded everything he did not think himself immediately concerned to notice, and that his understanding made no greater progress than his vanity.[210]

For Dobruska, men in the state of nature are neither only good, as for Rousseau, nor only hostile and warlike, as for Hobbes. They do not have any peculiar moral qualities. On the contrary, in their natural state, human beings, as we have just seen, are selfish; they only think of themselves, they act in their own interest and they owe nothing to others.

It should be noted that Dobruska, when speaking of the *être-homme*, never seems to consider women. The female world does not have a specific space in his intellectual horizon.

During the years of the French Revolution, women played an important role; in the eighteenth century there were also important thinkers, both in

---

208 Raymond Aron, *Les étapes de la pensée sociologique. Montesquieu, Comte, Marx, Tocqueville, Durkheim, Pareto, Weber*, 81.

209 Rousseau, *Discours sur l'origine et les fondements de l'inégalité*, 1–2 (Idem, *A Discourse on a Subject*, 174).

210 *Ibidem*, 84–85: [Concluons qu'errant dans les forêts sans industrie, sans parole, sans domicile, sans guerre, et sans liaisons, comme sans nul besoin de ses semblables, comme sans nul désir de leur nuire, peut-être même sans jamais en reconnaître aucun individuellement, l'homme sauvage sujet à peu de passions, et se suffisant à lui-même, n'avait que les sentiments et les lumières propres à cet état, qu'il ne sentait que ses vrais besoins, ne regardait que ce qu'il croyait avoir intérêt de voir, et que son intelligence ne faisait pas plus de progrès que sa vanité] (Idem, *A Discourse on a Subject*, 203).

France – think Olympe de Gouges (1748–1793) – and in England – think Mary Wollstonecraft (1759–1797). Dobruska doesn't seem to have been influenced in any way by this.

4.3 The Social Contract

Dobruska conceives in a different way from Hobbes the motivation that pushes men to leave the state of nature, live in society and sign the social contract. He believes that, with the signing of the pact, men become members *first and foremost* of a society, and not, as Hobbes thought, of a political corpus. For Dobruska, this society is equivalent to a "social ego" (*moi sociale* – Rousseau called it *moi commun*[211]).

The drive to sign the social pact comes from the lack of self-sufficiency and autonomy which characterizes human beings in the state of culture. Out of the autonomy they enjoyed in the state of nature, individuals need their peers to ensure self-preservation, or "individual biological existence".[212] On the other hand, living in society offers human beings two great and significant advantages. Only in the state of society do they have the opportunity to develop and strengthen their desires and intellectual and material abilities at the highest levels.

As we know, for Hobbes, the drive towards society was of a completely different origin. The social pact was necessary in order to guarantee stability to the State and to avoid the strong conflict between men, who are ready to subdue or even eliminate their fellow men in order to achieve their own goals. Hobbes conceives men both as thirsty for power and glory, as well as having a strong need for security. We read about it in the *Leviathan*:

---

211 Rousseau, *Du contrat social*, I. 6: [À l'instant, au lieu de la personne particulière de chaque contractant, cet acte d'association produit un corps moral et collectif composé d'autant de membres que l'assemblée a de voix, lequel reçoit de ce même acte son unité, son moi commun, sa vie et sa volonté] (Idem, *The Social Contract*, 15: "At once, in place of the individual personality of each contracting party, this act of association creates a moral and collective body, composed of as many members as the assembly contains votes, and receiving from this act its unity, its common identity, its life and its will"). Cf. Tracy B. Strong, *Jean-Jacques Rousseau. The Politics of the Ordinary* (Lanham: Rowman & Littlefield, 2002, I ed. 1994), 80.
212 George H. Sabine, *A History of Political Theory*, revised by T. Landon Thorson, Fourth edition, (Hinsdale: Dryden Press, 1973) (I. ed. 1937), 463.

> So that in the first place, I put for a generall inclination of all mankind, a perpetuall and restlesse desire of Power after power, that ceaseth onely in Death. And the cause of this, is not alwayes that a man hopes for a more intensive delight, than he has already attained to, or that he cannot be content with a moderate power: but because he cannot assure the power and means to live well, which he hath present, without the acquisition of more.[213]

For Dobruska, individuals derive a second benefit from living in society: they become citizens, equal bearers of inviolable rights such as the right to freedom and equality.

The contrast with naturalist thinkers of the past, such as Hobbes and Locke, is remarkable. The latter considered that the individuals who adhered to the pact had natural rights, which they had to renounce, as a result of the choice to establish themselves as a community (*pactum unionis*), to give life to the political society (*pactum subiectionis*). For Dobruska, along with Rousseau, individual rights are not transferred *in full* to the Sovereign. Rousseau affirms in his *Social Contract*:

> From whatever side we approach our principle, we reach the same conclusion, that the social compact sets up among the citizens an equality of such a kind, that they all bind themselves to observe the same conditions and should therefore all enjoy the same rights. Thus, from the very nature of the compact, every act of Sovereignty, *i. e.* every authentic act of the general will, binds or favors all the citizens equally.[214]

4.4 The State of Society

According to the doctrine expressed in the *Philosophie sociale*, with the exit from the state of nature and the institution of a civil society, through the social contract, man becomes a social being, that is "a man who lives together with his fellow human beings".[215]

Man lives with other individuals and interacts with them. Thanks to this social interaction, the human being is able to survive and overcome the concurrent lack of autonomy and self-sufficiency. But not just that. It is in society – in

---

213 Hobbes, *Leviathan*, 47 (I. 11).
214 Rousseau, *Du contrat social*, II. 4: [Par quelque côté qu'on remonte au principe, on arrive toujours à la même conclusion; savoir, que le pacte social établit entre les citoyens une telle égalité qu'ils s'engagent tous sous les mêmes conditions, et doivent jouir tous des mêmes droits. Ainsi par la nature du pacte, tout acte de souveraineté, c'est-à-dire tout acte authentique de la volonté générale oblige ou favorise également tous les citoyens] (Idem, *The Social Contract*, 28–29).
215 Dobruska, *Philosophie sociale*, 82.

the state of culture – that the individual succeeds in developing and fulfilling his desires and abilities, intellectual and material, until he reaches the highest levels, through the exchange with other human beings:

> His love for property, the sweetness of fortune, his taste, his appetitive faculty, make him unable to rejoice now in his primitive stage, and to settle for it. He needs society for the development of his appetizing faculty. He is no longer a sovereign being, self-sufficient, totally independent outside himself; he has become a dependent member of the great body of society.[216]

In this social body, which is society, man has the duty to provide for his own sustenance, but also the right to evolve according to his abilities, which for Dobruska vary from individual to individual.

At the same time, however, he must relate to others, also considering their needs and requirements. He can't act selfishly. He cannot only take from others to achieve his own selfish ends, but must also give, so that his fellow beings can in turn develop and evolve. In other words, social interactions between individuals in a democratic society must be based on the ethical principle of reciprocity, which we will discuss in more detail in the following chapter.

Therefore, the social man is also a moral being. He has two moral faculties: reason and feeling.[217]

Society, in Dobruska's vision, is a new whole or rather a sovereign and independent whole, spontaneously composed of the union of primitive individuals, who depend on each other for their livelihood and for the development of their material and intellectual capacities.[218] People are all equal in terms of natural and inalienable rights. They are all social men and, at the same time, holders of rights.

4.5 Social Context and Socialization Process: From the Individual Self to the Social Self

Moses Dobruska's sociological gaze is fixed both on individuals, understood as members of a society, and on society as a whole.

---

216 *Ibidem*, 128: [L'amour des propriétés, les douceurs de la fortune, son goût, sa faculté appétitive développée, le rendent incapable de jouir maintenant de son état primitif, et de s'en contenter. Il a besoin de la société par ce développement de sa faculté appétitive, il n'est plus un être souverain, se suffisant à lui-même, totalement indépendant hors de soi, il est devenu un membre dépendant du grand corps de la société].
217 *Ibidem*, 115.
218 *Ibidem*, 134–135.

This is a view that we can rightly define as "sociological", aimed at portraying individuals and society as they *are* and not as they *should be*, whereas the prescriptive character is instead proper to social philosophy.

This knowledge about the human being as a social being is multifaceted, complex and articulated on several levels, which we could call, using the terminology of today's sociology, micro, meso and macro.

The unit of analysis from which the sociological reflection of Dobruska starts – close in this respect to the liberal philosophical tradition – is the individual and not the group of individuals. Our author never speaks of social groups or movements as collective actors, although he denounces abuses of power and privileges based on belonging to certain social classes. Dobruska sees the individual, in a democratic society, not as a passive but as an active actor, capable of expressing his needs and desires and of fulfilling them.

The individual is also in a constant relationship and exchange with his fellow human beings, who are necessary for his material sustenance (his "self-preservation") and for the improvement of his abilities, which today we will call self-realization.

This subject is not the rational actor of the liberal Adam Smith, who is free to act in different areas of social life, as if he were a single atom. On the contrary, he is strongly rooted in a specific socio-cultural context, regulated by very precise social norms. The set of these social norms, which for Dobruska represents what today we would call "structure", influences the behavior of individuals.

Let's now take a closer look at the three levels of analysis: the micro level focused on the individual, then the meso level, which focuses on the interrelationships between individuals and, finally, the macro level, which explores the influence of the social structure of the wider context in which the individual lives.

4.5.1 At the Micro Level

The individual with whom Dobruska concerns himself is the one who is active in the public sphere, both in the productive (working) and the political sphere. The analysis of men in the private sphere, in particular in the family, is almost completely omitted. This, at least in part, is why women remain in the background, if not absent (alas), in his work. With the distinction between the "public sphere" and the "private sphere", which was emerging in the intellectual debate at the end of the eighteenth century, women were relegated to the private sphere, in the role of wives and mothers.[219] With a few exceptions – think of the already mentioned Olympe de Gouges and Claire Démar (1799–1833) – they disappeared from the public scene for almost a century, until the rise of feminist emancipation movements at the end of the nineteenth century.

Although Dobruska considers men to be endowed with the same rights, he is very careful to preserve individuality, which distinguishes one subject from another, in terms of needs, capacities, and desires. Some human beings may reach the highest perfection of their abilities, while others may not aspire to such a high goal. Some individuals will pursue the improvement of their economic situation until they achieve a life in luxury. Others, on the other hand, will prefer a more modest life in terms of material wealth, with a greater propensity towards the development of their own spirituality.[220] This capacity for human development and improvement is only possible in society. Although Dobruska starts from the individual, his theoretical approach cannot be conceived within methodological individualism.

4.5.2 At the Meso Level

Since individuals in society lose their autonomy from the state of nature, they are obliged to rely on others for their own livelihood and survival.

According to Dobruska, individuals as social beings are forced to interact with each other, both for reasons of mere material survival and for the improvement of their intellectual and creative potential.

Our author emphasizes the importance of relationality, which for him becomes a duty. With a rhetorical question, Dobruska asks himself: "In the social state, is man bound by the duty of relationship towards his fellow men?". And the answer is, unfailingly, "Yes".[221]

This conception of the individual has its roots in the Spinozian model. Spinoza had already placed an emphasis on the relationship, thus overcoming an essentialist approach to the human being, without embracing a holistic vision.[222]

---

219 Higonnet, *Sociability, Social Structure, and the French Revolution*, 101.
220 Dobruska, *Philosophie sociale*, 209.
221 *Ibidem*, 93: [Dans l'état social l'homme est-il tenu au devoir de la relation envers ses semblables? Oui].
222 See Ronald Breiger, *Baruch Spinoza. Monism and Complementarity*, in *Sociological Insights of Great Thinkers: Sociology through Literature, Philosophy, and Science*, ed. Christofer Edling and Jens Rydgren (Santa Barbara, CA: Praeger, 2011), 255–262; Emauele Costa, "Uno Spinoza

As Juliana Merçon points out, Spinoza can be presented as a systemic thinker *lato sensu:*

> The relational ontology that Spinoza proposes with his anti-substantialist vision of modal realities allows us to think of the individual as an open microsystem, whose existence depends on the interaction it maintains with other individuals.[223]

For the development of daily life and the stability of society, the interactions and bonds that the individual builds with his fellow human beings, in particular with those belonging to his generation, but also with those of past generations, are of crucial importance.

Although Dobruska never uses the term "family" in his entire work, and does not specifically analyze the functioning of it, he briefly dwells on the bonds between parents and children. These links are an important element of cohesion for society, not only because of the affective bond they express, but also because they pass on knowledge from one generation to the next. In this spirit, Dobruska cites *The Spirit of the Laws* of Montesquieu, which states that, in order to educate children, parents must be educated. In his attention to the transmission of knowledge from one generation to the next one, the influence of the Jewish world, from which our author comes, is also evident. According to Dobruska, parents have the task of directing and controlling the formation of children, telling them what they should read and what they should avoid. They should be aware of the content of the Universal Constitution, which represents "social education", while avoiding pseudo-philosophical essays:[224]

> Fathers and mothers remove from the hands of your children these learned and harmful stupid things. Almost all of these books are full of twists gargles and contradictions, of truths and fairy tales, of light and darkness.[225]

The text that children must feed on is the Universal Constitution. In the last chapter of the *Philosophe sociale*, Dobruska states that the democratic regime will remain stable where the most suitable and capable representatives have been chosen to govern:

---

sistemico. Strumenti per un'interpretazione sistemica del pensiero di Spinoza," *Rivista di Filosofia Neo-Scolastica* 106 (2014): 525–535.

223 Juliana Merçon, "La filosofía de Spinoza y el pensamiento sistémico contemporáneo," *Revista de Filosofía* (Universidad Iberoamericana) 133 (2012): 87.

224 Dobruska, *Philosophie sociale*, 74.

225 *Ibidem*, 73: [Pères et mères, ôtez des mains de vos enfans ces doctes et dangereuses niaiseries. Presque tous ces libres sont tellement remplis d'entortillage et de contradiction, de vérités et de fables, de lumière et d'obscurité].

The father is born again in the son, the mother is born again in the daughter. Some generations die, others reproduce them; but man is always man, his regime is always the same, as stable as the earth.[226]

4.5.3 At the Macro Level

Dobruska understands very well how the social and cultural context, in which the envied were born and live, influences beliefs, behaviors, and habits, as well as the ways people interact with one another. It is the set of social and moral norms that prevails within a specific social organization that guides and forms the beliefs of individuals, their behaviors and their lifestyles, as we would say today. Among other things, the *Philosophie sociale* shows how, in the theocratic social organizations, in which the normative system coincided with the corpus of religious precepts of the sacred Scriptures, there were very different behaviors regarding, for example, sexual relations between men and women, and relations between genders, as well as culinary habits.

In other words, the set of religious precepts – which can be considered as an independent variable – has a direct influence in shaping the behavior of individuals, in regulating the daily life of individuals and in assigning specific social roles:

The inhabitants of Mecca may be Christians, just as the inhabitants of Rome may be Mohammedans, but the difference between Christ and Muhammad, the only difference between these two men, between the system of the Gospels and the Koran, is also the difference between the people of Rome and the people of Mecca; It is thus that even in the Indies, between peoples of one and the same nation, of one and the same character and climate, only the Gospels and the Koran produce the differences between them; since the missionaries of the Gospel made some Christians, while the missionaries of the Koran made others Muslims.[227]

---

226 *Ibidem*, 235: [. . . car le père renaît dans son fils. La fille fait revivre la mère; des générations meurent, d'autres les reproduisent; mais l'homme étant toujours homme, son régime est toujours le même et demeure stable comme la terre].

227 Dobruska, *Philosophie sociale*, 196: [Les habitans de la Mecque pouvoient être des Chrétiens, aussi bien que les habitans de Rome pouvoient être des Mahométans; mais la différence entre le Christ et Mahomet, la seule différence entre ces deux hommes, entre le système de l'Évangile et du Koran, constitue la différence entre le peuple de Rome et le peuple de la Mecque; c'est ainsi, que même dans les Indes, entre des peuples d'une seule et même nation, seul et même caractère et climat, l'Évangile et le Koran seuls produisirent la différence entre eux, en ce que les Missionnaires de l'Évangile firent chrétiens les uns, et les Missionnaires du Koran firent musulmans les autres].

In this passage Dobruska highlights well how there is no "extrinsic essence" that distinguishes the inhabitants of one nation from another. The same individual born in Rome in a Christian religious context would become a Muslim if he were born in a country where the official religion was the Islamic one and not the Christian one. This same individual would believe and act in his daily life according to the dictates of the Koran, not the Gospels. In other words, it is clear to our author that, in primitive theocratic social organizations, religions and their spiritual leaders ("the legislators") play a crucial role in what we today call "secondary socialization", that is, in the internalization, by the individual, of the beliefs, values, and social norms defined by religion and its charismatic leaders.

Dobruska emphasizes very clearly how the identities of individuals and their behaviors are built socially and culturally through the internalization of the religious normative corpus. It is the intuition of a more general sociological law, according to which the set of beliefs and the normative corpus – be it religious, metaphysical, or based on the "laws of nature" – influence and determine in part the behaviors and rules of daily life.

The set of rules, regulations and social sanctions therefore has an impact on individual behavior, customs, and practices in everyday life. On the other hand, such a context allows the individual what in the "state of nature" would not have been possible: the possibility to develop himself at the highest levels, to reach perfection, to increase and expand his appetite both material and intellectual. That is why the individual needs society:

> I mean [. . .] to explain myself better: when I take away from man, whose instinct has been formed by culture, all the benefits of society and art, I send him back to his forest, to his cave, I force him to feed again on his roots and his acorns. Through the restitution of all the ancient benefits of the old state of nature, will he be able to concretely achieve his goal, the supreme good, the object of his research? Of course not. He needs bread now and not roots. His love for property, the sweetness of fortune, his taste, his developed appetitive faculty, make him unable to rejoice now in his primitive state and to settle for it. He needs society for the development of his appetitive faculty, he is no longer a sovereign being, which is enough to himself, totally independent with respect to everything that is outside him; he has become a member dependent on the great body of society, conforming to nature, all his rights and his advantages belong entirely to the new sovereign (society) and his individual preservation is thus transformed into the conservation of society.[228]

---

228 *Philosophie sociale*, 128 : [je veux dire [. . .] pour m'expliquer mieux: quand je retire à l'homme formé par la culture de son instinct, quand je lui retire tous les bénéfices de la société et de l'art., que je le renvoie à sa forêt, à sa caverne, que je le force a se nourrir de nouveau de ses racines et de ses glands. Par cette restitution de tous les bénéfices de l'ancien état de

In other words, man obtains from society the possibility to expand his own capacities and material and intellectual desires. Here we have an echo of the thought of Jean-Jacques Rousseau in the *Social Contract*, about the advantages that man obtains when he passes from the state of nature to the state of civilization:

> The passage from the state of nature to the civil state produces a very remarkable change in man [. . .] Although, in this state, he deprives himself of some advantages which he got from nature, he gains in return others so great, his faculties are so stimulated and developed, his ideas so extended, his feelings so ennobled, and his whole soul so uplifted, that, did not the abuses of this new condition often degrade him below that which he left, he would be bound to bless continually the happy moment which took him from it forever, and, instead of a stupid and unimaginative animal, made him an intelligent being and a man.

> Let us draw up the whole account in terms easily commensurable. What man loses by the social contract is his natural liberty and an unlimited right to everything he tries to get and succeeds in getting; what he gains is civil liberty, and the proprietorship of all he possesses.[229]

For both Dobruska and Rousseau, the passage, through the social contract, from the state of nature to the state of culture (or civilization, according to the expression of Rousseau) means the loss of some faculties and some rights but, at the

---

nature, pourroit-il actuellement atteindre son but, le souverain bien, objet de ses recherches? Non certes. Il lui faut désormais du pain et non pas des racines. L'amour des propriétés, les douceurs de la fortune, son goût, sa faculté appétitive développée, le rendent incapable de jouir maintenant de son état primitif, et de s'en contenter. Il a besoin de la société par ce développement de sa faculté appétitive, il n'est plus un être souverain, se suffisant à lui-même, totalement indépendant hors de soi, il est devenu un membre dépendant du grand corps de la société, conformément à la nature, tous ses droits et avantages appartiennent aujourd'hui en entier au nouveau souverain, (la société) et sa conservation individuelle se trouve ainsi changée en la conservation de la société].

229 Rousseau, *Du contrat social*, I. 8: [Ce passage de l'état de nature à l'état civil produit dans l'homme un changement très remarquable [. . .] Quoiqu'il se prive dans cet état de plusieurs avantages qu'il tient de la nature, il en regagne de si grands, ses facultés s'exercent et se développent, ses idées s'étendent, ses sentiments s'ennoblissent, son âme tout entière s'élève à tel point que, si les abus de cette nouvelle condition ne la dégradaient souvent au-dessous de celle dont il est sorti, il devrait bénir sans cesse l'instant heureux qui l'en arracha pour jamais et qui, d'un animal stupide et borné, fit un être intelligent et un homme. Réduisons toute cette balance à des termes faciles à comparer. Ce que l'homme perd par le contrat social, c'est sa liberté naturelle et un droit illimité à tout ce qui le tente et qu'il peut atteindre; ce qu'il gagne, c'est la liberté civile et la propriété de tout ce qu'il possède] (Idem, *The Social Contract*, 18–19).

same time, allows the achievement of some advantages, not only in terms of personal development.

There is no doubt that Dobruska follows Rousseau here, although he does not mention his name. However, he differs from Rousseau's model in terms of the content of losses and gains that are made by moving from one state to another. On the one hand, for Rousseau, during the transition from the state of nature to civilization, man is transformed from a substantially "deficient" being into an intelligent one, who advances spiritually. In addition, in exchange for the loss of natural freedom and the right to everything he craves and desires to achieve, he obtains civil liberty and the right to property. For Dobruska, on the other hand, the man who passes from the state of nature to that of culture loses his independence and the ability to stay alone. He becomes dependent on his fellow men, with whom he is forced to enter into a relationship to ensure his survival. As Durkheim will say much later, with his concept of organic society in the *De la division du travail social* of 1893,[230] societies are formed because no individual is self-sufficient and autonomous any more: everyone depends on the other. In other words, according to Dobruska's conceptualization of multiple needs, each individual has different material or intellectual needs and will be able to contribute to society according to his or her abilities.

Through interaction with other individuals and societal institutions (schools, universities, cultural and political associations) the individual has the opportunity to fulfill all his desires and to develop faculties, both material and intellectual. His being can progress until it reaches the perfection of its material and intellectual skills.

Unlike Rousseau, who remains a political philosopher, and affirms the dichotomy between individual and State, Dobruska emphasizes the duality between individual and society. For this reason, too, Dobruska should be counted among the founding fathers of sociology.

Now that we have outlined our author's theory on the individual and on society, we will deepen in the following pages the different types of interactions between human beings living in a democratic society and we will ask ourselves what, in the *Philosophie sociale*, is the element of cohesion that holds a society together.

---

230 Emile Durkheim, *De la division du travail social. Étude sur l'organisation des sociétés supérieures* (Paris: Félix Alcan, 1893).

4.6 Forms of Social Interactions between Individuals: From Selfishness to Reciprocity

The sociological thought of Dobruska conceptualizes different forms of exchange between individuals living in society. As we have just mentioned, interrelationships between members of society are necessary because, having abandoned their natural state, people are no longer autonomous, and are unable to provide for their own preservation and livelihood.

Dobruska theorizes two great models of interrelationships, which in Max Weber's (1864–1920) words we would now call two ideal-types: selfishness and reciprocity. These two models of interrelationships have antithetical characteristics and have completely opposite impacts both on other members of society and on society as a whole.

Reflection on forms of social interaction has been a fundamental theme of sociological thought, from classical authors to the present day.[231] Special attention has been paid by many authors to reciprocity, understood as "the provision of services or the supply of material goods, with the expectation of having subsequently a return of services or goods in ways, quantities and timescales

---

231 In sociological thought, the concept of reciprocity has been a fundamental theme for various authors from the nineteenth century to the present day. Think for instance of Georg Simmel (1858–1918), who underlined the fundamental social meaning of reciprocity: "Aller Verkehr der Menschen beruht auf dem Schema von Hingabe und Äquivalent. Nun kann für unzählige Hingaben und Leistungen das Äquivalent erzwungen werden. Bei allen wirtschaftlichen Tauschen, die in Rechtsform geschehen, bei allen fixierten Zusagen für eine Leistung, bei allen Verpflichtungen aus einer rechtlich regulierten Beziehung erzwingt die Rechtsverfassung das Hin- und Hergehen von Leistung und Gegenleistung und sorgt für diese Wechselwirkung, ohne die es keine soziale Balance und Zusammenhalt gibt" [Georg Simmel, *Soziologie. Untersuchungen über die Formen der Vergesellschaftung* (Leipzig: Duncker & Humblot, 1908), 590]. Karl Polanyi (1886–1964) dwells on three fundamental forms of integration defined as reciprocity, redistribution, and market exchange. Alvin W. Gouldner (1920–1980) analyzed the relationship between reciprocity and morality, but also the role that the stabilization of a social system fulfilled by reciprocity fulfills. For Gouldner, not only does the rule of reciprocity serve to stabilize the function of groups, offering additional motivation and reinforcement to behaviors of compliance with social roles, but it is also a starting mechanism, i.e. a mechanism, which helps to initiate new social interactions, functional in the early stages of formation of certain groups, before they develop. Howard Becker conceptualizes the *homo reciprocus*. Randall Collins considers reciprocity as the basic process that makes exchange possible and as an equivalent to the pre-conceptual solidarity of Durkheim. See Linda D. Molm, David R. Schaefer and Jessica L. Collett, "The Value of Reciprocity," *Social Psychology Quarterly* 70 (2007): 199–217.

fixed by cultural norms"[232] In sociological discourse, a distinction is generally made between two types of reciprocity: generalized and balanced.

"Generalized reciprocity", which takes place mainly within the family, "has no precise content, does not set time limits and does not even require that what is returned has the same economic value as what has been given".[233] "Balanced reciprocity", which takes place outside the family networks, on the other hand, means "the exchange which provides for an equivalent refund in value calculated very precisely".[234] A good example is the return of the invitation to dinner of friends, who welcomed us with respect and affection at home.

Let's take a closer look at these two antagonistic models of interrelation and the impact on individuals and the community as a whole.

4.6.1 Selfishness

After a detailed analysis of man and society, and their rights and duties, Dobruska focuses on the interrelationships between individuals. The first question is what selfishness is, what its distinctive features are, and why in the long run it is harmful to the community:

> I also define selfishness as individual preservation. But let me explain: selfishness is a state that seeks to achieve its purpose. I mean, [the selfish person] satisfies his appetite on others while refusing to allow others to exercise it on him. The selfish person makes his ego the center of the relationships of all external and foreign activities; but it refuses to others the same exercise on him; thus an active state must be explained, which is not passive except for all that is outside of him. In a few words, in order to achieve his goal, [the selfish person] tries to be relative for others, and is not relative to them, that is to say, he rejects the reciprocity of the relationship.[235]

---

232 Arnanldo Bagnasco, Maurizio Barbagli and Alessandro Cavalli, *Corso di sociologia* (Bologna Il Mulino, 1997), 491.

233 *Loc. cit.*

234 *Ibidem*, 491–492.

235 Dobruska, *Philosophie sociale*, 95–96: [Je définis aussi l'égoïsme *conservation individuelle*. Mais je m'explique: l'égoïsme est un état qui cherche à atteindre son but: je veux dire satisfaire sur autrui sa faculté appétitive, pendant qu'il refuse à cet autrui l'exercice de la même. L'égoïsme fait de *son moi* le centre des relations de toutes les activités extérieures et étrangères: mais il refuse aux autres le même exercice sur lui, ainsi doit-il être expliqué un état actif qui n'est passif que pour ce qui est hors de lui. En un mot, qui pour arriver à son but, cherche a être relatif pour les autres, et à ne pas l'être envers eux, c'est-à-dire, qu'il refuse la réciprocité de la relation].

And again:

> Selfishness is also individual preservation. However, the one who rejects the reciprocity of a relationship also rejects his duty and thus does not follow the law. Individual preservation is therefore the eternal principle, the fundamental basis of all justice and injustice.[236]

As I have argued in the previous pages, the man who lives in society, according to Dobruska's theory, needs his fellow human beings, and has the duty to enter into a relationship with them, for his own sustenance and to satisfy his appetite. The person who establishes a relationship in selfish terms is helped by other members of society to survive and to fulfill his material and intellectual desires, but when asked to return the services or goods obtained, rejects any kind of relationship. In other words, this person is able to take from others what he needs, but does not want and does not feel obliged to return the services or material, emotional, or intellectual goods that he received. And this way of interrelating with others is not only against the right enshrined in the Universal Constitution but is also a profoundly immoral action.

In the third chapter of the Universal Constitution, dedicated to *Principle, Law and Selfishness,* we read:

> And as, in the state of society, man needs the relationship with his fellow men for individual preservation, and satisfaction of the fully developed appetitive faculty, the need establishes the duty of the relationship on his side and makes of this necessary reciprocity a right.[237]

Therefore, the person who refuses to interact reciprocally with others places himself outside the law. In so doing, he will, in the long term, be able to obtain goods and services that are greater than he would need. This amounts to an abuse of wealth and power by one individual against others, with the risk of creating a society in which one group dominate the remaining components and ask them to sacrifice their individual self. According to Dobruska, selfishness is an abomination because it "destroys the divinity of a common interest".[238]

---

236 *Ibidem*, 98: [L'égoïsme est aussi la conservation individuelle, mais qui refusant la réciprocité de la relation, refuse son devoir, n'est pas en droit. La conservation individuelle est donc le principe éternel, la base fondamentale de toute justice et injustice].

237 *Ibidem*, 97: [Et comme, dans l'état de société, l'homme a besoin de la relation de ses semblables pour la conservation individuelle, et la satisfaction de la faculté appétitive développée, le besoin établit le devoir de la relation de son côté, et fait un droit de cette réciprocité nécessaire].

238 *Ibidem*, 99: [l'égoïsme, principe infâme, [. . .] dont il détruit la divinité d'un intérêt commun].

After destroying the common interest of the community, the selfish person pursues only his partial interest, with harmful consequences:

> By introducing the hell of a partial interest, the true right is swallowed; and, by vomiting the abhorrent right of the strongest in society, one becomes guilty, and the other miserable, it confuses error with truth, obscures the simple path of nature and reason, complicates social philosophy, and deceives humanity in the science of living.[239]

To put this even more precisely:

> Why, what does selfishness do? [The selfish person] refuses the right of others to himself; for this refusal, the duty of obedience to the principle of others is lost; therefore, his refusal is a true usurpation of the rights of others. So selfishness, this criminal substitution of rights, is really the usurpation of the rights of others [. . .] Morality is the opposite of selfishness, because the principle gains through morality itself, and loses through selfishness.[240]

In addition to usurping the rights of others, the selfish person also commits, according to Dobruska, an immoral action. Refusing to support another individual in their moment of need is a serious immoral act, regardless of the type of need: it could be a need linked to daily life but also to an event of exceptional drama, such as a natural disaster or an accident.

What's more, it is not just an immoral act that affects the individual, but one which affects society as a whole. More precisely, it causes the immorality of the State. We have observed that, for Dobruska, "the morality of the State is the consequence of individual morality".[241] Therefore, selfish action is not just action against the law but is deeply unfair: it is action against social justice.

4.6.2 Reciprocity

Selfish action, which refers only to itself and rejects the duty of the relationship, is countered by acting according to the model of reciprocity.

---

239 *Loc. cit.*: [. . . et en introduisant l'enfer d'un intérêt partiel, engloutit le droit véritable; et en vomissant l'exécrable droit du plus fort dans la société, rend l'un coupable, et l'autre misérable, confond l'erreur avec la vérité, obscurcit le sentier simple de la nature et de la raison, en compliquant la philosophie sociale, et en trompant l'humanité dans la science de vivre].

240 *Ibidem*, 104: [Car, que fait l'égoïsme? Il refuse le droit d'autrui sur lui; or, par ce refus, le devoir de l'obéissance au principe d'autrui, perd; donc son refus est vraie usurpation des droits d'autrui [. . .] Ainsi l'égoïsme, cette substitution criminelle des droits d'autrui [. . .] La moralité est l'opposé de l'égoïsme, en ce que le principe gagne par elle, et perd par l'égoïsme].

241 *Ibidem*, 108: [La moralité d'état est la conséquence de la moralité individuelle].

By reciprocity, Dobruska means the exchange in which an individual provides services, goods, information, or emotional assistance in support of a fellow human being, or for his material or intellectual development. The assumption is that the other, sooner or later (usually in a rather short time), will reward him with similar goods and services. This obligation to reciprocate is a duty, which over time strengthens social ties.

The need for reciprocity arises from living in society. In this context, the needs of various kinds, which each individual has, are multiple and increasingly extend throughout life. The satisfaction of these needs can only take place thanks to continuous interrelation, based on reciprocity. We read in the *Philosophie sociale*:

> In the social state, in which the multiple and more extensive needs cannot be satisfied or contained without the reciprocal and mutual assistance of all the members, everyone must contribute with all his means to the needs and to the satisfaction of the whole. No one can have the privilege of being dispensed from it, no one should interfere with it by preference, and no one can remain in a state of inertia or guilty neutrality, when it comes to the same interest in relation to the purpose (the principle): and certainly no one will remain a detached spectator, if he is awakened by an interest, which is the same as that of all the other members.[242]

In other words, all members of society, without exception, are expected to contribute to this mutual exchange, based on reciprocity, which serves to achieve the general interest of society. As I already mentioned, the ultimate goal of society is its self-preservation and the happiness of its individual members.

The obligation to reciprocate, the duty of relationships, is necessary, since "the conservation of each individual depends on the conservation of the entire social body".[243]

In conclusion, according to Dobruska, reciprocity performs important functions for a social system: it guarantees the preservation of the individual self and the social one, it allowsfor the satisfaction of the multiple needs of individuals, it represents an antidote to the immorality of both the individual and the State, and it makes possible social cohesion and a society's stability over time.

---

242 *Ibidem*, 157: [Dans l'état social où des besoins multipliés et plus étendus ne peuvent être *prévenus ni contenues* que par le concours réciproque et mutuel de tous les membres, tous doivent concourir de tous leurs moyens aux besoins, et au contentement du tout. Aucun ne peut avoir le privilège de s'en dispenser, aucun ne doit s'y immiscer par préférence, et nul ne peut rester dans une inertie ou neutralité coupable ; quand il s'agit de l'intérêt égal relativement *au but,* (le principe) et certainement personne ne restera spectateur de sang froid, s'il est éveillé par un intérêt égal á celui de tous les autres membres].
243 *Ibidem*, 100.

4.7 Society and Its "Social Treasure"

In his reflections on society, Dobruska seems to us to anticipate, even before Comte and Durkheim, what in sociology will be called, in the twentieth century, the "school of functionalist thought" or "functionalism" *tout court*. It will not be useless to recall here the definition of this theoretical orientation:

> [Functionalism is] the analysis of cultural and social phenomena in terms of the *functions* they perform in a sociocultural system. In functionalism, society is conceived as a set of inter-connected parts, in which no part can be understood if it is isolated from the others. Any change in one of the parts is considered to cause a certain imbalance, which in turn produces further changes in other parts of the system and even a reorganization of the system itself. The development of functionalism is based on the model of the organic system that we find in the biological sciences.[244]

Dobruska conceives society as a group of individuals, who are not to be considered as isolated, independent and only rational atoms, but are interconnected with each other, dependent on each other for their livelihood and for the satisfaction of their needs. They are individuals capable of acting according to morality, following their own rationality but also their own feelings.

Although he does not use the term "function", Dobruska always stresses the ways in which each party – the members of society and society itself – interacts, the obligations and duties it must fulfil to meet the needs of individuals, to ensure happiness, and to keep the social system in balance.

Our author wonders how it is possible that the social system could remain stable, and immune to the *mélanges monstreux* of the society of the past, characterized by the absolute monarchy. This is a central theme in his reflection, as it will be for his successors, first for Comte and then for Durkheim:

> Representative democracy, the only regime of the primitive sovereign, is also the only healthy one. The reason lies in this perfect balance, according to which each of its members – whatever their strength and capacity – receives a portion of nourishment equal to their own needs; that is to say, that there exists in the whole body a balance or an equilibrium of strictly identical interest, which assures them [i.e. the parties] a state of strength and health; from this also comes an advantage and the general good, which is nothing more than the sum of all the goods gathered by each one. We must therefore conclude that the regime (government) in which the general will is carried out relentlessly and representatively by the most capable and appropriate members is the only legitimate one.[245]

---

244 George A. Theodorson and Achilles S. Theodorson, eds., *A Modern Dictionary of Sociology* (New York: Crowell, 1969), 167.
245 Dobruska, *Philosophie sociale,* 234–235: [La démocratie représentative, seul régime du souverain primitif, est aussi le seul salutaire. On en découvre la raison dans cette pondération

From this brief quotation we see how Dobruska compares society to a body composed of different parts, each with different needs. Thanks to the democratic process of representation, all members of this social system receive exactly what they need to meet their needs – no more, no less, *quantum sufficit*. The stability of the democratic regime over time is granted by the representatives of the citizens, who have been selected from among the most capable and most suitable individuals: they are perfectly familiar with the Universal Constitution and know what their citizens want.

While individuals are dependent on each other for social action, this is not the case under the law. In this context, individuals are to be considered as sovereign and independent entities, all having the same rights. Everyone has the right to citizenship. It is in no way acceptable for one individual to have more rights than another.

What is society's duty to itself? What are its assets, its "treasures" – what are its capitals, as we would say using the terminology of contemporary sociology? And how do these treasures differ from those of individuals? What are the obligations and functions of society towards its members, towards its citizens? In the *Philosophie sociale* we see the following:

> What are the duties of the new sovereign, society, towards itself? They consist of the contribution of all cultural resources, together with the natural resources of each member, so as achieve the fullest satisfaction of the appetitive faculty, perfected and developed, the instinct formed by the principle, means whose union represents the property of the new sovereign, namely the social treasure, and which are obliged to lend each other mutual assistance with regard to the purpose required by the principle, that is, to be able to preserve themselves in the state of culture.[246]

---

parfaite, d'après laquelle, quelle que soit leur force ou – leur capacité, chacun des membres reçoit une portion de nourriture égale à ses besoins; c'est-à-dire, qu'il existe dans ce corps entier, un balancement ou équilibre d'intérêt rigoureusement égal, lequel assure leur état de force et de santé; d'où proviennent aussi l'avantage et le bien général, qui n'est autre, que la somme des biens réunis d'un chacun. Il nous faut donc conclure, que le Régime (gouvernement) dans lequel la volonté générale et sans cesse exécutée représentativement, par le membre le plus capable et le plus propre, est le seul légitime].

246 *Ibidem*, 138: [En quoi consistent les devoirs du nouveau souverain, la société, envers lui-même? Ils consistent dans la contribution de tous les moyens de culture réunis aux moyens naturels de chacun de ses membres, afin, d'arriver par elle à la satisfaction la plus entière de la faculté appétitive perfectionnée et développée, l'instinct formé pour le principe, moyens dont la réunion présente la propriété du nouveau souverain, c'est-à-dire le *trésor sociale*, et qui sont obligés de se prêter un secours mutuel relativement au but exigé par le principe, c'est-à-dire, pour pouvoir se conserver dans l'état de culture]. This text is available also in the fragmentary German draft. See Appendix 3.

Society is therefore obliged to support the development of all resources, both the cultural and natural assets of each individual, in order to achieve a very specific goal: to satisfy the desires of those who live together and to perfect their material and intellectual faculties.

In another passage of his work, Dobruska expands the concept of social treasure, that is, of the ownership of the new sovereign, affirming that it consists in the whole of "all the forces and means of culture which are added to the forces and natural means which preceded each individual", that is, to the forces and natural means which the individuals possessed in the state of nature, before entering to live in society (in the state of culture).[247]

What exactly do the "forces and means of nature" possessed by each individual and the "forces and means of culture" consist of? In *Philosophie sociale*, these terms are not precisely defined. Rather, the author seems to take them for granted. It can be assumed, therefore, that they refer to a philosophical debate, well known at the time, between *philosophes* and revolutionaries. A debate that Dobruska could not but know.

We start with the individual and his "natural means" (*moyens naturels*) or natural resources. In order to get closer to the meaning of this concept in Dobruska's work, it seems useful to compare it with a text entitled *Abrégé des principes de l'économie politique* (*Synthesis of the principles of political economy*), attributed to the "Margrave de Bade", and published in Paris in 1772. It is a synthesis, authored by Karl Friedrich von Baden (1728–1811), of the *Leçons oeconomiques* of Victor de Riqueti, Marquis of Mirabeau (1715–1789). Both the lexicon and the main ideas are rather close to Dobruska's conceptions, and it is likely that the book was part of his readings. In the first section of the *Abrégé*, the natural needs (*besoins naturels*) and the natural means of man (*moyens naturels de l'homme*) are analyzed. The needs of man are manifold and follow a very precise hierarchy. The text first distinguishes between "needs" (*nécessité*), which in contemporary language are often referred to as "primary needs", followed by "necessities" (*les besoins*). The needs of man are essentially three: i) subsistence, ii) rest, which implies the need for security, and finally, iii) reproduction of the species. In addition to these three needs, there are two other categories of needs: iv) clothing; v) education to improve industry, and to use force according to the type of goods that are offered to us or that escape us.[248]

---

247 *Ibidem*, 143: [La propriété du nouveau souverain de la société, consiste dans toutes les forces et moyens de culture, qui se réunissent aux forces et moyens naturels antérieurs de chacun de ses membres].
248 Karl Friedrich von Baden, *Abrégé des principes de l'économie politique* (Paris: Chez Lacombe, 1772), 83.

The natural means of man *(moyens naturels de l'homme)* are the constitutive means which belong to a person as an individual. These are divided into two types. First of all, the (physical) strength of man and all that follows from it, such as constancy in work, temperance, agility, must be considered. The second natural means is intelligence and everything that derives from it (such as industry, that is, being ingenious and industrious), combined with memory *(souvenirs)*, and together with all activities and creations related to ingenuity and memory.

Such ideas, exhibited in the *Abrégé des principes de l'économie politique,* seem to us particularly suited to shed light on the term "natural forces and means".

Like the *Abrégé*, the *Philosophie sociale* also start from the needs of the individual and those of society, to arrive at the natural means of individuals, and those of culture, that are necessary to satisfy these needs.

Dobruska argues that in society there are multiple needs *(besoins multipliés)*, which cannot be foreseen or fully met. That is, we have a hierarchy of needs, which must be briefly explained.

Initially, the needs for individual conservation must be met, which coincide with the first five needs exposed in the *Abrégé* – subsistence, rest, safety, reproduction, clothing. However, unlike Mirabeau, summarized by Karl Friedrich von Baden, who sees individuals as autonomous, rational and detached from the social context in which they live, for Dobruska – as a good "sociologist"-men, when they live in society, are no longer autonomous entities. They therefore have another urgent need: to forge links with other members of society in order to survive and to achieve their highest goals.

This brings us to the last need, that of developing intellectual and material faculties, of perfecting our ingenuity until we reach the highest peaks – making human potential blossom – thanks to social life.[249]

---

249 Dobruska seems to anticipate by two hundred and fifty years the famous theory of the hierarchy of needs, elaborated by the psychologist Abraham Maslow (1908–1970) starting from the Forties of the last century. He has shown how individuals who have once managed to meet basic needs are driven to develop their inner potential and self-fulfillment. The levels of the hierarchy of needs are, according to Maslow's model, five: i) basic needs (food, water, sleep, sexual relations); ii) stability and security; iii) love, affection and sense of belonging to the community; iv) self-esteem including the need for prestige; v) development of one's own potential and self-realization. See Abraham H. Maslow, "A Theory of Human Motivation," *Psychological Review* 50 (1943): 370–396; Idem, *Motivation and Personality* (New York: Harper & Row Verlag, 1970); Andrew B. Trigg, "Deriving the Engel Curve. Pierre Bourdieu and the Social Critique of Maslow's Hierarchy of Needs," *Review of Social Economy* 62 (2004): 393–406. However, unlike Maslow, for whom the needs are innate and above all psychological, Dobruska emphasizes social needs. He also argues that the development and realization of human

However, the analysis of Dobruska's needs does not end here: just as there is a hierarchy of needs for individuals, there is also one for society. Society first and foremost needs to survive over time, but also to be defended against external attacks.

Both the needs of individuals and those of society must be met, both by natural forces and means and by means of culture, the "social treasure". In fact, all individuals, through mutual assistance and mutual exchange, are required to contribute to the satisfaction of collective needs with all their means (*moyens*).[250]

We can now answer, with more knowledge of the historical and intellectual context, the question from which we started: what exactly are these forces and means of nature and culture?

We know that, through his passage into the state of culture, man partly maintains the faculties he had in the state of nature, but in addition broadens his expressive potential. The properties of man in nature, defined in the *Philosophie sociale* as the "primitive sovereign", consist of "all natural forces and means, which can lead man to his goal, required by the principle",[251] that is, individual conservation. These forces and means are the physical strength and intelligence and ingenuity necessary for survival. Here, too, we see how the *Abrégé* helps us to shed light on the terms used by Dobruska. As I said above, the natural means, listed in the *Abrégé*, are made up of the force possessed by man and his intelligence, understood in the broadest sense (being rational, ingenious, able, having mnemonic abilities): in all likelihood, this is precisely the reference scheme through which we must also interpret the "means" put in place by nature in the *Philosophie sociale*.

As for the "means of culture", our author shows that they are all resources that allow material and intellectual development, such as housing, health care facilities, and buildings for education, but also education as such and wider cultural heritage. At this point we could see in Dobruska a precursor of functional-structuralism, since he is interested in identifying the conditions and structures that satisfy individual needs. In the *Philosophie sociale*, these conditions are given by the set of all the natural resources of each individual, to which are

---

intellectual and material faculties can only occur in society through social interaction with other individuals and through the cultural means of society.

250 Dobruska, *Philosophie sociale*, 157.

251 *Ibidem*, 143: [La propriété du souverain primitif de l'homme, dans l'état de nature, consiste dans toutes les forces et moyens naturels qui peuvent conduire l'homme à son but, exigé par le principe].

added the resources or cultural assets that Dobruska defines, for the first time in the history of sociological thought, as "the social treasure" of society.[252]

Dobruska's final reflection on this "social treasure" concerns its distribution:

> It is well demonstrated that no individual isolated in his "particular", or any other corporation, that exists in some new adopted unit, cannot acquire in society an unfair and more important interest. The new sovereign has no right to give or transfer to an isolated individual this new unfair and most important interest, whoever this individual is, not even to any corporation, under any title, i.e. the new sovereign can not abuse his "social treasure".[253]

The social treasure should not be distributed unfairly among members of society, favoring certain individuals or certain corporations, but fairly among citizens.

4.8 Society: Rights and Duties

4.8.1 Public Contributions

According to the *Philosophie sociale*, the new sovereign (society) can ask its citizens for various public contributions of a physical, moral, or patrimonial nature, but under two conditions.

The first condition is that contributions are required only for a specific purpose, namely for the preservation of society as a whole and for the full happiness

---

252 The idea that both the community and individuals can possess certain "treasures" or "capital" anticipates lines of thought, which in sociology will only be developed much later. Think of this in relation to the thought of Karl Marx (1818–1883) up to Pierre Bourdieu (1930–2002). Marx theorizes in *Capital* the different forms of capital that the two major social classes possess in a capitalist society – the capitalists have the economic and technological capital for the production of goods and services while the proletarians possess their mere "workforce" that they sell to the capitalists in exchange for a salary. The French sociologist Pierre Bourdieu expanded this conceptualization. According to him, in addition to economic capital, there are also cultural, social, and symbolic capitals.

253 Dobruska, *Philosophie sociale*, 146: [Quoiqu'il soit bien avéré qu'aucun individu isolé en son particulier, ni toute autre corporation sous quelque unité nouvelle adoptée qu'elle subsiste, ne puisse pas acquérir dans la société un intérêt inégal et plus important. Il n'est pas moins constant que ce nouveau souverain lui-même, n'a pas le droit de céder ou transporter à un individu isolé ce nouvel intérêt inégal et plus important, quelque soit cet individu, ni même à une corporation quelconque, sous quelque dénomination qu'elle existe, c'est-à-dire que le nouveau souverain ne peut abuser du trésor social].

of its members. No public contribution may be required for other purposes, such as for a particular interest of an individual or an association.

The government will not be able to demand contributions that hinder luxury or that are detrimental to personal needs. As we shall see later, Dobruska does not condemn luxury as a source of happiness for some members, nor does he propose any redistributive principles. The State is not obliged to redistribute economic and social resources, but has the task of guaranteeing equal rights. If the government were to demand the renunciation of luxury or need by an individual, it would be a tyranny.[254]

The second condition for a government's claiming a contribution is that it must be based on law. Moreover, the government cannot usurp the private assets of its citizens that serve their livelihood or their personal defense. For example, the government cannot require the individual to give up arms which serve his personal defense.[255]

4.8.2 Defending Society: The Supremacy of the Strongest and Deception

Dobruska considers whether the supremacy of the strongest and/or the use of deception are permissible instruments in a democratic society, or whether they should be bannedoutright.

The supremacy of the strongest and deception, which can represent an abuse of reason, are sacred rights, when they intervene "in defense of the principle", that is, for the preservation of the collective self (*moi social*). In this case, it is a possible course of action to sacrifice a minority of society in order to defend society as a whole.

If, on the other hand, the supremacy of the strongest and deception are used against the principle of the collective ego, they correspond to a murder, a true tyranny.

4.8.3 Unit of Interest: The Ultimate Goal of Society

The fifteenth chapter of the Universal Constitution sets out the principles that a legislator must follow with regard to the interests of the individual and of the State, so that his actions can be judged healthy and good for the whole of society.

---

254 *Ibidem*, 153.
255 *Loc. cit.*

For legislation to be effective, it is necessary for the interest pursued by the State to be simple and unitary. The "legislator-philosopher" should not consider different corporations, groups, or social classes, but should start from individual human beings (*être homme*), who, as Dobruska has pointed out, are distinguished by the climate in which they live, by the food they eat, and by the habits they follow in their daily lives.

Although men are so different, they are brought together by an identical desire, which is constantly renewed. And this desire is the greatest possible prosperity. This prosperity is composed of the sum of the happiness of individuals:

> It is indisputable that there is not a State that is perfectly happy in its entirety and in the parts that make it up, except that in which each member, individually and in itself, enjoys happiness, and whose analysis represents only the fundamental and natural basis of the uniformity of interests in the scale that is its responsibility, multiplied in an equal and generic manner, that is to say, general prosperity is but the sum of the happiness of each individual.[256]

In short, the State must pursue a single interest, namely social prosperity, consisting of the sum of the happiness of individuals.

Why, in many States, do we not enjoy the prosperity that the people of Europe so long for?

> States that distinguish between public and individual interests are not prosperous. More precisely, these are States that pursue an interest that does not correspond to the sum of the happiness of their citizens. And this happens when new interests emerge from groups of people such as, for example, the interest of a part of the legislative body, of a king, constitutional or not, of any privileged caste. If the state also pursues these interests, then the overall interest will be different from the sum of the happiness of individuals.[257]

What happens if a State does not follow the natural principle but rather opposes it? What happens when two conflicting interests form the fundamental basis of legislation and the form of government? In this case there is a conflict of interest: the interest of the State is in opposition to that of individuals, and vice versa, bringing strong and inevitable tensions within society.[258]

---

256 *Ibidem*, 226–227: [Il est donc incontestable, qu'il n'y a d'état entièrement et parfaitement heureux dans son ensemble, et dans les portions qui le composent; que celui où chaque membre individuellement et en son particulier, jouit du bonheur, et dont l'analyse, ne présente que la base fondamentale et naturelle de l'uniformité d'intérêt dans son échelle, multipliée d'une manière égale et générique, c'est-à-dire, la prospérité générale, n'est que la somme réunie du bonheur de chacun des membres qui le composent].
257 *Ibidem*, 227.
258 *Ibidem*, 224–225.

According to Dobruska, a truly democratic State, which wants to avoid continuous conflicts, must pursue the only general interest, prosperity, given by the sum of the happiness of individual citizens.

4.9 Morality and Immorality of the Individual and Society

The morality of the individual and that of society are the subject of the fourth and fifth chapters of the Universal Constitution.

According to Dobruska, the individual must not only be put in a position where he can support himself, but also one in which he can satisfy his desires and his material and intellectual appetite. The task and duty of society is to enable the citizen to achieve these fundamental rights.

People act to satisfy their desires and passions or to ensure their survival. But they can also act for moral reasons. The moral faculties of man lie both in rational discernment (*la raison*) and in feelings. Not always, however, do feelings and reason want the same things. If man listened only to his feeling, he would not perform certain actions, which he would by listening only to his own intellect, and vice versa. Indeed, feelings and reason are often at odds with each other.[259]

Dobruska defines morality as follows: "A voluntary partial relationship to the principle of the individual self of another".[260]

Morals must be distinguished from law, that is to say, from the rules required by the State. We have seen that, for its own preservation, society imposes a specific rule on the individual: the duty of the relationship. In fact, the preservation of the individual depends on the preservation of the whole body of society.

When an individual asks for something from another individual for his own preservation, a voluntary relationship is established between them. Therefore, "he who gives to the poor food or clothing, does a moral action, because its preservation does not depend on his gift".[261]

If, on the other hand, an individual voluntarily sacrifices himself to defend society, he is not carrying out a moral action but acts according to the law, according to a rule that is recognized and sanctioned by the law. Why is that? Because his conservation, that of the individual in the state of culture, depends on the conservation of society (see Fig. 4). An individual citizen's moral behavior is only possible towards another citizen, not towards society as a whole.

---

259 *Ibidem*, 115.
260 *Ibidem*, 100: [*Une relation volontaire, partielle, pour le principe du moi individuel d'un autre*].
261 *Loc. cit.*

Selfishness is against morality, since the selfish man takes from others without giving anything in return.

Fig. 4: The Mutual Interdependence between the Conservation of the Individual and that of Society.
Source: author.

We now come to the morality of society. As we have already mentioned, Dobruska believes that "the morality of the State is the consequence of individual morality".[262] He continues his argument in this way:

> Let me explain: if an individual has voluntarily saved another from the claws of a ferocious beast, if he has snatched him from the flames, if he has prevented him from being swallowed up by the force waves of a raging wave, if, finally, he has preserved his life from any other imminent danger, and if society rewards the individual for this particular voluntary act, this reward is a moral act of the society of the State.[263]

Therefore, the morality of the State is what recognizes and rewards individual moral action. This represents "the highest virtue of humanity, which it honors itself".[264] If the State does not recognize and reward individual morality, then it acts immorally.

4.10 The Boundaries of Freedom Between Self-Preservation and Lawlessness

For Dobruska, the great adventurer who, from a provincial Jewish family, was able to climb the highest peaks of Viennese society and then throw himself into the intellectual fray of Paris, the ability to live as unhindered as possible and without external constraints is an essential principle. In his turbulent life,

---

262 *Ibidem*, 108: [La moralité d'état est *la conséquence de la moralité individuelle*].
263 *Loc. cit.*: [Je m'explique: si un individu en a sauvé volontairement un autre des griffes d'une bête féroce, s'il l'a arraché aux flammes, s'il t'a empêché d'être englouti sous les flots d'une onde couroucée; enfin, s'il a préservé ses jours de tout autre péril éminent, et que la société récompense cet individu de cet acte de relation volontaire particulière, cette récompense est un acte moral de la société d'état].
264 *Ibidem*, 111.

he managed to transcend the limits of faith, wealth and, cultural horizons. His idea of freedom has traits in common with John Locke's thinking, but at the same time it differs from it by more than one point. The English philosopher, for whom Dobruska has a deep respect, speaks of freedom with an emphasis on the dimension of power. Freedom, for Locke, is the power to do or refrain from a particular action. In *An Essay Concerning Human Understanding*, Locke writes:

> So that the *Idea of Liberty*, is the *Idea* of a Power in any Agent to do or forbear any particular Action, according to the determination or thought of the mind, whereby either of them is preferr'd to the other; where either of them is not in the Power of the Agent to be produced by him according to his *Volition*, there he is not at *Liberty*, that Agent is under *Necessity*. So that *Liberty* cannot be, where there is no Thought, no Volition, no Will; but there may be Thought, there may be Will, there may be Volition, where there is no *Liberty*.[265]

According to Dobruska, a freedom that is not anchored in the law does not apply to everyone. Only the physically and morally strongest citizens will be able to be free men, while the weakest and least capable spirits will be not only limited in their actions but also subject to the will of the strongest.

We read in the *Philosophie sociale*:

> It is impossible that freedom, which Lo[c]ke defines as power, is a freedom that brings happiness to the masses of society, because nature has not given each of its members physical or moral power in equal measure; on the contrary, strength and weakness are unequally distributed.

> From Lo[c]ke's definition we should conclude that the weakest in spirit and body would not have the same right to freedom. Since, according to his definition, freedom is power, a universal freedom cannot be understood, and it must necessarily be considered as individual freedom. But a freedom that is an individual prerogative, in society, is a tyranny, and a freedom that goes too far is lawlessness; Lo[c]ke could have said in the same way: freedom is tyranny, freedom is lawlessness.[266]

---

265 Locke, *An Essay*, II. 21. 6 (Idem, *An Essay*, edited by Peter H. Nidditch, 237–238).
266 Dobruska, *Philosophie sociale*, 174: [Il est donc impossible que la liberté, que Lo[c]ke définit puissance, soit une liberté qui fasse le bonheur de la masse de la société, puisque la nature n'a point donné à chacun de ses membres, une mesure égale de puissance soit physique ou morale, et qu'au contraire, la force et la foiblesse sont inégalement partagées entre eux. Toutefois, d'après la définition de Lo[c]ke, il nous faudroit conclure que les plus foibles d'esprit et de corps, n'auroient pas le même droit à la liberté. Or, puisque d'après sa définition, liberté est puissance, on ne peut entendre une liberté universelle, il faut nécessairement qu'il n'ait voulu définir qu'une liberté individuelle ayant pouvoir de tout faire. Mais une liberté prérogative individuelle, dans la société, étant une tyrannie, et une liberté poussée trop loin, étant *licence*; Loke pouvoit dire aussi justement: liberté est tyrannie, liberté est licence].

For Dobruska, the foundation on which individual freedom must rest is law, equal for all citizens. Only in this way can a democratic society guarantee individual freedom for everyone, regardless of their social class, religion, or level of education:

> Law is the duty of the relationship according to the principle, where the principle is individual conservation. As a result, freedom is based on the principle of law, and anything that hurts freedom is necessarily contrary to the principle, and therefore not a right.[267]

Dobruska therefore makes two important reflections on the boundaries of freedom.

The first boundary, or demarcation line, of the individual's freedom, is self-preservation. It is a question of defining the selection criteria that an individual has at his disposal in a democratic society.

In other words, the *Philosophie sociale* considers whether the individual can act according to his own tastes, inclinations, and in pursuit of pleasure, or whether social action should be delimited on the basis of some ethical principle.

A free individual has the possibility to choose between different behaviors and different activities. Some do him good and improve his well-being, while others do him harm.

As we have seen, freedom must be based on law, which in turn emanates from a very specific ethical principle, individual conservation. Consequently, on the basis of this principle, the freedom of choice of the subject is restricted. He cannot act only on the basis of his taste and his will. There is a very clear and distinct line of demarcation between what an individual can do and what a democratic society prohibits him from doing. In fact, there is an obligation not to harm oneself or, even more so, other individuals: "freedom in law consists in the choice between different beneficial things, and between non-harmful things".[268]

The free citizen cannot choose that which jeopardizes his physical or mental constitution. He is not allowed to choose between destructive options. This would be contrary to the ethical principle of individual conservation, the principle on which the Universal Constitution drawn up by Dobruska is based. The

---

267 *Ibidem*, 177: [Droit est devoir de la relation pour le principe, donc le principe est la conservation individuelle. Il en résulte, que la liberté se fonde sur le principe du droit, et que tout ce qui blesse la liberté, est nécessairement contraire au principe, n'est pas droit].

268 *Ibidem*, 192: [Mais si nous avons une fois trouvé cette ligne de démarcation, alors nous verrons, que la liberté en droit ne consiste en autre chose que dans le choix *entre les differens bons*, et les *différens non nuisibles*].

example given in the *Philosophie sociale* concerns the choice of a sick person in convalescence, in front of a variety of meals. Among the foods you can choose from there are those that support your recovery, and that do not harm your health, or those that are tasty but that damage and prevent the healing process. If, as in Locke, the principle of freedom were independent of the ethical principle of self-preservation, the patient in question could easily choose the food that seriously affects his health. No one could stop him, he would act according to his will. According to Dobruska, this example clearly shows how the exercise of mere will can turn into an abuse of power – in this case against oneself – or into a license, that is, for example, a special preference given to a particular citizen or corporation.

The choice of a harmful food by the patient is a bad act, as it endangers his health and his life. In the chapter dedicated to freedom, Dobruska thus concludes his reasoning:

> . . . bad choice becomes an act, an obedience against the principle, against the right, crime; freedom degenerates into license, the power to commit this act becomes tyranny, therefore it is necessary that [this act] be stopped by law and brought back to the beginning.[269]

The second boundary to individual freedom is the abuse of power, by one individual against others, or by the institutions of society, which, in doing so, contravene the law. A license then occurs.

One example of a license, on which Dobruska dwells more closely, is the one concerning religious institutions and, in particular, the imposition by a majority of their own religion.[270] His criticism is directed against the Christian religion, which in eighteenth-century Europe was the most widespread religion. It is not the words of Christ, towards whom Dobruska shows deep respect, that are being targeted, but the ecclesiastic dogmas, instituted by the "priests, successors of Christ" (*les prêtres, successeurs du Christ*[271]).

According to the *Philosophie sociale*, the teachings of priests, according to which the kingdom of heaven had an absolute value and priority over the

---

269 *Ibidem*, 187–188: [. . . le mauvais choix devient un acte, une obéissance contre *le principe, contre le droit. Un crime*; la liberté dégénère en licence, la puissance de commettre cet acte devient tyrannie, donc il faut qu'il soit arrêté là par la loi, et ramené au principe].
270 *Ibidem*, 181.
271 *Ibidem*, 46.

earthly world, "teach to die and not to live".[272] Dobruska is convinced that "there is no doctrine that is more dangerous for society, nothing that more hurts the principle of conservation of the self, both in the state of nature and in the social order. Yes, this religion is a clear usurpation of the rights of society, a murder of the principle".[273]

---

272 *Ibidem*, 180: [Celle-ci enseigne à mourir, mais non à vivre ; pour elle le ciel est tout; la terre n'est rien].

273 *Loc. cit.*: [Certainement il ne peut exister de doctrine plus dangereuse pour la société, nulle ne blesse autant le principe de la conservation du moi, dans l'état de nature et dans l'ordre social; oui, cette religion est une usurpation manifeste sur les droits de la société; un assassinat du principe].

5 Democracy, Aristocracy, or Monarchy? Representative Democracy

In the penultimate chapter of the Universal Constitution, Dobruska reflects on three different political models – democracy, aristocracy and monarchy. He wants to establish which is the best government for the future society that is born from the collapse of the *Ancien Régime*. It should be noted that the term "government" is understood in the eighteenth century in a manner similar to what is found, for example, in *The Spirit of the Laws* of Montesquieu,[274] that is its the sense of "political regime", and not in its contemporary meaning of "organ of executive power".

Let's stick to the metaphor of society as a body composed of different members, and imagine what can happen if some members are privileged over others, if they are fed and cared for more than the rest:

> In fact, if the blood flows faster, or heads towards the head more abundantly than usual, the eyes acquire a more vivid sparkle, the cheeks are more colorful, but it is an advantage that lasts little. Since nature has determined, for each part of the body, a portion of the juices necessary for its growth and maintenance, if you increase the supply to one part of the body to the detriment of the others, this produces the destruction of everything else. This apparent improvement [of a part of the body] is only a trap; this external brilliance hides the disease, and death watches over its victim.[275]

It's a clarifying metaphor. If a society adopts an aristocratic and monarchic regime, it privileges certain social groups or individuals at the expense of the great mass. In the long run, these regimes will destroy society itself.

If we move from the body to aristocratic and monarchic regimes, "the appearance is no less deceptive; the outward opulence of a small group hides from us the

---

274 The first thirteen books of *The Spirit of the Laws* of Montesquieu are devoted to the three types of government, which Raymond Aron calls a political sociology. It is "un effort pour réduire la diversité des formes de gouvernement à quelques types, chacun de ceux-ci étant défini, tout à la fois, par sa nature et son principe" (Aron, *Les étapes de la pensée sociologique*, 30). In the second book entitled *On the laws that derive directly from the nature of the government* Montesquieu begins by noting that "there are three species of governments: *republican, monarchical,* and *despotic*": See Montesquieu, *The complete Works of M. de Montesquieu*, 9.

275 *Philosophie sociale*, 233: [En effet, si le sang flue plus vite, ou se porte vers la tête en plus grande abondance que de coutume, les yeux acquièrent un éclat plus vif, les joues sont plus animées, mais cet avantage dure peu. La nature ayant déterminé pour chaque partie du corps, la portion de sucs nécessaire à sa croissance et à son entretien, l'augmentation de recette d'une partie au détriment des autres, produit la destruction de toutes; car cette apparence de mieux, n'est qu'an piège; cet extérieur brillant cache la maladie, et la mort veille sa victime].

misery of a million individuals; and the imminent death of the whole body is the inevitable consequence of this abusive and destructive regime".[276]

5.1 Representative Democracy

According to the *Philosophie sociale*, the compass that allows one to orient oneself in one's choice of political regime is always the primitive sovereign in the state of nature.[277] Representative democracy is the only healthy political regime for society, precisely because it is the one followed by the primitive sovereign in the state of nature.

In fact, only democracy can give each member, or individual, whatever his or her strength and ability, a portion of food commensurate with his or her needs.[278] In other words, in a representative democratic regime there is a balance or, if you like, a strictly fair balance of interests, which ensures the strength and health of the State. From this balance comes the general benefit and well-being which is given by the sum of the assets of each member:

> In the primitive state of pure nature, all members contribute to the needs and content-ment of the whole body; none [of the members] is dispensed from this task on the basis of a privilege; no member is preferred and no one can dwell in a state of guilty neutrality when it comes to the common interest in relation to the purpose, the principle.

> The stomach asks for food; the eye discovers it; the feet take it to the refreshing source, the nourishing root, which the hands promise to take immediately. If the hand finds a resistance, a dispute follows immediately. It overcomes the obstacle or rejects the oppo-nent who has less strength; and if it has more strength, the animal escapes and its paws save it from danger. In this situation, there is no struggle for functions, between the eye and the hand, the foot and the ear. Each of these members involuntarily and with all their means, shall co-operate in the defense and mutual assistance of the other. Each member uses all his knowledge in favor of the supreme one (the body).[279]

---

276 *Ibidem*, 234: [Ici l'apparence n'est pas moins trompeuse; l'opulence extérieure d'un petit nombre, nous cache la misère d'un million d'individus: et la mort prochaine du corps entier, est la suite inévitable de ce régime abusif et destructeur].
277 *Ibidem*, 233.
278 *Ibidem*, 234.
279 *Ibidem*, 156: [Dans l'état primitif de pure nature, tous les membres concourent aux be-soins et au contentement de tout le corps; aucun ne s'en dispense par privilège; aucun ne s'y porte par préférence, et nul ne peut demeurer dans une coupable neutralité, quand il s'agit de leur égal intérêt relativement au but, le *principe*. L'estomac demande des alimens, l'œil les dé-couvre; les pieds portent à la source rafraîchissante, à la racine nutritive, que la main prend aussitôt le soin d'arracher. Si elle trouve une résistance, s'il survient une dispute, elle

Here, society is conceived as a "social body" similar to what happens in the natural state, and democracy is the only system that satisfies the principle of harmonic distribution of resources, so as to maintain the vital balance of society.

The democracy to which the *Philosophie sociale* refers is the representative one, which differs from the direct one. If in direct democracy decisions for the community are taken by the holders of political rights, in representative democracy they are not taken by all citizens with the right to vote, but by the representatives that the citizens elect.

5.2 The Three Powers: Legislative, Executive, and Judicial

The *Philosophie sociale* questions the principles that allow the functioning of representative democracy. Dobruska substantially takes up the political theory of the division and separation of the three powers – the legislative, executive and judicial – elaborated almost half a century earlier by Montesquieu in *The Spirit of the Laws* (1748), an immense and fundamental work, which Montesquieu himself considered as "the fruit of the reflections of a lifetime".[280]

In the sixth chapter of the eleventh book, *On the laws that form political liberty, with regard to the constitution,* Montesquieu affirms the need for a division of powers within the State:

> In every government there are three sorts of power: the legislative; the executive in respect to things dependent on the law of nations; and the executive in regards to matters that depend on the civil law.

> By virtue of the first, the prince or magistrate enacts temporary or perpetual laws, and amends or abrogates those that have been already enacted. By the second, he makes peace or war, sends or receives embassies, establishes the public security, and provides against invasions. By the third, he punishes criminals, or determines the disputes that

---

surmonte l'obstacle ou repousse l'adversaire inférieur en forces; et s'il est supérieur, l'animal fuit, et ses jambes le sauvent du danger. Dans cette situation, point de lutte dans les fonctions, entre l'œil et la main, le pied et l'oreille, mais chacun de ces membres concourt involontairement et de tous ses moyens, à la défense et assistance réciproque de l'autre conclusion, chaque membre déploie tout son avoir en faveur du tout principal (le corps)].

280 Charles-Louis de Montesquieu, *Pensées – Le Spicilège*, edition established by Louis Desgraves, Paris: Laffont, 1991, nr. 1868: [Cet ouvrage est le fruit des réflexions de toute ma vie, et, peut-être, que, d'un travail immense, d'un travail fait avec les meilleures intentions, d'un travail fait pour l'utilité publique, je ne retirerai que des chagrins, et que je serai payé par les mains de l'ignorance et de l'envie].

arise between individuals. The latter we shall call the judiciary power, and the other, simply, the executive power of the state.[281]

As is well known, Montesquieu's theory, which has become the fulcrum of modern democracies, provides not only for the division of powers, but also for their separation.

Only with this separation is it possible to avoid tyranny and guarantee what is most desirable in a State, the freedom of individuals and the possibility for them to have control over their own lives:

> When the legislative and executive powers are united in the same person, or in the same body of magistrates, there can be no liberty; because apprehensions may arise, left the same monarch or senate should enact tyrannical laws, to execute them a tyrannical manner.

> Again, there is no liberty if the judiciary power be not separated from the legislative, the life and liberty of the subject would be then the legislator. Were it joined to executive power, the judge might behave with violence and oppression.

> There would be an end of every thing, were the same man, or the same body, whether of the nobles or of the people, to exercise those three powers, that of enacting laws, to exercise those three powers, that of enacting laws, that of executing the public resolutions, and of trying the causes of individuals.[282]

---

281 Montesquieu, *L'esprit des lois*, I. 11. 6 (Idem. *Tutte le opere*, 1219: [Il y a, dans chaque État, trois sortes de pouvoirs; la puissance législative, la puissance exécutrice des choses qui dépendent du droit des gens, et la puissance exécutrice de celles qui dépendent du droit civil. Par la première, le prince ou le magistrat fait des lois pour un temps ou pour toujours, et corrige ou abroge celles qui sont faites. Par la seconde, il fait la paix ou la guerre, envoie ou reçoit des ambassades, établit, la sûreté, prévient les invasions. Par la troisième, il punit les crimes, ou juge les différends des particuliers. On appellera cette dernière la puissance de juger; et l'autre, simplement la puissance exécutrice de l'État]. See Idem, *The complete Works of M. de Montesquieu*,198.

282 *Loc. cit.* (Montesquieu, *Tutte le opere*, 1220): [Lorsque, dans la même personne ou dans le même corps de magistrature, la puissance législative est réunie à la puissance exécutrice, il n'y a point de liberté; parce qu'on peut craindre que le même monarque ou le même sénat ne fasse des lois tyranniques, pour les exécuter tyranniquement. Il n'y a point encore de liberté, si la puissance de juger n'est pas séparée de la puissance législative, et de l'exécutrice. Si elle était jointe à la puissance législative, le pouvoir sur la vie et la liberté des citoyens serait arbitraire; car le juge serait législateur. Si elle était jointe à la puissance exécutrice, le juge pourrait avoir la force d'un oppresseur. Tout serait perdu, si le même homme, ou le même corps des principaux, ou des nobles, ou du peuple, exerçaient ces trois pouvoirs; celui de faire des lois, celui d'exécuter les résolutions publiques, et celui de juger les crimes ou les différends des particuliers]. See Idem, *The complete Works of M. de Montesquieu*, 199.

5.3 Legislative Power and the Enactment of Laws

It is on the basis of the premises laid down by Montesquieu that Dobruska, in the seventh chapter of his Universal Constitution, questions legislative power.

The task of legislating is entrusted to the legislative body (*le corps législatif*). According to the *Philosophie sociale*, this body is made up not of all the people, but of one part only of them. The holders of political rights elect their representatives, to whom they entrust the task of representing moral faculties, sentiment and reason, to seek and express determination through the principle and for the principle·[283]

This means that the legal bases of the law must be based on the moral faculties of individual citizens, in view of the general interest (the principle), which is the preservation of the social self.

For Dobruska, the law is "the expression of the determination of moral faculties, directed from the principle and for the principle".[284] In other words, the law expresses the moral faculties of a part of the members of the people – the elected representatives in the assembly. It must be based on the principles of the Universal Constitution.

What are such moral faculties, whether they be held by the legislative body or by elected citizens? According to our author, "man essentially possesses two moral faculties: reason and feeling".[285] However, these two faculties are not always in agreement with each other; on the contrary, they often disagree. Sometimes reason wants something that repels feeling, and vice versa. It is conscience that will determine whether man should listen to his own feeling or reason.

The law is the result of a process, in which the various members of the legislative body propose certain rules of conduct. These are the rules of conduct of the moral faculties, of reason and of the sentiment of the legislators.

When discussing the definition of a new law, the members of the legislative body should reflect on the needs of the social self, starting with the individual man:

> See, feel and reason about the needs of the great social self, according to the individual man, according to your judgment and your insights. Work, in such a way that your legislation reflects what happens in yourself, where the voices of reason and feeling alternately

---

283 Dobruska, *Philosophie sociale*, 20: [Le corps législatif est le délégué du peuple, pour représenter les facultés morales, *le sentiment* er *la raison* pour chercher et pour exprimer la détermination par le principe et pour le principe].

284 *Ibidem*, 119: [La loi est l'expression de la détermination des facultés morales, dirigées par le principe, et pour le principe].

285 *Ibidem*, 115.

become higher and more powerful; in a word, that each of you, according to his conscience, alternately relies on that of the two faculties which results to him as the most useful and the most applicable for the principle.[286]

The mediating authority will end the discussion and debate during the lawmaking process and determine the final law.

From what we have just said it is clear that, for Dobruska, the "legislative body is delegated by the people, to represent moral faculties, feeling and reason, so as to ensure the self-preservation of individual citizens and society".[287]

It should be pointed out that, if the legislative body ceases to represent the moral faculties of the people, its mission is null and void, because it has not achieved its aim.

In the *Philosophie sociale*, the justification and foundation of the legislator deviate from those of the political philosophy of Jean-Jacques Rousseau. If, for the latter, the foundation of the legislator resides in the general will (and not in the will of all), which has as its object the common good of the deliberative body,[288] for Dobruska it must instead be based on law.

Not only "the laws must be based on law but, in turn, law can only be based on the principle by which it is determined".

5.4 Executive Power

After analyzing the legislative power, the *Philosophie sociale* briefly mentions the executive power, which is interconnected with the legislative one. Once the legislature has defined its laws and behaviors, it is necessary for the executive to implement what has been decided.

It is clear that, for Dobruska, there is a direct link between the legislative and executive powers. And, in fact, he states that there is only one power, "both legislative and executive".[289]

---

286 *Ibidem,* 118: [Voyez, sentez et raisonnez sur les besoins du grand moi social d'après l'homme individuel, d'après votre jugement et vos lumières. Travaillez, de manière qu'il en soit dans votre législation ainsi que chacun de vous voit arriver en lui-même, ou la voix de la raison et du sentiment devient alternativement plus haute et plus puissante; en un mot, que chacun de vous fasse suivant sa conscience, dominer alternativement celle des deux faculté qui lui résultera comme la plus utile et la plus applicable pour le principe].
287 *Ibidem*, 120.
288 Alessandro Ferrara, "Autenticità, normatività dell'identità e ruolo del legislatore in Rousseau", in *La filosofia politica di Rousseau*, eds., Giulio Maria Chiodi and Roberto Gatti (Milano: Franco Angeli, 2012), 29.
289 *Ibidem,* 119.

5.5 The Judicial Power: Of Penalties and Crimes

Once the legislature has enacted the laws and the executive has put them into practice, a function and specific bodies must also be provided for in order to determine whether the laws have been correctly applied or whether an infringement has been committed. In the latter case, if citizens fail to comply, they must be punished with penalties.

Although Dobruska does not dwell on the judiciary and its main organs, such as the judiciary or the public prosecutor's office, he devotes a brief chapter – the fourteenth of his *Philosophie sociale* – to "punishments and crimes".[290]

The title naturally evokes the masterpiece of the Milanese Illuminist Cesare Beccaria, *Dei delitti e delle pene*, published in 1764 in Livorno[291] and translated a year later into French.[292]

Given the wide diffusion and recognition that Beccaria's work had among the *philosophes* throughout Europe, including French intellectuals – Diderot, Helvétius, Buffon, d'Holbach, d'Alembert and up to Voltaire, who dedicated an important *Commentary* to it in 1766[293] – it is very likely that Dobruska also knew the book.

Dobruska asks himself: "What criteria should be used to punish a person who commits a crime?". His answer is clear: the penalties for those who commit a crime must be based on the nature and proportionality of the crime committed. In other words, if the violation of the law concerns the civil sphere, a penalty enshrined in the civil code will follow. If the infringement concerns criminal matters, then criminal law will have jurisdiction. For a very slight transgression, there will also be a slight sanction; for a serious transgression there will be a severe penalty.[294]

In the case of a very serious crime, is it permissible to sentence the offender to the death penalty? According to the Universal Constitution, the death penalty

---

290 *Ibidem*, 218–119.

291 Cf. Cesare Beccaria, *Dei delitti e delle pene* (Livorno: Coltellini, 1764). The essay by the jurist and philosopher Cesare Beccaria proposed an important reform of criminal law. It was meant to introduce a "reduction in repressive intervention (today we would say "minimum penalty law"), [. . .] refusal of torture and request for a general reduction in penalties". See Alberto Burgio, "Tra diritto e politica. Note sul rapporto Beccaria-Montesquieu," *Rivista di Storia della Filosofia* 51 (1996): 661.

292 Cesare Beccaria, *Traité des Délits et des Peines, traduit de l'italien d'après la troisième édition, revue et corrigée et augmentée par l'auteur, avec des additions de l'auteur qui n'ont pas encore paru en italien* (Lausanne [but Paris] 1766. The translator was André Morellet (1727–1819).

293 Burgio, "Tra diritto e politica," 659.

294 Dobruska, *Philosophie sociale*, 219.

can only be imposed on those who have jeopardized the security and existence of the entire social body.

The proximity to Beccaria's thought is obvious. The Milanese jurist, in fact, theorized a drastic reduction of the death penalty to two cases: "when the 'power' and 'relationships' of a citizen represent threats to the 'security of the nation' and when 'his death is the only real brake to divert others from committing crimes'".[295]

According to Dobruska, the argument for this principle (the death penalty for those who endanger the safety of society as a whole) derives from the observation of what is happening in nature. In fact, the man who puts his own security at risk, risks dying, that is, "to be punished with death".[296]

5.6 Election of Civil Servants

Having defined the political regime and the three types of power, the second set of principles concerns the election of civil servants.

The first principle of this set concerns public officials, who are true representatives of the people, and whose election takes place in two different ways: (i) directly, by the people themselves, or (ii) through an electoral body, elected with general consent, and endowed with powers for the election of officials.[297]

The second principle concerns government representatives:

> The election of each member of the legislative body, of all officials, however modest their task may be, shall be made by roll call aloud. No official will be able to obtain any post without this formal procedure.[298]

The third principle is to determine who should represent the people:

> [. . .] the most capable and most suitable members must be employed as representatives by unanimous choice of all the other members in defense of and at the service of society as a whole since the government must assimilate its functions according to the regime of nature, which is the only just and precise form of government.[299]

---

295 Burgio, "Tra diritto e politica," 662.
296 Dobruska, *Philosophie sociale*, 218–219.
297 *Ibidem*, 160.
298 *Ibidem*, 169: [L'élection de chaque membre du corps législatif inclusivement, tous les fonctionnaires, si petit que soit leur emploi, se doit faire par appel nominal à haute voix, et aucun fonctionnaire ne pourra parvenir à aucune place sans cette formalité].
299 *Ibidem*, 158: [C'est ainsi que doit se conduire le gouvernement du nouveau corps (la société) dans chaque circonstance, les membres les plus capables, et les plus propres doivent être employés représentativement par le choix unanime de tous les autres, à la défense et au service du grand tout car le gouvernement doit assimiler ses fonctions au régime de la nature, qui

For Dobruska, the members who deserve to be elected as representatives of the government (political regime) are those who have developed and perfected their intellectual faculties.[300]

Moses Dobruska finally reflects, in the fourth group of principles, about the duration of the mandate of the government representatives. Mandates should last for as little time as possible, to avoid one of the social pathologies of the *Ancien Régime*, that is, the abuse of power by those who govern. Moreover, it is not acceptable for representatives of the people to be confirmed for life, that is, for an unlimited period of time.[301]

In order to prevent abuse of power by public officials, even during their term of office, it is the duty of the people to monitor their activities. In fact, "the people are always at the same time monarch and subject".[302]

5.7 The Defense of the State and the Just War

In the seventh chapter of the Universal Constitution, Dobruska asks whether war is just or unjust, and whether the use of armed force by a state is permissible and ethically acceptable.

It is right that a State should use armed force when it wants to defend a society that fights for freedom and equality of rights for each citizen, and that seeks to satisfy the appetite, developed at the highest levels. The use of war, on the other hand, is ethically unjust when it is not motivated by the general interest, which we have outlined here. It would then be a tyrannical war, contrary to the general interest and to to the founding principle of the Universal Constitution.[303]

5.8 Social Education

Dobruska has presented us with his Universal Constitutions. In each chapter, a specific theme has been examined in depth, and at the end of the chapter the

---

est l'unique forme du gouvernement juste et exacte, ou chaque fonctionnaire est un véritable représentant du corps entier, et ou l'élection de chaque membre se fait par le consentement du corps entier].

300 *Ibidem*, 159.
301 *Ibidem*, 169.
302 *Ibidem*, 170: [C'est ainsi que le peuple reste toujours en même-terms le monarque et le sujet].
303 *Ibidem*, 129.

principles, or rather the regulatory rules necessary to build a representative democratic society, have been set out. The set of all the principles forms the framework (*tableau*), which is to be exhibited in the assemblies of the popular sections and the legislative body. Every people, taking into account its geographical and climatic situation, will find in the *tableau* freedom and happiness, indispensable to realize the second part of the Constitution. Since, as we know, the first part of the Constitution is the guarantee on which the second part rests, the people will no longer have to fear oppression or abuse.

We have already briefly discussed the educational value of the Universal Constitution. It is a concept, one of pedagogy at the service of law and democracy, which already finds full expression in Montesquieu. In the fifth chapter of the fourth book of *The Spirit of the Laws*, which bears the significant title of *Education in the Republican Government*, we read the following:

> It is in a republican government that the whole power of education is required. [. . .]

> This love is peculiar to democracies. In these alone the government is intrusted to private citizens. Now, the government is like every thing else: to preserve it, we must love it. [. . .]

> Every thing, therefore, depends on establishing this love in a republic; and to inspire it ought to be the principal business of education: but the surest way of instilling it into children is for parents to set them an example.[304]

The difference between Montesquieu's approach and what is found in the *Philosophie sociale*, in terms of democratic education, lies rather in the motivations that are called upon to implement the educational process. Montesquieu appeals to the concept of virtue:

> Virtue in a republic is a most simple thing; it is a love of the republic; it is a sensation, and not a consequence of acquired knowledge; a sensation that may be felt by the meanest as well as by the highest person in the state. When the common people adopt good maxims, they adhere to them steadier than those we call gentlemen. It is very rare that corruption commences with the former: nay, they frequently derive from their imperfect light a stronger attachment to the established laws and customs.

---

304 Montesquieu, *L'esprit des lois*, IV. 5: [C'est dans le gouvernement républicain que l'on a besoin de toute la puissance de l'éducation [. . .] Cet amour est singulièrement affecté aux démocraties. Dans elles seules, le gouvernement est confié à chaque citoyen. Or, le gouvernement est comme toutes les choses du monde; pour le conserver, il faut l'aimer [. . .] Tout dépend donc d'établir, dans la république, cet amour; et c'est à l'inspirer, que l'éducation doit être attentive, mais, pour que les enfans puissant l'avoir, il y a un moyen sûr; c'est que les pères l'aient eux-mêmes] (Idem, *Tutte le opere*, 976–978). See Idem, *The complete Works of M. de Montesquieu*, 43–44.

The love of our country is conducive to a purity of morals, and the latter is again conducive to the former. The less we are able to satisfy our private passions, the more we abandon ourselves to those of a general nature. How comes it that monks are so fond of their order? It is owing to the very cause that renders the order insupportable. Their rule debars them all those things by which the ordinary passions are fed; there remains, therefore, only this passion for the very rule that torments them; the more austere it is, the more it curbs their inclinations, the more force it gives to the only passion left them.[305]

The strategy proposed by Dobruska is partly different, in focusing on "interest" as a concrete benefit of democracy, rather than on an idealistic call for democratic pietas:

In a word: the form of democratic government must have real charm and advantages: either yes or no. If it did not have them, it would be worth nothing, it would have to be rejected and it would not deserve for us to deal with it; but if it has them, as is true, we only have to say: the form of republican democratic government has advantages, real and sublime beauties, which are freedom, equal rights.[306]

For the liberalist Dobruska, citizens must have a clear understanding of the benefits of democratic freedom. The benefits of freedom – such as the enjoyment of private property, freedom of the press, freedom of religion – must be understood through a cognitive process that also involves emotions. Think of the joy of owning a house, the happiness of being able to express one's ideas, the feeling of peace and trust of those who do not suffer discrimination because of their religious faith:

---

305 *Ibidem*, V. 2: [La vertu dans une république est une chose très simple: c'est l'amour de la république; c'est un sentiment, et non une suite de connoissances: le dernier homme de l'Etat peut avoir ce sentiment, comme le premier. Quand le peuple a une fois de bonnes maximes, il s'y tient plus long-tems, que ce qu'on appelle les honnêtes-gens. Il est rare que la corruption commence par lui. Souvent il a tiré, de la médiocrité de ses lumières, un attachement plus fort pour ce qui est établi. L'amour de la patrie conduit à la bonté des mœurs, et la bonté des mœurs mène à l'amour de la patrie. Moins nous pouvons satisfaire nos passions particulières, plus nous nous livrons aux générales. Pourquoi les moines aiment-ils tant leur ordre? C'est justement par l'endroit qui fait qu'il leur est insupportable. Leur règle les prive de toutes les choses sur lesquelles les passions ordinaires s'appuient: reste donc cette passion pour la règle même qui les affligent. Plus elle est austère, c'est-à-dire, plus elle retranche de leurs penchans, plus elle donne de force à ceux qu'elle leur laisse" (Idem, *Tutte le opere*, 994–996). See Idem, *The complete Works of M. de Montesquieu*, 52.
306 Dobruska, *Philosophie sociale*, 211: [En un mot: il faut que la forme du gouvernement démocratique ait oui ou non, des charmes et des avantages réels. Si elle n'en n'avoit pas, elle ne vaudroit rien, il fauchoit la rejeter, et elle ne mériteroit point que l'on s'en occupât; mais si elle les a, comme il est très – véritable, nous n'avons qu'à dire: la forme du gouvernement démocratique républicain à des avantages, des beautés réelles et sublimes, qui sont la liberté, l'égalité des droits].

All we need is to develop these real and sublime advantages into a constitution, to bring them to the feeling and reason of youth, and thus sow the seeds of human dignity for the true democrat. By only this means, by this unique vessel of light, this only true principle of a democratic republic, will disappear the fear of seeing a large part of our fellow French citizens, drag on, so to speak, aristocratic principles, and transmit them from generation to generation, according to the great number of aristocrats who are still among us.[307]

For Dobruska, therefore, education is the knowledge of the interests and advantages that democratic principles, contained in the Constitution, confer on citizens (Fig. 5). The first and main of these advantages is undoubtedly freedom, which allows the individual to develop their own desires, material and intellectual.

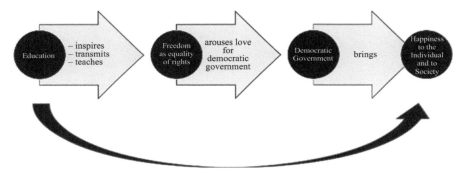

Fig. 5: The Formative Process and the Goals of Education, according to the *Philosophie Sociale* of Moses Dobruska.
Source: author.

In order to educate young people on democratic principles, the Universal Constitution must be an inspiring one. Like Montesquieu, Dobruska is convinced that learning is a process that also deeply involves emotionality. That is why

---

307 *Ibidem*, 217: [On n'a besoin que de développer ces avantages réels et sublimes dans une constitution, de les porter au sentiment et à la raison de la jeunesse, et de semer ainsi le germe de la dignité de l'homme, pour le vrai démocrate. Par ce seul moyen, par cette bâse unique de lumière, ce seul vrai principe d'une république démocratique, disparoîtra la crainte de voir une grande partie de nos concitoyens François, s'éterniser pour ainsi dire dans les principes aristocratiques, et les transmettre de génération en génération, d'après la grande quantité d'aristocrates qui sont encore parmi nous].

the principles must be "felt" and internalized emotionally. It is interesting to remark that this emotional dimension of learning, which we see emerging in the *Philosophie sociale,* will only be deepened in the social sciences from the 1980s onwards.[308]

308 Tina Hascher, "Learning and Emotions. Perspectives for Theory and Research," *European Educational Research Journal* 9 (2010): 13–27. On the subject of emotions in sociological research, see Helena Flam, *Soziologie der Emotionen. Eine Einführung* (Konstanz: UVK, 2002); Katharina Scherke, *Emotionen als Forschungsgegenstand der deutschsprachigen Soziologie* (Wiesbaden: Springer, 2009); Massimo Cerulo, *Sociologia delle emozioni* (Bologna: Il Mulino, 2018).

6 Happiness

6.1 The Telos of the Future Democratic Society: The Happiness of Citizens

Moses Dobruska's philosophical-social thought has not only a vocation of social criticism and evaluation of all the dysfunctions of the *Ancien Régime*, but also a proactive vision, which places the emphasis on all the advantages of the society of the future.

Dobruska is well aware of the model of society that he intends to build, and of the purpose that this society will have to pursue. He wants a democratic society in which citizens can be happy.

Happiness is therefore the great cornerstone of his Universal Constitution. It is the ultimate goal, it is the *telos* of the future society, it is the longed-for goal that justifies the difficult battle against the absolutist monarchical society. The *Philosophie sociale* therefore also has a teleological angle.

We know that, for the social philosophers of the nineteenth century, and again for those of the first half of the twentieth century, happiness has a rather marginal role. At the theoretical centre is the idea of economic and social progress, or the idea of a communist society, based on equality and overcoming private ownership of the means of production.

The situation is different in the eighteenth century, where the search for happiness is not only fashionable, but sometimes takes on tones of obsession.[309] And this is not only in the salons of the *philosophes*, writers, cultivated women, and novelists, locked up in their beautiful castles or élite circles – happy, it will be said, about their privileges, and far from the daily life of the peasant population, which instead struggles, day by day, for physical survival. The concern for happiness also affects revolutionary circles and political activists, in France as in America, who sought a radical change in a society that is largely still semi-feudal.[310]

---

309 Louis Trénard, "Pour une histoire sociale de l'idée de 'bonheur' au XVIIIe siècle," *Annales historiques de la Révolution française* 35, 173 (1963): 309.

310 Laurent Loty, *Que signifie l'entrée du bonheur dans la Constitution*, in *Le bonheur au XVIIIe siècle*, texts gathered and presented by, Guilhem Farrugia and Michel Delon (Rennes: Presses Universitaires de Rennes, 2015), 79–86: 81.

Suffice it to recall the second paragraph of the *Declaration of Independence of the United States of America* of 1776,[311] which states that "the pursuit of happiness" is an inalienable right of man:

> We hold these Truths to be self-evident, that all Men are created equal, that they are endowed by their Creator with certain unalienable Rights, that among these are Life, Liberty, and the Pursuit of Happiness – That to secure these Rights, Governments are instituted among Men, deriving their just Powers from the consent of the Governed, that whenever any Form of Government becomes destructive of these Ends, it is the Right of the People to alter or to abolish it, and to institute new Government, laying its Foundation on such Principles, and organizing its Powers in such Form, as to them shall seem most likely to effect their Safety and Happiness.[312]

In France, too, the *Declaration of the Rights of Man and of the Citizen* of 1789,[313] which was partly inspired by that of the United States of America, states that the ultimate goal of the new Constitution is to achieve the happiness of citizens, considered equal before the law.

---

311 The *Declaration of Independence*, drawn up on July 2, 1776 and entered into force two days later, sanctioned the independence of thirteen British colonies in North America.

312 *A Declaration by the Representatives of the United States of America*, 4 July 1776.

313 The *Declaration of the Rights of Man and of the Citizen* was approved by the National Assembly on 26 August 1789 and would also be the preamble to the liberal Constitution of 1791. I recall the first paragraph, which stresses that the purpose of any political institution is to maintain the Constitution and reach universal happiness. *Déclaration des droits de l'homme, et articles de Constitution présentés au Roi, avec sa réponse*, Paris: chez Baudoin, imprimeur de l'Assemblée Natonale, 1789, [1]-2: [The Representatives of the French People constituted in the National Assembly, considering that ignorance, oblivion, or contempt for human rights are the only causes of public misfortune and corruption of governments, have decided to set out, in a solemn declaration, the natural, inalienable, and sacred rights of man, so that this declaration, constantly present to all members of the social body, reminds them incessantly of their rights and duties; so that the acts of the legislative power, and those of the executive power, which can be compared at any time with the purpose of any political institution, are more respected; so that the complaints of citizens, now based on simple and indisputable principles, always turn to the maintenance of the Constitution and the happiness of all (Les Représentants du Peuple Français, constitués en Assemblée Nationale, considérant que l'ignorance, l'oubli ou le mépris des Droits de l'Homme sont les seules causes des malheurs publics et de la corruption des Gouvernements, ont résolu d'exposer, dans une Déclaration solennelle, les droits naturels, inaliénables et sacrés de l'Homme, afin que cette Déclaration, constamment présente à tous les Membres du corps social, leur rappelle sans cesse leurs droits et leurs devoirs; afin que les actes du pouvoir législatif, et ceux du pouvoir exécutif pouvant être à chaque instant comparés avec le but de toute institution politique, en soient plus respectés; afin que les réclamations des Citoyens, fondées désormais sur des principes simples et incontestables, tournent toujours au maintien de la Constitution, et au bonheur de tous)].

From now on, individuals will no longer be subjected, oppressed by unjust and tyrannical political regimes, but citizens capable of building political institutions that make them happy. The kind of happiness which is pursued is not only a happiness of the individual but also of the community as a whole. As Laurent Loty states, "these constitutional preambles reveal that the so private and individual question of happiness is inseparable from a collective dimension, of an ideological and political order".[314]

It should be remembered that only a couple of years later, in September 1791, The *Declaration of the Rights of Women and of the Female Citizen,* by the writer and feminist Olympe de Gouges (1748–1793) was published. In the preamble, it is stated that women must also be able to enjoy the same rights as men, so as to achieve the same happiness:

Mothers, daughters, sisters, representatives of the nation, ask to be constituted in a national assembly. Considering that ignorance, oblivion, or contempt for women's rights are the only causes of public misfortunes in the corruption of governments, they have resolved to set out in a solemn declaration the inalienable and sacred natural rights of women, so that this declaration, which is constantly present to all members of the social body, may incessantly remind them of their rights and duties, so that the acts of the power of women and those of the power of men, being able to be confronted at any time with the purpose of any political institution, are more respected, so that the complaints of the citizens, now based on simple and indisputable principles, are always directed towards the maintenance of the constitution, good morals and the happiness of all.[315]

---

314 See Loty, *Que signifie l'entrée du bonheur*, 79: [Ces préambules constitutionnels révèlent aussi que la question si privée et individuelle du bonheur est inséparable d'une dimension collective, d'ordre idéologique et politique].

315 *Déclaration des droits de la femme et de la citoyenne*, (Paris: 1791), 6: [Les mères, les filles, les sœurs, représentantes de la nation, demandent d'être constituées en assemblée nationale. Considérant que l'ignorance, l'oubli ou le mépris des droits de la femme, sont les seules causes des malheurs publics et de la corruption des gouvernements, ont résolu d'exposer dans une déclaration solennelle, les droits naturels inaliénables et sacrés de la femme, afin que cette déclaration, constamment présente à tous les membres du corps social, leur rappelle sans cesse leurs devoirs, afin que les actes du pouvoir des femmes, et ceux du pouvoir des hommes pouvant être à chaque instant comparés avec le but de toute institution politique, en soient plus respectés, afin que les réclamations des citoyennes, fondées désormais sur des principes simples et incontestables, tournent toujours au maintien de la constitution, des bonnes mœurs, et au bonheur de tous]. Olympe de Gouges was a French writer of novels, plays, and political essays, and a political activist, who fought for the recognition of the inalienable rights of women as well as men. An *ante litteram* icon of feminism whose writings have long been forgotten. She was guillotined on November 3, 1793. It is said that before climbing the gallows she said: "If the woman is given to climb the gallows, she will be given to climb the stands too". For further information see Sophie Mousset, *Women's Rights and the French Revolution. A Biography of Olympe de Gouges* (New Brunswick: Transaction, 2007).

With this statement, for the first time in such a clear and explicit way, women express their will to enter fully into history as active subjects, and not as subjects dependent on their father's or husband's power. However, we know that the path of women towards full citizenship will be much longer and more difficult than that of men.

The Constitution of the French Republic, promulgated on June 24, 1793, also takes up the preamble of the Declaration of the Rights of Man and of the Citizen, slightly modifying it and reaffirming the concept of happiness in the first article:

> The French people, convinced that oblivion and contempt for the natural rights of man are the only causes of the misfortunes of the world, have decided to set out in a solemn declaration these sacred and inalienable rights, so that all citizens, being able to constantly compare the acts of government with the purpose of each social institution, do not allow themselves to be oppressed and discouraged by tyranny, so that the people always have before their eyes the foundations of their freedom and their happiness, the magistrate the rule of his duties, the legislator the object of his mission. Consequently, it proclaims, before the Supreme Being, the following declaration of human and citizen's rights.
>
> Art. 1. – The purpose of society is common happiness. – The government is set up to ensure that man enjoys his natural and inalienable rights.[316]

It is noteworthy that the preface to the *Philosophie sociale* is dated June 26, two days after the publication of the Constitution of 1793. This is not a random coincidence, but a desire on the part of Dobruska to join the constitutional debate, which has engaged French politics for many months. Even with regard to the

---

316 *Acte constitutionnel du Peuple Français avec le Rapport, la Déclaration des Droits et le Procès-verbal d'inauguration*, Paris: Imprimerie nationale, 1793, 17: [Le Peuple Français, convaincu que l'oubli et le mépris des droits naturels de l'homme sont les seules causes des malheurs du monde, a résolu d'exposer, dans une déclaration solennelle, ces droits sacrés et inaliénables, afin que tous les citoyens, pouvant comparer sans cesse les actes du gouvernement avec le but de toute institution sociale, ne se laissent jamais opprimer, avilir par la tyrannie; afin que le peuple ait toujours devant les yeux les bases de sa liberté et de son Bonheur, le magistrat la règle de ses devoirs, le législateur l'objet de sa mission. En conséquence, il proclame, en présence de l'Être suprême, la déclaration suivante des droits de l'homme et du citoyen. Article premier. Le but de la société est le bonheur commun. Le gouvernement est institué pour garantir à l'homme la jouissance de ses droits naturels et imprescriptibles]. On the Constitution of June 24 see *La Constitution du 24 juin 1793. L'utopie dans le droit public français?*, texts collected by Jean Bart, Jean-Jacques Clère, Claude Courvoisier and Michel Verpeaux, coordinated by Françoise Naudin-Patriat (Dijon: Editions universitaires, 1997). As for the constitutional draft promoted by the Gironde, and then shelved after the prevalence of the Jacobins, see Andreas Kley and Richard Amstutz, *Gironde-Verfassungsentwurf aus der französischen Revolution vom 15./16. Februar 1793 deutschsprachige Übersetzung mit einer Einleitung und kommentierenden Anmerkungen* (Zürich: Nomos, 2011).

happiness of citizens, which is the ultimate goal of the constitutional effort, the closeness between our author's project and the official document is significant.

Although Dobruska tends to be rigorous in his definitions, we do not find throughout the *Philosophie sociale* a clear distinction between individual and public happiness (*félicité publique*).[317] However, we can deduce six basic elements of happiness.

First, Dobruska theorizes a subjective dimension to happiness. As I have already pointed out, for our author, human beings are different from each other in terms of physical, moral,[318] and intellectual strength. Nature has never produced two identical beings.[319] In fact, it loves the infinite nuances that it strives to create. Precisely because human beings are so different, they want different things. As a result, each of them seeks happiness in their own way. Note how Dobruska never starts from a metaphysical vision of *ex ante* happiness, but from the "almost empirical" observation of individuals in their social and cultural context, in effect anticipating future social sciences.

Secondly, Dobruska links happiness to the idea of "individual progress", a thesis now more relevant than ever in various schools of thought in the social sciences.[320] Let us remember that Dobruska defines man as "a living being whose instinct is susceptible to the highest development and the greatest perfection". Developing one's material and intellectual desires, expanding one's potential, perfecting oneself (*perfectibilité*) and freely using one's faculties – all these progressive attitudes allow man to achieve coveted happiness. On this theme, Dobruska says:

> Since what the individual owes to society is reduced to the development of his appetite, which in no way represents a real benefit, without the freedom to use all his faculties to satisfy his highest desires, and since individuals are in absolutely the same situation as regards the free exercise of their faculties to achieve happiness, problems can only arise when the exercise of that freedom degenerates into excess.[321]

---

317 Dobruska, *Philosophie sociale*, vi.
318 *Ibidem*, 174.
319 *Ibidem*, 208.
320 Think, for example, of positive psychology or the concept of *empowerment*. See, e.g., Norbert Herriger, *Empowerment in der Sozialen Arbeit. Eine Einführung* (Stuttgart: Verlag W. Kohlkammer, 2019) (I ed. 2002).
321 *Philosophie sociale*, 86: [Or, comme tout ce que l'individu doit à la société se réduit au développement de sa faculté appétitive, qui n'est point un bénéfice réel, sans la liberté de faire usage de toutes ses facultés pour satisfaire ses désirs développés, et comme tous les individus sont absolument dans le même cas par rapport à cet exercice libre de leurs facultés pour atteindre le bonheur désiré, il n'y peut exister d'inconvénient que lorsque l'exercice de cette liberté dégénère en licence].

Here we can see a great closeness to the thought of the Jacobin Robespierre, influenced in turn by Rousseau. At the National Convention, which took place in the Tuileries Palace, in the session of May 10, 1793, just a month before the publication of the *Philosophie sociale*, Robespierre began his speech on the *Constitution* with these words:

> Man was born for happiness and freedom, and he is always a slave and unhappy! Society has as its aim the maintenance of his rights and the perfection of his being, and everywhere society degrades and oppresses him! The progress of human reason has prepared this great revolution, and it is your duty to accelerate it.[322]

For Dobruska, as for Robespierre, man must aspire to his own happiness, thanks to the perfection of his being, supported by society, of which I will say more in the chapter dedicated to the social determinants of happiness.[323] This progress is naturally also linked to rational abilities, to reason. As Robert Mauzi points out, happiness "symbolizes the triumph over destiny [. . .] Thanks to progress, happiness ceases to be a dream and becomes a certainty. From motionless abstraction or inconsistent chimera, it is transformed, in a decisive way, into a *project*".[324] This project of perfectibility should be understood as a becoming, a movement, and not as rest or tranquility of the soul.

Thirdly, the project of expansion and perfectibility of man, which leads to happiness, is realized in the social reality of everyday life. It is therefore an earthly happiness and not a religious one.

Among the *philosophes* of the eighteenth century there was a wide debate about whether happiness was earthly or spiritual. That is, whether it could be achieved in earthly life or only in the afterlife, as claimed by many authors, especially in the first half of the century. Some, such as Madame Aubert, conceived of happiness in close relation to religious practices, without renouncing worldly life. In this regard, Madame Aubert, an author of whom no biographical

---

322 Maximilien de Robespierre, *Œuvres de Robespierre*, collected and annotated by Auguste Jean- Marie Vermorel (Paris: F. Courmol, 1866), 276 (cf. Maximilien de Robespierre, *Pour le bonheur et pour la liberté. Discours*, selected and presented by Yannick Bosc, Florence Gauthier and Sophie Wahnich (Paris: La Fabrique 2000): [L'homme est né pour le bonheur et pour la liberté, et partout il est esclave et malheureux! La société a pour but la conservation de ses droits et la perfection de son être; et partout la société le dégrade et l'opprime! Le temps est arrivé de le rappeler à ses véritables destinées; les progrès de la raison humaine ont préparé cette grande révolution, et c'est à vous qu'est spécialement imposé le devoir de l'accélérer].
323 See below, 6. 2.
324 Robert Mauzi, *L'idée du bonheur dans la littérature et la pensée françaises au XVIIIe siècle* (Paris: Colin, 1965), 570: [Elle symbolise le triomphe de celle-ci sur le destin. [. . .] Grâce au progrès, le bonheur cesse d'être un rêve pour devenir certitude. D'abstraction immobile ou inconsistante chimère, il se change résolument en *projet*].

detail is known,[325] explains in the preface to her 1730 essay *Les charmes de la société du chrétien* how it is precisely sociability, the aptitude to live in society, that leads to happiness.

According to the author, the Christian religion plays a very important social role in this regard because it creates solid bonds that bring satisfaction. "Only the Christian believer is able to open paths that lead to a solid happiness".[326] As Mauzi points out:

> The Christian is no longer, as in the past, the tortured ascetic, the lost mystic, or the militant of faith. Now he becomes an honest man, perfumed and courteous, sweet to his fellow men, who knows how to live wonderfully.[327]

For his part, Dobruska certainly does not have in mind a happiness linked to religious practices, let alone to Christian ones, but a happiness that can only be achieved in earthly life, thanks to the bonds of reciprocity between individuals.

This brings us to the fourth characteristic of happiness. In addition to being linked to the rationality necessary for the development of appetizing, material, and intellectual faculties, the happiness theorized in the *Philosophie sociale* is combined with feeling, the ability to listen to one's heart and to feel empathy for other human beings. The "seed of happiness resides in the hearts of peoples".[328] The feeling that leads to happiness is born from one's relationship with others, thanks to the social interaction that individuals have with their fellow human beings. As far as the achievement of individual and public happiness is concerned, in short, there is no duality between reason and feeling.

A fifth meaning of the term is that of moral happiness. In this way, we enter into the broad eighteenth-century debate about the link between morality, called "virtue" by many authors, and happiness.[329]

Virtue here means "to grant an advantage in view of the happiness of another person over one's own happiness".[330] In other words, virtue is doing good, being a benefactor, not harming others. For Augustin Rouillé d'Orfeuil (17–18 century),

---

325 Cfr. Gauvin A. Bailey, *The Spiritual Rococo. Decor and Divinity from the Salons of Paris to the Missions of Patagonia* (Farnham: Ashgate, 2014), 35.

326 "Madame" Aubert, *Les charmes de la société du chrétien* (Paris: Jacques Estienne, 1730), 22.

327 Mauzi, *L'idée du bonheur*, 185: [Le chrétien n'est plus cet ascète torturé, ni ce mystique éperdu, ni ce militant de la foi, qu'il lui arrivait d'être naguère. Il devient un honnête homme, parfumé et courtois, doux pour ses semblables, et sachant merveilleusement vivre].

328 Dobruska, *Philosophie sociale*, 4.

329 A subject that has already been widely addressed by the philosophers of antiquity. Think of the fourth book of the *Republic of* Plato: cf., e.g., Richard D. Parry, "Morality and Happiness. Book IV of Plato's "Republic," *The Journal of Education* 178 (1996): 31–47.

330 Mauzi, *L'idée du bonheur*, 580.

virtue "is love for truth and good. Every man who knows all the qualities that really constitute good, desires, loves them, and necessarily follows them".[331]

At first glance, virtue and happiness may seem in opposition to each other: if you give an advantage to another person, increasing his happiness, or if you act in the general interest, instead of for your own sake, as Luc de Clapiers, Marquis of Vauvenargues (1715–1747),[332] says, you do not act in view of your own happiness.

A more in-depth examination, however, shows that the need for happiness is not in contradiction with the moral need. On the contrary, it implies it. To the extent that "virtuous actions contribute to the peace of the soul, being virtuous means working for one's own happiness".[333] According to Dobruska, the moral actions that one person carries out towards another do not only benefit the person directly concerned (the beneficiary) but also those who carry out this action.

An example of moral action, reported in the *Philosophie sociale,* is the help that a person offers to two unfortunate people, who risk drowning in a river: "he sacrifices his own rest, in throwing himself into the waves to grab the unfortunate from the abyss, which already opens under their inert bodies".[334] From the sentence I have just quoted, it emerges how the benefactor renounces his own rest in order to perform a selfless action. Unlike other 18th century authors, such as the Catholic bishop Jean-Baptiste Massillon (1663–1742),[335] Dobruska does not, however, analyze the link between rest and happiness. Rather, our author notes the link between happiness and moral action toward

---

331 Augustin Rouillé d'Orfeuil, *L'alambic moral, ou, Analyse raisonnée de tout ce qui a rapport à l'homme.* [but Paris?] : Maroc, 1773, 535: [Vertu . . . est l'amour de la vérité et du bien . . . tout homme qui connoit toutes les qualités qui constituent réellement le bien, le désire, l'aime et le suit nécessairement].

332 Luc de Clapiers de Vauvenargues, *Œuvres complètes* (Paris: Hachette, 1968, vol. 1), 64: [La préférence de l'intérêt général au personnel, est la seule définition qui soit digne de la vertu, et qui doive en fixer l'idée. Au contraire, le sacrifice mercenaire du bonheur public à l'intérêt propre, est le sceau éternel du vice]; cf. Mauzi, *L'idée du bonheur,* 580.

333 *Loc. cit.*

334 Dobruska, *Philosophie sociale,* 102: [un don de son propre repos de se jeter dans les flots pour arracher des malheureux à l'abyme qui s'ouvre déjà sous leurs corps abattus].

335 In the eighteenth century a great debate, which animated the *philosophes,* concerned whether happiness arose from rest and inner life or from action, in particular from virtuous or moral action. According to Massillon, for example, happiness "is not to be found in splendor or power, but in innocence, in the quiet of the soul purified of passions and satisfied with itself". Mauzi, *L'idée du bonheur,* 603.

other people – acting for the good of others. The reward for these moral actions consists of a sense of fullness, which can lead to happiness.

A final meaning of the term "happiness", theorized in the *Philosophie sociale*, is what we could define as "sociological happiness". I propose this definition based on the "philosophical happiness" of which Mauzi speaks in the eighteenth century.[336] The reference is to the "science of happiness", of which the Age of Enlightenment is in search, starting from the knowledge of human nature and of the "laws of feeling". The premise of this science is the existence of a "universal human being", whose inner mechanisms of the "heart" can be known. On the basis of these mechanisms, it will be possible to "know" what makes a man happy and what makes him unhappy.

Alexander Pope is the philosopher who, more than any other, expresses the morality of universal man, whose ultimate goal is happiness. In Pope's *Essay on Man*, man's destiny is no longer taken to be determined by God. Man determines his place in the universe and builds his happiness. We have already noticed Dobruska's debt to Pope, also expressed by the quotation from the *Essay on Man* on the frontispiece of the *Philosophie sociale*. Unlike the English philosopher, however, our author does not focus on the universal man, but on the man who lives with other individuals in society.

Dobruska does not pursue a "philosophical happiness", starting with universal man. His objective is instead a "sociological happiness", which is about being social. The *Philosophie sociale* investigates the social, cultural, and political conditions that allow, or prevent, the achievement of happiness in society.

In conclusion, we can say that, for Dobruska, happiness is not an unreachable chimera, but a condition within the reach of many, thanks to the support of society.

6.2 The Social Determinants of Happiness

Dobruska believes in the possibility of scientifically studying happiness. Its purpose is not to provide a simplistic explanation or some moral rules for the achievement of a "universal and abstract philosophical happiness", defined *ex ante*. Rather, our author asks himself what are the political, social, and cultural factors that allow man to develop, to satisfy his material and intellectual desires, and to act morally, that is to say, to move towards the achievement of happiness.

---

336 *Ibidem*, 216–268: *Le bonheur philosophique*.

These are the elements that, in today's sociological literature, we would define as the "social determinants" of happiness, or all those political, legal, cultural, economic, and social conditions that can support, or prevent, the achievement of individual happiness. This is a theme that, since the nineties of the twentieth century, has again been of great interest among social scientists, from psychologists to sociologists.[337]

Dobruska identifies four kinds of factors that promote happiness: political factors (democratic regime and universal rights), legal factors (the Constitution, the law, and the hierarchy of sources), cultural factors (education) and, finally, economic and social factors (the distribution of material wealth among the social classes).

6.2.1 Political Factors Supporting the Achievement of Happiness

Only a democratic regime, based on the universal right to freedom, defends man "from devastation and the invasion of licenses",[338] as well as tyranny, all of which prevent him from expressing himself and moving freely in society. It is thanks to the equality of rights – freedom – that man is allowed to develop all his faculties, the source of happiness. It can well be said that, in the *Philosophie sociale*, the first determinant of happiness is political: without democracy, there can be no happy life for all citizens.

6.2.2 Legal Factors

It is not difficult to anticipate the answer that Dobruska offers in specifying the legal conditions that support the achievement of happiness of individuals in a

---

337 For a first overview of the social determinants of happiness (and dissatisfaction) see Karl-Siegbert Rehberg, "The Fear of Happiness. Anthropological motives," *Journal of Happiness Studies* 1 (2000): 479–500; Alfred Bellebaum and Robert Hettlage, eds., *Glück hat viele Gesichter. Annäherungen an eine gekonnte Lebensführung* (Wiesbaden: VS Verlag, 2010); Silvana Greco, Mary Holmes and Jordan McKenzie, "Friendship and Happiness from a Sociological perspective," in *Friendship and Happiness. Across the Life-Span and Culture*, ed. Melikşah. Demir (New York: Springer 2015), 19–35; Andrew E. Clark, Sarah Flèche, Richard Layard, Nattavudh Powdthavee and George Ward, "The Key Determinants of Happiness and Misery," in *World Happiness Report 2017*, eds. John Helliwell, Richard Layard and Jeffrey Sachs, (New York: Sustainable Development Solutions Network, 2017), 122–143 (with further bibliography).
338 Dobruska, *Philosophie sociale*, 76.

democratic society. The realization and then the application of a good Constitution are the best guarantee for universal human rights: the freedom of individuals, equality, and the abolition of the privileges of some social groups over others.

As we know, once the Constitution has been implemented, it guarantees the people freedom, an inalienable right already enshrined in the second article of the *Declaration of the Rights of Man and of the Citizen* of August 26, 1789.

After the Universal Constitution, the second condition, of a legal nature, which allows the attainment of happiness by individual citizens and society as a whole, is represented by the laws: "The laws – we read in the *Philosophie sociale* – are therefore and should only be the guarantee of freedom and equality, or the right to exercise all efforts, to achieve supreme happiness in society".[339]

Thanks to the hierarchy of normative sources, which I already discussed, laws will be able to guarantee the freedom of individuals, and thus, the achievement of happiness.

6.2.3 Cultural Factors

The cultural condition that allows happiness to be achieved is education. The purpose of education is to achieve both the individual and the general well-being of the society in which the individual is placed.

Dobruska writes:

> How simple and easy this measure of sanctions will be with men raised and nourished by the Constitution itself! Then it will be impossible to take away their freedom and the benefits of the principle, that not only do they feel it but that they know it. Indeed, all education must be directed towards a goal that makes the individual happy, and the good of the society in which he lives. However, the first part of the Constitution, which is nothing other than the principle itself and the base of general happiness, will naturally lead him to this goal.[340]

---

339 *Ibidem*, 89: [Les loix ne sont donc et ne doivent être que la garantie de la liberté et de l'égalité, ou du droit de l'exercice de tous ses efforts, pour atteindre le suprême bonheur dans la société].

340 Dobruska, *Philosophie sociale*, 67: [Combien sera simple et facile cette mesure de sanction avec des hommes élevés et nourris par la Constitution elle-même! Alors il sera impossible de leur ravir la liberté et les bienfaits du principe, que non-seulement ils sentent y mais qu'ils savent. En effet, toute éducation doit être dirigée vers un but qui fasse le bonheur de l'individu, et le bien de la société dans laquelle il vit. Or, la première partie de la Constitution, qui n'est autre chose que le principe lui-même et la base du bonheur général, le conduira naturellement à ce but].

6.2.4 Economic and Social Factors

After reviewing these political, regulatory and cultural conditions, Dobruska focuses on the economic and social conditions that can affect individual happiness and that of the community.

This brings us to one last condition, which has been the subject of great debate, from the time of the Enlightenment to, one might say, the present day. Even today, many social scientists, particularly sociologists of the structuralist school, conduct empirical research on the role that social stratification and the distribution of socio-economic resources play in achieving well-being.

To answer the question about the link between economic and social conditions and happiness, our author must first establish whether happiness is subjective.

As I already pointed out, according to Dobruska, both in the state of nature and in the state of culture, there are no identical individuals, with equal faculties, abilities, and desires. As a result, what makes one individual happy may differ from what satisfies a different person. And this satisfaction is not always linked to economic and social conditions.

Dobruska denies the link between happiness and economic and social resources, following for example the work of Montesquieu, for whom happiness is achieved subjectively, thanks to an attitude of the soul, without economic and social conditions having any effect.[341] Moreover, already in 1705, Formentin, an author of whom we have no biographical details, wrote in his *Traité du bonheur* that one can be happy at any age, in all conditions and situations of life.[342]

According to the *Philosophie sociale*, however, the improvement of economic and social conditions – from poverty to wealth – can help to achieve happiness.

Dobruska joins the *philosophes* who advocate a hedonistic and materialistic view of life, according to which wealth is a source of happiness, since it is able to increase the pleasant sensations of individuals. Not only can wealth increase individual happiness, but also the happiness of the community as a whole. In other words, "the happiness of a nation is in function of the material goods in circulation".[343]

---

341 Cf. Mauzi, *L'idée du bonheur*, 149.
342 *Ibidem*, 150: *Traité du bonheur*, by [?] Formentin (Paris: J. Guilletat 1706 [but 1705]): see Pierre M. Conlon, *Prélude au siècle des lumières en France, répertoire chronologique de 1680 a 1715*, 5 vols. (Genève: Droz, 1970–1974: vol. 3), 406.
343 Mauzi, *L'idée du bonheur*, 157.

Already Voltaire had argued, in his *Dictionnaire philosophique*, that luxury "is a state of fact, a moment of civilization, which brings pleasure. To condemn luxury is to reject history".[344]

Dobruska distanced himself from the moralists, who condemned hedonist worldliness in favor of a frugal life, far from material goods and the excesses of wealth. According to these thinkers, as wealth increased, the possibility of being happy diminished, for several reasons. For political writer and moralist Henri de Feucher Artaize, the rich are unhappy because they lack imagination, because their souls are no longer moved by the pleasures to which they have become accustomed, because they can no longer grasp the magic that binds the soul and the things of the world. In his book *Réflexions d'un jeune homme*, published in 1786, De Feucher states:

> In this way, the first malaise of wealthy people is to have only the pleasures linked to the senses; to possess only what they possess, without embellishing it. The heart, the imagination, do not produce anything for them, they remain cold, dead in their enjoyment. This is also the most fruitful source of our pleasures.[345]

Dobruska, on the other hand, rejects any law that restricts luxury and wealth, as it would damage an inalienable human right, which is that of private property:

> Every law that prescribes compulsory sacrifices, which concern luxury, abundance (except in difficult moments, when they are necessary for the common good or required by public health), is an attack on individual property, is oppressive, vexatious, criminal, and is repudiated by the principle [of the Constitution].[346]

If wealth and luxury are protected, the ideal of poverty is firmly rejected:

> Even more disastrous is the political chimera of some legislators and philosophers, who seek the fortune of a people in the equality of poverty and indigence of all its members.[347]

---

344 *Ibidem*, 159. The entry *Luxe* in Voltaire's *Dictionnaire philosophique* begins in the following ironic way: "On a déclamé contre le luxe depuis deux mille ans, en vers et en prose, et on l'a toujours aimé".

345 Henri de Feucher Artaize, *Réflexions d'un jeune homme* (London [but Paris]: Chez Royez, 1786), 115.

346 *Philosophie sociale*, 212: [Chaque loi qui exige des sacrifices involontaires, concernant le luxe, l'abondance (excepté dans les momens impérieux, où ils sont exigés par la nécessité pour la salut public), est attentatoire à la propriété individuelle, est oppressive, vexatoire, criminelle, est repoussée par le principe].

347 *Ibidem*, 207: [Plus funeste est encore la chimère politique de quelques législateurs et philosophes, qui cherchent la fortune d'un peuple, dans l'égalité de la pauvreté et de la *mal aisance* de tous ses membres].

Poverty, according to Dobruska, not only does not make people happy, but causes them to feel uneasy. Although he is aware of the close link between economic resources and happiness, both individual and collective, our author departs from thinkers who see social inequalities as bad for society, and who advocate the need for a fairer distribution of resources.

The reasons why Dobruska, convinced as he is that inequalities are not necessarily bad for society, opposes the redistribution of wealth (*fortunes*) and possessions (*possessions*), are essentially four, as we will see.[348] From this point of view, Dobruska's thinking distances itself from that of the Jacobin Robespierre, who, as we have just seen, is in favor of a more egalitarian distribution of economic resources.

It is clear that, in the *Philosophie sociale*, the State must not intervene directly in the management and redistribution of individual wealth, but must limit itself to guaranteeing the mechanisms of representative democracy.

The important thing is that everyone receives what he needs to meet his needs and desires. However, this does not mean that economic and social resources are distributed equally. In fact, there will be more materialistic people who wish to obtain more economic resources and others who are less ambitious or more spiritual.

---

348 Mauzi, *L'idée du bonheur*, reminds us that many writers, philosophers and economists, including Voltaire (1694–1778) and Turgot (1727–1781), did not believe that social inequality was an evil for society or "an unjust survival" of the feudal past, but interpreted it as "an important factor for the progress" of society. For example, for Paul Henri Thiry d'Holbach (1723–1789), a thinker known for his great erudition as well as for his atheism, inequality does not harm society at all. In fact, it keeps it alive. He stated: "Society, like nature, establishes a necessary and legitimate inequality between its members. This inequality is just, because it is based on the invariable goal of society, I mean its preservation and happiness (La société de même que la nature, établit une inégalité nécessaire et légitime entre ses membres. Cette inégalité est juste, parce qu'elle est fondée sur le but invariable de la société, je veux dire sa conservation et son bonheur)" (d'Holbach, *Politique naturelle*, in Mauzi, *L'idée du bonheur*, 154). The economist and politician Turgot goes so far in this reasoning as to argue that inequality is not an evil but even a "happiness for human beings" (Turgot, *Lettre à M.me de Graffigny sur les Lettres péruviennes*, in Mauzi, *L'idée du bonheur*, 153). Social inequalities are explained as consequences of inequalities in nature. In nature there are no two identical beings. Consequently, given that society is an agglomeration of people, who have different abilities, it is unthinkable that economic resources should be equally distributed. These different skills of individuals are very useful to society, however, because if properly used through the social division of labor, they allow the preservation and development of society itself. The most deserving, capable and ambitious individuals will occupy the most coveted positions in society for which they will obtain economic wages and social recognition, and they will be paid the most, while the least capable and able will occupy the least remunerated positions.

The first argument, according to which economic inequalities are not a bad thing but even a push towards happiness, sees in the state of necessity a stimulus capable of "awakening the dormant talents" of individuals, pushing them to satisfy their needs.

If, in a given society, there is a fair distribution of resources, it would even be necessary to redistribute them unfairly, in order to introduce abundance, mediocrity and poverty again:

> equal goods should be collected and distributed unequally, to reintroduce abundance, mediocrity and even poverty, in order to awaken the sleeping talents of all individuals in their own interest, and to satisfy their appetite, which is the principle, so as to make everyone happy through hope, desire and activity.[349]

Hope would be born from need, and even from indigence, this great promoter of fortunes, and a source of happiness:

> What would then be man's greatest happiness? Hope. It is hope which shows man a more distant purpose, to sweeten the pains of the past, the anxieties of the present, through the enjoyment of a future that he has not yet tasted.[350]

The second argument in favor of an unfair distribution of wealth is of a moral nature. If all resources were equally distributed, it would not be possible for people to act ethically. They wouldn't know they needed each other:

> Finally, how many moral actions would be lost if all human beings enjoyed the same fortune, and if they no longer needed each other.[351]

The third argument against an equitable redistribution of resources is linked to the role of the democratic State. If the State intervened to redistribute resources, this would mean an abuse of power. It would no longer be the exercise of power for the common good and for the happiness of the individual, but a license. If the State intervened, it would restrict individual freedom and seriously damage it, with the consequent annulment of the social contract:

---

349 Dobruska, *Philosophie sociale*, 211: [. . .] il faudroit accumuler les possessions égales, les distribuer d'une manière inégale, pour introduire de nouveau l'abondance, la médiocrité, et même la pauvreté, afin d'éveiller les talens endormis de tous les individus pour leur propre intérêt, et pour la satisfaction de leur faculté appétitive, qui est le principe, afin de faire ainsi le bonheur de chacun par l'espérance, l'appétit et l'activité].

350 *Ibidem*, 208: [où seroit alors la félicité plus grande de l'homme ? l'espérance. Elle qui montre à l'homme un but plus éloigné, pour lui adoucir les peines du passé, les inquiétudes présentes, par la jouissance d'un avenir qu'il n'a pas encore goûté].

351 *Loc. cit.*: [Enfin combien d'actions morales perdroient leur existence, si tous les humains jouissoient d'une fortune égale, et que l'un n'eût pas alternativement besoin de l'autre].

even the slightest sacrifice required of the individual by society, by the legislature, or by the legislator, would be a tyranny, an act against nature, which bears the odious imprint of a liberticidal plot, trickery, or ignorance. And this tyranny, this act against nature, entails the nullity of the social contract.[352]

6.2.5 Political and Cultural Factors that Prevent Happiness

After analyzing the conditions that favor the attainment of individual and public happiness, Dobruska also highlights in his work all those structural conditions – political, legal and social – that, on the contrary, prevent the attainment of the desired well-being.

Political factors include all illiberal regimes, which do not guarantee the right of citizens to freedom and equality:

> In such a regime, tyranny can only be a mortal enemy of general happiness, and as such, condemned to public execration; but it can always, in the angelic form of freedom, usurp the happiness of a society, from which it takes away equality of rights by its simple dominance, which it kills with the poisoned tip of its scepter.[353]

The targets of this invective are not only regimes that ignore the rights of individuals, but also systems of government that conceive freedom in terms of power. I have already recalled John Locke's definition of freedom as "the power to do or not to do according to one's will". If this power does not gain regulatory legitimacy (under the law), it cannot be exercised by all. It follows that only the physically and morally strongest citizens can be said to be free, while the weakest and least capable individuals are subject to the will of the strongest:

> It is therefore impossible that freedom, which Locke defines as power [*puissance*], is a general freedom, a freedom that makes the happiness of the masses of society, because

---

352 *Ibidem*, 206–207: [le moindre sacrifice exigé de l'individu par la société, par le corps législatif, ou par le législateur, seroit une tyrannie, un acte contre nature, portant l'empreinte odieuse d'un attentat liberticide, de l'astuce ou de l'ignorance, laquelle tyrannie, lequel acte contre nature frappent le contrat social de nullité].

353 *Ibidem*, 176: [dans tel régime, la tyrannie ne peut y être que comme une liberticide, une ennemie mortelle du bonheur général, et comme telle, vouée à l'exécration publique; mais elle peut toujours, sous la forme angélique de la liberté, usurper le bonheur d'une société dont elle dépouille l'égalité des droits par sa simple prépondérance, et qu'elle tue avec la pointe empoisonné de son sceptre].

nature has not endowed each member with the same power, both physical and moral. On the contrary, strength and weakness are unfairly distributed.[354]

The second category of factors that stand in the way of achieving happiness is of a cultural nature. In particular, Dobruska focuses on false morality:

> Wise men of the earth, you who truly and sincerely want the happiness of mankind, at last overthrow the profane temple of false morality, whose basis, instead of being built on principles, rests only on consequences, and on a painful mixture of truth and falsehood, depending on whether ineptitude or dishonesty deem them necessary for such a building.[355]

---

354 *Ibidem*, 174: [Il est donc impossible que la liberté, que Lo[c]ke définit puissance, soit une liberté générale, une liberté qui fasse le bonheur de la masse de la société, puisque la nature n'a point donné à chacun de ses membres, une mesure égale de puissance soit physique ou morale, et qu'au contraire, la force et la foiblesse sont inégalement partagés entre eux].
355 *Philosophie sociale*, 46–47: [Sages de la terre, qui voulez véritablement et sincèrement le bonheur du genre humain, renversez enfin tout-à-fait le temple profane de la fausse moralité; dont la bâse, au lieu de porter sur les principes, ne repose que sur des conséquences, et un mélange pitoyable de vérités et de faussetés, suivant que l'ineptie ou l'improbité les jugeoient nécessaires à cet édifice].

7 Reception and Influence of the *Philosophie Sociale*

It is now time to analyze how the *Philosophie sociale* has been received by contemporaries, and up to the present day, and what influence it has had, in particular, on social philosophers and sociologists.

Despite having aroused a certain amount of interest between the end of the eighteenth century and the first decades of the nineteenth century in the revolutionary circles and among the liberal Enlightenment thinkers, Dobruska's *Philosophie* was largely forgotten in the twentieth century. It must be said that the diffusion of the text had been hindered by several factors, first among them the fate of the author, imprisoned a few months after publication, with the infamous accusation of having conspired against the revolution. After Dobruska's death at the guillotine in April 1794, even his book, published anonymously, found cautious readers only, not inclined to remember a thinker who had fallen into political disgrace.

However, the book was read with interest, as demonstrated by the fact that it was reprinted, in an edition that until now had escaped the attention of scholars, with the sole exception of the Italian historian Luciano Guerci.[356] In 1797, the *Philosophie sociale* was printed by Moutardier in Paris, with a new frontispiece. It was no longer dedicated *au peuple françois* (French people), but with a new and more universalistic inspiration, *à tous les peuples, par un citoyen de tout pays.*[357] One wonders who promoted this publication, indeed if it could have been someone related to the family circle to which Dobruska had turned in his "will" on the eve of the execution.[358] Or was the initiative to circulate the book due to some

---

356 Luciano Guerci, "Per una riflessione sul dibattito politico nell'Italia del Triennio repubblicano," in *Universalismo e nazionalità nell'esperienza del giacobinismo italiano, (1796–1799)*, eds., Luigi Lotti (Rosario Villari, Roma-Bari: Latreza, 2003), 320 note 10.

357 *Philosophie sociale, dédiée à tous les peuples, par un citoyen de tout pays*, Paris, imp. de Mutardier, 1797: copies at the Bibliothèque Nationale de France and at the Aargauer Kantonsbibliothek (Aarau, Switzerland). The announcement of the publication of the volume appears in some bibliographic reviews of the time: *Verkündiger oder Wochenschrift zur Belehrung, Unterhaltung und Bekanntmachung fur alle Stände* 2 (1798); *Neue allgemeine Deutsche Bibliothek* 1799; *Intelligenzblatt der Allgemeinen Literatur-Zeitung* 1798; *Journal général de la littérature de France* 1 (1798); *Magasin encyclopédique, ou Journal des sciences* 5 (1799).

358 A sort of brief spiritual testament, addressed by Dobruska / Frey to his son Joseph ("Peppi"), is preserved in a copy of the 1793 edition of the *Philosophie Sociale*, auctioned in Paris a few years ago and now in a private collection: cf. Scholem, *Du frankisme au jacobinisme*, 88–89; Laurence Sigal-Klagsbald in *Exposition Juifs et Citoyens* (Paris: A.I.U., 1989), 69–73 no. 188, and, recently, Saverio Campanini, "Da Giacobbe ai Giacobini," in *Le tre vite di Moses Dobrushka, Le tre vite di*

Parisian political circle?[359] In fact, in a letter written immediately before the execution, which was kept in a copy of the first edition of the *Philosophie sociale*, Dobruska invited his son Joseph ("Peppi"), the addressee of the message, to reprint the work, adding the name of the author. This latter wish was, however, not fulfilled in the reprint of 1797.

As I will show in the following, it is clear that social theorists of great importance, first among them Henri de Saint-Simon and Auguste Comte, read the *Philosophie sociale* and drew inspiration from it. However, they carefully avoided publicly expressing their debt to a "foreigner", a subject of the Austrian empire suspected of espionage and, as if that were not enough, a converted Jew. Moses Dobruska and his extraordinary biographical adventure was brought to light in 1979/1981 by the great Gershom Scholem, scholar of Jewish mysticism, who was born in Berlin and subsequently emigrated to Israel. Scholem's study, originally published in French, re-evaluated Dobruska's esoteric interests, Masonic commitment, and adventurer's attitudes, but almost completely overlooked the intellectual significance of *Philosophie sociale*. Even the few fleeting hints of *Philosophie* found in specialist literature in more recent years have not changed this situation of underestimation and substantial misunderstanding. Cited more for its title than for its contents, within attempts to reconstruct the history of the concept of

---

Moses Dobrushka, by Gershom Scholem, ed., with an essay by Saverio Campanini, trans., by Elisabetta Zevi (Milano: Adelphi, 2014), 161–165 and plates. Here is the French text of the letter: [Dieu! Liberté! innocence! Peppi mon Enfans chérie, unique et tendre fils, que cette devise sacrée soit gravée dans ton cœur pour jamais! c'est le seul héritage que je te laise après moi, c'est la bénédiction d'un père mourant. Sois si heureux, que j 'étois malheureux ! Sache que mourir n'est rien, mais qu'il est cruel d'être méconnu, et de ne pas pouvoire continuer à travailler pour la Liberté. Lorsque tu seras parvenue à un âge mûr et que tes connoissance[s] égaleront ton patriotisme, tu feras réimprimer cet ouvrage, dont j 'etois empêché de remplir plusieurs lacunes essentielles, par la triste sorte que j 'ai subi. Fais y mettre mon nom, et justifie ainsi mon memoir, et par tes connoissances et par tes vertus, et par la promulgation d'un ouvrage dont l'auteur ne sera jamois soupçonné de la Postérité d'avoir pu conspirer contre la Liberté. Mon cher fils, tu as un penchant pour l'état militaire, les derniers paroles d'un père te défend de t'y engager, si ce n'est pas la loi t'appelle, il est prudent pour toi de rester inactive jusque à la paix, car on pourrait te soupçonner jusque dans tes Vertus, et il faut conserver ta vie pour consoler ta tante ma malheureuse et vertueese soeur, que je te recomende à l'aimer et à respecter, il faut qu'après la paix tu cherche[s] ta mère ma pauvre femme (que j'adore jusque au tombeau) et tes deux soeurs mes pauvres Enfans. Il faut leur faire l'étonnant Recit de mon malheur et de mes vertus méconnues, il faut les engager malgré tous ce que j 'ai soufert pour la Liberté de venir habiter avec toi la France Republicaine et de quitter le sol impur des tyrans d'Autriche, je n'ai qu'un seul Regret, de ne pas avoir eu la bonheur de voir consolider la Liberté de ce peuple imortel pendant ma vie. Adieu mon tendre fils / fils chér à mon cœur / ton père mourant / junius frey / Paris le 29 Ventose l'an 2 de la Repl.].
359 Cf. already Guerci, *Per una riflessione,* 320: [sarebbe anche interessante sapere da chi fu rimesso in circolazione [il libro di Dobruska]".

social philosophy, Dobruska's book was still waiting for an exhaustive examination. The present book is the first attempt to give the work of the learned, elusive, unfortunate Moses his rightful place in the history of social thought in modern Europe, including through a meticulous reconstruction of his traces that can be found in much better-known thinkers.

7.1 In the Eighteenth Century: From François Chabot to Immanuel Kant

7.1.1 François Chabot: Protector, Friend, Admirer

The Jacobin parliamentarian François Chabot, who was Moses Dobruska's political patron, married his sister Léopoldine and shared his misfortune, ending up on the gallows on the same day, compared his friend in enthusiastic terms to "Europe's greatest thinker". Certainly, the doubt arises that this is a rhetorical exaggeration, due to personal closeness, even if Chabot, who had completed excellent studies and had been part, in his youth, of the Capuchin order, enjoyed a good intellectual reputation in his time.[360] Chabot seems to have been among the first to read a draft of the *Philosophie sociale* while it was still in gestation, as he himself recalls, in a brilliant passage referring to January 1793:

> At the beginning of the Convention [established on September 21 1792], Junius Frey often came to the petitions desk alone or with his brother and nephew. He was closely linked to Richard, Bentabole, Gaston, Simon of Strasbourg, Proly, and other Montagnards. I used to say hello sometimes. Finally, Richard took me to dinner at his house in early January 1793. I was disturbed by food and smoke. Richard retired and the Frey brothers gave me a philosophical essay on freedom and equality to read. I left, accompanied by Emmanuel Frey, the younger brother. He thought I was drunk. The next day, they came to see me and marveled at the profit I had made from their dissertation, which they thought I wouldn't even understand on an empty stomach, let alone the state of drunkenness in which they thought I was [. . .] From that moment on, I became involved with the Frey brothers, I dined very often at their house, while they came even more often to eat at my house. I urged them to have their essay on freedom and equality printed, and they told me that it was taken from a great philosophical work, that they were preparing for the French people and that it should give freedom to the universe. Later they read the work to me, and I appreciated it very much.[361]

---

360 Although not without defects, the broadest profile of Chabot is still that offered by the old study of Louis Gabriel A. de Bonald, *François Chabot, membre de la Convention (1756–1794)* (Paris: Émile-Paul Éditeur, 1908).

361 [François Chabot], "Histoire véritable du mariage de François Chabot avec Léopoldine Frey en réponse à toutes les calomnies que l'on a répandues à ce sujet," ed. Albert Mathiez,

Interestingly, in this text, the *Philosophie sociale* is presented as the joint work of the two brothers Dobruska/Frey. It is possible that Emmanuel, who remained in the shadow of his older brother throughout his life, actually played an important role, at least in the first phase. It must be said, however, that Chabot himself, on other occasions, and also Robespierre, of whom I will say more below, indicate only Moses/Junius as the author. This is what happened at the meeting of the "Jacobin Society" on Sunday, August 4 1793, when Chabot took the floor to praise the *Père Nicaise* and the *Philosophie sociale* and propose its dissemination at the expense of the State:

> The author of the *Père Nicaise* or the *Antifédéraliste* and the *Philosophie Sociale* offers these two works to the Society. Chabot asks that honorable mention be made of these two works, the first of which, in the style of the *Père Duchesne*, contains happy allusions to the reach of the people, to the present circumstances; it can and must be of great use to our lost brothers, but in good faith, who seek education; they will see what federalism is and whoever preaches it, they will know the mountain [i.e. the Jacobins] and what they have done for the people, they will learn all their duties. The second, made only for deep thinkers, comparable to the most valuable writings on politics – Montesquieu, Rousseau – needs to be spread among the enlightened men of all departments, as the other must be among the least educated people. Chabot wrote twice to the Minister of the Interior to urge him to spread this excellent work, but apparently, he adds, my letters have remained in Mr. Champagneux's offices, I have not received a reply. The general meeting decides on the civic mention.[362]

Annales révolutionnaires 7 (1914): 248: [Au commencement de la Convention Junius Frey venait souvent au banc des pétitionnaires seul ou avec son frère et son neveu. Il était fort lié avec Richard, Bentabole, Gaston, Simon de Strasbourg, Proly et autres Montagnards. Je le saluais quelquefois. Enfin Richard me mena diner chez lui au commencement de janvier 1793. J'y fus incommodé par le poêle et la pipe. Richard se retira et les frères Frey me donnèrent à lire une dissertation philosophique sur la liberté et l'égalité. Je me retirai accompagné d'Emmanuel Frey le cadet. Il me crut ivre. Le lendemain ils vinrent me voir el furent étonnés du profit que j'avais fait de leur dissertation qu'ils croyaient que je n'avais pas comprise même à jeun et à plus forte raison dans l'état d'ivresse où ils me croyaient [. . .] Dès ce moment, je me liai avec les frères Frey, je dînais chez eux très souvent et ils déjeunaient chez moi plus souvent encore. Je les exhortai à faire imprimer leur dissertation sur la liberté et l'égalité, ils me dirent que c'était extrait d'un grand ouvrage philosophique qu'ils préparaient pour le peuple français qui devait donner la liberté à l'Univers. Ils me lurent successivement leur travail dont je fus fort content] (see also above, 2. 7).

362 François Chabot, *Journal des débats et de la correspondance de la Société des Jacobins*, 464, August 6, 1793, 2: L'auteur du Père Nicaise ou l'Antifédéraliste et de la Philosophie sociale fait hommage de ces deux productions a la société. Chabot demande qu'on fasse mention honorable de ces deux ouvrages, dont le premier, dans le genre du père Duchêne, contient des allusions heureuses et parfaitement à la portée du peuple, sur les circonstances présentes; il peut et doit être de la plus grande utilité à nos frères égarés, mais de bonne foi, qui cherchent à s'instruire; ils y'verront ce que c'est que le fédéralisme et ceux qui le prêchent, ils y connaisseront la montagne

The *Philosophie sociale* is placed here on a par with the great texts of Montesquieu and Rousseau, a high *pedigree*, which supports the fame of our Dobruska and gives him, I believe, a certain celebrity in the Republic of Letters, at least for a few months, during the summer of 1793. Still, in his defensive memoir written in prison, between the end of 1793 and the beginning of 1794, Chabot has only praise for the work of his brother-in-law:

> I don't have the madness to compare the second part of my memoir to the *Philosophie sociale* of Junius Frey, whom a virtuous philosopher calls Frey Locke, since he read this book that will survive the memory of all our persecutors. However, my pride is flattered by the conformity of his principles with those of the leading European thinker, and my vanity is even more flattered by being joined to him by the heart of a virtuous woman, worthy of being his sister. The principle of my dissertation on the expenses of the Republic, or rather on the constitution, which we had to adapt to this principle, so well developed in the *Philosophie sociale*, was finally established in the revolutionary government, decreed in Billaud's Report. My brother-in-law and I had the glory of having established it first of all, raising against the idolatry of the moment, which made it impossible to think differently from the immortal Jean-Jacques [Rousseau]. But I don't claim to advance government science. All I want is [government's] stability, based on the laws of nature. I leave to my brother-in-law the glory of studying politics in books and fighting their mistakes through the efforts of his genius.

> Today it is said that he is a conspirator and that the sacrifices he made in Strasbourg and Paris, that his sister and his nephew, who led with his younger brother, that his demonstrations in favor of the Jacobins against the "Feuillants", that his status as a federation of the Lower Rhine, that his courage under the walls of the Castle of the Tuileries, his apparent zeal against Austria and Prussia in August and September, the adoption of a son of the Republic, the maintenance of an old man, the war he declared to all the realists, "Feuillants" and other enemies of the people, were only means to better capture the trust of the patriots. Yes, of course, he is an extraordinary conspirator, because he conspires since childhood against every kind of error and tyranny, and there is not a page of his *Philosophie sociale* that is not a conspiracy against prejudices and despotism of all kinds. What I say: each page is a death sentence against him before the court of all oppressors of mankind. The foreign conspirators go in groups: he stays in his room and sees no one but at the table or at the Jacobins. Conspirators preach to people to deceive or seduce them, if possible: Junius Frey cannot be

---

et ce qu'elle a fait pour le peuple, ils apprendront tousleurs devoirs. Le second, fait seulement pour les penseurs profonds, comparable à ce qu'on écrit de plus précieux sur la politique, Montesquieu, Rousseau a besoin d'être répandu parmi les hommes éclairés de tous les départemens, comme l'autre doit l'être parmi le peuple moins instruit. Chabot écrivit deux fois au ministre de l'intérieur pour l'engager à répandre cet excellent ouvrage; mais apparemment, ajoute-il, que mes lettres sont res tées dans les bureaux de Mr. Champagneux, je n'en ai point eu de réponse. L'assemblée arrête la mention civique (a slightly different version of the same text also in *Journal de la Montagne* 66, 424, Tuesday August 6, 1793 – meeting of 4 August).

heard, friends, he composes books: for whom? For the most profound wise, for the legislators able to refute his mistakes and to feel the depth of his principles.[363]

---

363 "François Chabot, représentant du peuple, à ses concitoyens qui sont les juges de sa vie politique. Mémoire apologétique publié pour la première fois", ed. Albert Mathiez, in *Annales révolutionnaires* 6 (1913) 533–550, 681–706; 7 (1914), 224–247: 547–548: [Je n'ai pas la folie de comparer la seconde partie de mon mémoire à la *Philosophie sociale* de Junius Frey, qu'un philosophe vertueux appelle Frey Locke depuis qu'il a lu cet ouvrage qui survivra à la mémoire de tous nos persécuteurs, mais mon orgueil est flatté de la conformité de ses principes avec ceux du premier penseur de l'Europe et ma vanité est plus flatté encore de lui être uni par le cœur d'une femme vertueuse digne d'être sa sœur. Le principe de mon mémoire sur les dépenses de la République ou plutôt sur la constitution qu'il nous convenait d'adapter à ce principe, si bien développé dans la Philosophie sociale, vient enfin d'être consacré dans le gouvernement révolutionnaires décrété sur le rapport de Billaud. Mon frère et moi avions la gloire de l'avoir établi les premiers en nous élevant contre l'idolâtrie du jour qui ne permettait pas de penser autrement que l'immortel Jean-Jacques. Mais je n'ai pas la prétention de faire faire un pas à la science du gouvernement. Je n'ai que celle d'en désirer la stabilité en la basant sur les loix de la nature. Je laisse à mon beau-frère la gloire d'étudier la politique dans les livres et d'en combattre les erreurs par les efforts de son génie. L'on dit toujours que c'est un conspirateur et que les sacrifices qu'il fait à Strasbourg et à Paris que sa sœur et son neveu qu'il emmenés avec son cadet, que ses démonstrations en faveur des jacobins contre les feuillans, que sa qualité de fédéré du Bas-Rhin, que son courage sont les murs du château des Tuileries, son zèle apparent contre l'Autriche et la Prusse au mois d'août et septembre, l'adoption d'un enfant de la République, l'entretien d'un vieillard, la guerre qu'il a déclarée à tous les royalistes, feuillans et autres ennemis du peuple n'étaient que des moyens de mieux capter la confiance des patriotes. Oui, certes, c'est un conspirateur d'un genre extraordinaire; car il conspire depuis son enfance contre tous genres d'erreur et de tyrannie et il n'est pas une page dans sa *Philosophie sociale* qui ne soit une conspiration contre les préjugés et le despotisme contre le tribunal de tous les oppresseurs du genre humain. Les conspirateurs étrangers vont dans les grouppes: il reste dans son cabaret et ne voit personne qu'à table ou aux jacobins. Les conspirateurs prêchent aussi la liberté au peuple pour l'égarer ou le séduire si cela était possible: Junius Frey ne peut pas se faire entendre, amis il compose des livres: pour qui? pour les savans les plus les plus profonde, pour les législateurs capables de réfuter ses erreurs et de sentir la profondeur de ses principes]. The original text by Chabot continues with further details on Moses and Emmanuel Dobruska: [Je ne suis pas exact. Il a composé un ouvrage pour le peuple et cela à ma sollicitation. Il est l'auteur des *Aventures du Père Nicaise* et il en travaillait bien d'autres à l'époques de son arrestation, parce que je crois que c'est pour le peuple qu'il faut écrire aujourd'hui et qu'après avoir combattu les Brissotins il faut vulgariser tous les principes et toutes les connaissances pour n'avoir rien de commun avec cette faction scélérate dont nous avons purgé le sol de la liberté. Lui fera-t-on un crime de ce petit ouvrage intitulé *L'antifédéraliste* que le gouvernement a envoyé dans les départements les plus brissotinés et qu'il a rappelés ainsi à l'unité républicaine par le puissant mobile de l'intérêt particulier dans les tems que nos braves armées y réduissaient ceux que l'erreur avait armes d'un fer rebelle. Despotes et aristocrates, royalistes et fédéralistes vous sérés vengés de cet insolent prédicateur de l'unité républicaine. L'unité républicaine! Les nouveaus ennemis de notre liberté qu'il se préparait à combattre sont parvenus à le faire passer pour un de vos agens et à l'arracher aux soins d'une sœur vertueuse qui rétablissait une santé délabré par la fatigue des

I have included a long excerpt from this text because it confirms one of the aims of the *Philosophie sociale*, which is to provide a theoretical basis for the intellectual discourse of the time and, possibly, also for government action. The collaboration with Chabot made possible, albeit for a very short time, this transposition of the philosophical-social doctrines of Dobruska into parliamentary debate. Chabot presented his own *Memoir* on finances to the National Convention of February 27, 1793.[364] He says that he was inspired by the ideas being elaborated, and then printed, in the *Philosophie sociale*, or at least that he took them into account. It must be said that the subject of public expenditure, which the *Memoir* discusses in a technical way, is not expressly dealt with in the *Philosophie sociale*, and that therefore the contacts between the two texts are necessarily limited to some theoretical affinity. It should be noted, in particular, the insistence that Chabot places on the derivation of laws from principles, the only ones that guarantee legal legitimacy:

> Moreover, I have never judged the goodness of a law for the reasons of those who propose it [. . .] I judge the laws only on the immutable rule of principles: and our opponents are

---

combats que sa plume vigoureuse livrait à tous les ennemis de l'humanité. Il est dans les fers, et après avoir glorieusement combattu la tyrannies, il est juste qu'il meure sous son coups. O toi, qui déteste jusqu'à l'erreur et à l'hypocrisie de la modestie; toi qui te dis le quatrième parmi les sages amis des hommes: toi qui ne mets avant ton nom que celui de Jésus, de Socrate et de ton père, prépare-toi à le mériter par une mort aussi courageuse que celle des deux premiers et ton nom sera placé avant celui de ton père en dépit de ton respect filial. Mais non, Robespierre l'a dit, la cigue n'est pas si commune en France qu'à Athènes et les pharisiens de la liberté sont déjà démasques, le peuple ne sera beintôt plus leur dupe, ton innocence et la vertu seront enfin reconnues. Dans tous les cas, tu ne mourras pas tout entier, tu laisses des ouvrages immortels. Et toi aimable misanthrope [Emmanuel Frey], tu partagerais la gloire due à ton frère puisque tu as partagé ses périls, que tu peux l'honorer de tes blessures à la journée tu dix et du désespoir même que le cause la vue de tant de malheureux humains. Mais non, tu seras forcé d'aimer et d'estimer les hommes car ils vont te rendre justice ainsi qu'à toute sa famille. On a beau dire que vous êtes des cospirateurs. Il faut aujourd'hui le prouver et la lois frappe les faux témoins. Vous n'avez fréquenté que les plus chauds montagnards, les Simon, les Bentabole, les Richard, les Gaston et plusieurs excellents jacobins. On ne vous a vus qu'au milieu des plus chauds amis correspondance était un brevet de civisme à l'époque de mon mariage et vous n'êtes pas devenus sans double conspirateurs depuis votre union avec moi. Si cela, était, vous sériés les plus scélérates des hommes, car vous auriés trompé le plus chaud de vos amis et je serais volontiers votre bourreau. Mais que dis-je? L'offre que vous m'avez fait de la main de votre sœur lorsque je vous la demandais pour un de mes amis n'est-elle pas une preuve de plus votre dénouement à la cause des sans-culottes].

364 *Archives parlementaires de 1787 à 1860*, Première série, vol. 69, *Du 19 février 1793 au 8 mars 1793* (Paris: Imprimerie nationale, 1901), 302–314 (27 février 1793).

forced to agree that the suppression of ecclesiastical treatment is in accordance with the principles.[365]

The closeness to Dobruska's convictions is evident here, as it is similar in the *Memoir* of Chabot and in the *Philosophie sociale*: the call, indeed very optimistic, to the advent of a new and progressive religion in the future. If Dobruska defines this new creed as the *religion de la verité des principes*,[366] Chabot spoke of a *religion de la loi*, to which Catholic priests, enrolled for the occasion among the defenders of the Revolution, should also contribute:

> If I count less on the progress of philosophy, if I did not hope that the citizen priests will help us establish the religion of the law on the ruins of all idols and superstitions, especially when the awareness of their personal interest preaches to them in favor of this new cult; if I were not sure that the people, taking part in the legislation, will in a short time bind exclusively to the altar of the country, and will bind to it with the strongest bonds, with the bonds of its happiness and its own love.

> If I did not know that this religion of law is naturally the religion of those who contribute to its formation, because men have always venerated the god they have built themselves; if I were not certain that this religion would become universal, I would have feared that the principles of justice would be in conflict with those of freedom.[367]

7.1.2 Jacques-Nicolas Billaud-Varenne and the Provisional Constitution of December 4, 1793

But it is not only Chabot's thought, in that frenetic and fatal 1793, that is influenced by Dobruska's reflections. Echoes of the *Philosophie sociale* can also be

---

365 Chabot, in *Archives parlementaires*, vol. 69, 305: [Mais encore je n'ai jamais jugé de la bonté d'une loi par les motifs de ceux qui la proposent [. . .] Je n'è juge des lois que sur la règle immuable des principes: et nos adversaires sont forcés de convenir que la suppression des traitements ecclésiastiques est conforme aux principes].
366 Dobruska, *Philosophie sociale*, 50. See above 3. 11.
367 Chabot, in *Archives parlementaires*, vol. 69, 306: [Si je comptais moins sur les progrès de la philosophie, si je n'espérais que les prêtres citoyens nous aideront à établir la religion de la loi sur les débris de toutes les idoles et de toutes les superstitions, surtout lorsque la reconnaissance et leur intérêt personnel leur prêchent ce nouveau culte; si je n'étais as- suré que la part que le peuple va prendre à la législation, l'attachera exclusivement dans peu à l'autel de la patrie, et l'y attachera par les liens les plus forts, par les liens de son bonheur et de son amour-propre. Si je ne savais que cette religion de la loi est naturellement la religion de ceux qui con- courent à sa formation, parce que les hommes ont toujours adoré le dieu qu'ils se font eux- mêmes; si je n'étais assuré que cette religion va, devenir universelle, j'aurais craint que les principes de la justice ne fussent en opposition avec ceux de la liberté].

found in the *Billaud[-Varenne] Report* (Rapport de Billaud[-Varenne]), as Chabot himself defines it. Chabot claims a continuity of principles between his own reflections, the theories of Dobruska and the document edited by Jacques-Nicolas Billaud-Varenne (1756–1819), on which the based law of the 14 Frimaire of the year II (December 4, 1793) was based, a sort of provisional Constitution, promulgated by the National Convention to organize the government, which had the task of managing the Jacobin dictatorship.[368] A decree of October 10, 1793 *de facto* suspended the application of the Constitution of June 24 of the same year and established that "the government will be revolutionary until peace".[369] Given this situation, a provisional power structure was necessary, which Billaud-Varenne outlines in his text, in which clear assonances with concepts formulated by Moses Dobruska are evident. This link between the *Philosophie sociale* and revolutionary legislation has so far been completely ignored by specialist research, in part because of the convulsive nature of the political events that frame it. Billaud-Varenne presents his *Report* to the National Convention on November 18 (28 Brumaire), 1793. Moses Dobruska and his brother Emmanuel are still at large, but for a short time: they will be imprisoned on November 23.[370] Obviously, their political misfortune, and that of Chabot, have not yet obscured the theoretical novelties of the *Philosophie sociale*.

The parallels between the Billaud-Varenne Report and Dobruska's work are lexical and theoretical.

At the lexical level, Billaud-Varenne uses the lexeme *désorganis-er*, which we have seen to be characteristic of the *Philosophie sociale*. Disorganization is invoked, with a negative connotation, to describe the state of anarchy which the reorganization of the revolutionary government must remedy:

> In all respects, this order of things is therefore disorganizing social harmony, because it tends to break both the unity of action and the indivisibility of the Republic. Do not delude yourselves: it belongs to any central authority to which the territory, the population, and the accumulation of powers give a sufficiently strong consistency to exist on its own,

---

368 *Décret du 14 frimaire, précédé du rapport fait au nom du Comité de salut public sur un mode gouvernement provisoire et révolutionnaire par Billaud-Varenne, à la séance du 28 brumaire, l'an second de la République française, une et indivisible* (Paris: Imprimerie nationale 1793).

369 Louis Antoine de Saint-Just, *Rapport sur la nécessité de déclarer le gouvernement révolutionnaire jusqu'à la paix*, in Idem, *Œuvres choisies. Discours, rapports, institutions républicaines, proclamations, lettres* (Paris: Gallimard 1968), 168: "Le gouvernement sera révolutionnaire jusqu'à la paix."

370 See above 3. 11.

tending relentlessly to independence, by virtue of the pure gravitational force of its civil preponderance.[371]

In the face of the disorganization of social harmony, the *Report* opposes a centralization of power, which goes in the direction of Jacobin anti-federalism, reiterated by Dobruska in his *Père Nicaise*. Furthermore, the *Report* applies the principle, expressed in the *Philosophie sociale*, which sees the executive power as a purely passive continuation of the action of the legislative. As I have mentioned above,[372] Dobruska departs in this respect from what Rousseau recommends in the *Social Contract*. Rousseau sees in the legislator "the mechanic who invents the machine", while "the prince", that is, the executive power, is "the worker who assembles it and makes it go".[373] The *Philosophie sociale,* on the other hand, pronounces itself in total submission to the executive, which simply becomes a "machine" without autonomy, if not one which carries out what is ordered passively:

> Every deliberation and direction, however small it may appear, is a moral function, which belongs to the moral function, and cannot be separated from it without being followed by the harmful effects, which derive from all our actions, when they depart from the ways of nature, and therefore sin against the institutions of this regulating mother. The deliberative power, which guides a government based on the unshakable foundations of nature, can only be one. It is the moral legislative power, and, according to the comparison of Rousseau, the physical executive power can only be the act resulting from all decrees, resolutions, and directives, even the most insignificant of the legislative body, the only governing body. The executive officers are only the machine it directs. Soldiers fighting for the holy cause of the people, copyists working in their offices, couriers flying from one end of the Republic to the other for the public interest; individuals, artists, shopkeepers, workers, these are the real executive officials, the body, the machine.[374]

---

371 Billaud-Varenne, *Rapport*, in *Décret du 14 frimaire*, 11: [Cet ordre de choses est donc, sous tous les rapports, désorganisateur de l'harmonie sociale, car il tend également à rompre et l'unité d'action et l'indivisibilité de la République. Ne vous trompez pas: il est de l'existence de toute autorité centrale, à qui le territoire, la population et la cumulation des pouvoirs donnent une consistance assez forte pour exister par elle-même, de tendre sans celle à l'indépendance par la seule gravitation de fa prépondérance civile].

372 See above 3. 11.

373 Rousseau, *Du contrat social*, II. 7. 83 (Idem, *Il contratto sociale*, 51): [Mais s'il est vrai qu'un grand Prince est un homme rare, que sera-ce d'un grand Législateur? Le premier n'a qu'à suivre le modèle que l'autre doit proposer. Celui-ci est le mécanicien qui invente la machine, celui-là n'est quel l'ouvrier qui la monte et la fait marcher].

374 Dobruska, *Philosophie sociale*, 8: [Chaque délibération et direction, quelque petite qu'elle soit en apparence, est une fonction morale, qui appartient à la fonction morale, et n'en peut être séparée sans qu'elle ne soit suivie des funestes effets, qui résultent de toutes nos actions, alors qu'elles s'écartent des voies de la nature, et qu'elles pèchent ainsi contre les institutions de cette mère régulatrice. Le pouvoir délibérant, dirigeant dans un gouvernement fondé sur

This, which, at the time of the composition of the *Philosophie sociale*, is a theoretical statement, acquires, in the autumn of 1793, assertory value, and becomes a program of management of the State:

> In government, as in mechanics, everything that is not precisely assembled, both in number and size, achieves only an inaccurate movement, and causes endless interruptions. The obstructive resistances and the frictions that act as obstacles decrease by simplifying the gear. The best civil constitution is the one closest to the processes of nature. It admits in its movements only three principles: the pulsing will, the being that enlivens it, the action of such an individual on the surrounding objects: therefore, every good government must have a center to its will, levers that are immediately united to it, and the secondary organs on which these levers act, to extend the movement to the last extremities. With this precision, the action loses none of its strength or direction in a faster and better regulated communication. Everything that goes beyond [this] becomes exuberant, parasitic, without vigor and without unity.[375]

From the *Philosophie sociale*, Billaud-Varenne takes the metaphor of the executive machine, which does not allow waste in the methodical precision of its gears. His reference to the model of nature is likewise borrowed from Dobruska's text. Let us remember how proud Chabot was, in the passage quoted above, of the fact that the criticism of Rousseau had been received at the institutional level: "My brother-in-law [i.e. Moses Dobruska] and I had the glory of having established it [this principle of the passivity of executive power] first of all, raising us against the idolatry of the moment, which made it impossible to think differently from the immortal

---

les bases inébranlables de la nature ne peut être qu'un. C'est le pouvoir moral législatif, et selon la comparaison de Rousseau lui-même, le pouvoir physique exécutif ne peut être que l'acte résultant de tous les décrets, délibérations et directions, même les moins importantes du corps législatif, seul corps gouvernant, et dont les fonctionnaires exécutifs ne sont que la machine dirigée par lui. Des soldats combattant pour la sainte cause du peuple, des copistes travaillant dans ses bureaux, des courriers volant d'un bout de la République à l'autre pour l'intérêt public; des particuliers, des artistes, des commercans, des ouvriers, voilà les vrais fonctionnaires exécutifs, le physique, la machine].

375 Billaud-Varenne, *Rapport*, in *Décret du 14 frimaire* cit., 7–8: [En gouvernement comme en mécanique, tout ce qui n'est point combiné avec précision, tant pour le nombre que pour l'étendue, n'obtient qu'un jeu embarrassé, et occasionne des brisemens à l'infini. Les résistances entravantes, et les frottemens destructeurs, diminuent à mesure qu'on simplifie le rouage. La meilleure constitution civile est celle la plus rapprochée des procédés de la nature qui n'admet elle-même que trois principes dans ses mouvemens: la volonté pulsatrice, l'être que cette volonté vivifie, l'action de cet individu sur les objets environeans: ainsi, tout bon gouvernement doit avoir un centre de volonté, des leviers qui s'y rattachent immédiatement, et des corps secondaires sur qui agissent ces leviers, afin d'étendre le mouvement jusqu'aux dernières extrémités. Par cette précision, l'action ne perd rien de sa force ni de sa direction dans une communication et plus rapide et mieux réglée. Tout ce qui est au-delà devient exubérant, parasite, sans vigueur et sans unité].

Jean-Jacques [Rousseau]". It is a sad irony of fate that both Chabot himself and Dobruska fell victim to that machine of power that they had helped to create.

7.1.3 The Anonymous Review in the *Journal Encyclopédique*

Already in July 1793, a few weeks after the publication of the *Philosophie sociale*, the *Journal encyclopédique* (1756–1794) announced the novelty with a short anonymous statement – the collaborators of the newspaper did not sign their articles:[376]

> *Philosophie sociale, dédié au Peuple François,* par un citoyen de la section de la République Française, ci-devant du Roule, vol. in-8, de 240 pages, with this epigraph: *The proper study of Mankind is man.* POPE. A Paris. Chez Froullé, imprimeur-libraire, quai des Augustins, N. 39 – This work breathes a sweet philosophy worthy of a philanthropist: the principles would never spread sufficiently.[377]

In December of the same year, the same *Journal encyclopédique*, No 218, published a review of the *Philosophie sociale*, which was very articulate and extensive.

The anonymous author omits the first part of the work (that is, the revolutionary part, as Dobruska calls it, or *Research on some of the main subjects of social philosophy*), to concentrate on the second part, and then move on to some of the concepts and fundamental rights of the Universal Constitution, contained in the third part.

This thematic choice is also significant for us, because it allows us to grasp the impact of the *Philosophie sociale* on the readers of the time. The reviewer is interested in understanding the essence of Dobruska's constitutional proposal and the philosophical principles that inspire it. In the intellectual and revolutionary circles of the time this was a subject of great importance. Then he goes into the Universal Constitution underlining some salient concepts such as that

---

376 Pierre Rousseau (1716–1785) and his brother-in-law Karl August Wilhelm Weissenbruch (1744–1826), born in Saarbrücken, were the editors of the *Journal encyclopédique*, founded on January 1, 1756. For more information on Karl August Wilhelm Weissenbruch and Pierre Rousseau see Carl Helmut Steckner, "Karl August Wilhelm Weissenbruch (1744–1826), *Saarländische Lebensbilder*, ed. Peter Neumann (Saarbrücken: Saarbrücker Dr. u. Verl. 1989), 39–58.

377 *Journal encyclopédique*, July 1793, §424–425: [*Philosophie sociale, dédiée au Peuple François,* par un citoyen de la section de la République Française, ci-devant du Roule, vol. in-8, de 240 pages, avec cette épigraphe: The proper study of Mankind is man. POPE. In Paris. Chez Froullé, imprimeur-libraire, quai des Augustins, N. 39 – Cet ouvrage respire une philosophie douce et digne d'un philanthrope: les principes n'en sauroient être trop propagés].

of man, of law as a duty, and of freedom. The result is a rather precise picture of the philosophical and social conception of Dobruska, of which we can read this summary paraphrase:

> All legislators, except Jesus Christ, have sunk into the inextricable labyrinth of metaphysics to adapt their legislation to the faculties of the human soul, and have generated only systems where the imagination has played a preponderant role over reason. They brought nothing but unhappiness on to humanity, for not having understood that their speculations should have been based on precise notions about the fate of man. For what I have said and what I will report, we will see how our philosopher brings them back to their true purpose.[378]

The author of the review then quotes several passages from the second part of Dobruska's work, that relating to the form and essence of the Constitution. He highlights, among other things, how the foundations of the Constitution are truth and rationality, but also the "heart", or rather emotions. Rationality and emotionality cannot be completely separated and must interact with each other.

After discussing the third part of the *Philosophie sociale*, the reviewer concludes with a substantially positive judgment on the contents, although he is very critical about the style. The theory developed in the work is legitimate:

> There are good things in the work. The theory is true: there is no good legislation that is not based on the eternal principles of nature. [Nature] has done everything for the happiness of man, and he is unhappy only because he does not want to hear its voice or observe its precepts. We can see, therefore, that the author makes us think; what he lacks is the art of expressing his thoughts with the necessary clarity, especially when writing to instruct the people.[379]

After having presented the work in depth, the *Journal encyclopédique* strongly invites the author of the *Philosophie sociale* to review his text from a stylistic point of view. He also suggests that he should develop and articulate his ideas

---

378 *Journal encyclopédique*, December 1793, 220: [Tous les législateurs, excepté J. C., se sont enfoncés dans le labyrinthe inextricable de la métaphysique pour calquer leur législation sur les facultés de l'âme humaine, et ils n'ont enfanté que des systêmes où l'imagination a eu plus de part que la raison, et ils n'ont fait que le malheur de l'humanité pour n'avoir pas senti que leurs spéculations devoient reposer sur les notions précises de la destination de l'homme. Par ce que je viens de dire et ce que je vais rapporter, on verra que notre philosophe les ramène au véritable but].

379 *Journal encyclopédique*, December 1793, 234: [Il y a de bonnes choses dans son ouvrage. Sa théorie est vraie; point de bonne législation qui ne soit basée sur les principes éternels de la nature. Elle a tout fait pour le bonheur de l'homme. Il n'est malheureux, que parce qu'il ne veut, écouter sa voix, ni observer ses loix. On voit donc que l'auteur fait penser; il ne lui manque que l'art d'exprimer ses pensées avec cette clarté qui est nécessaire, surtout lorsqu'on écrit pour l'instruction du peuple].

more, that he should not be so tight in the elaboration of his concepts and theories.[380] *Brevis esse laboro, obscurus fio.* This precept of Horace, so well known, urges the reviewer, is certainly overlooked by the anonymous author. Even if he had wanted to take account of the criticism, in December 1793 Dobruska had concerns of a completely different and much more serious kind.

7.1.4 The Appreciation of Immanuel Kant

Habent sua fata libelli, says the old, wise Latin motto. And authors, too, *habent sua fata.* The fate of Dobruska, we know, was tragic. And by a very spiteful fate, on the same day as Dobruska's arrest in Paris, November 24, 1793, Immanuel Kant, the philosopher who our author venerated more than anyone else, spoke indirectly of him, praising his work. Since Johann Friedrich Hartnock, who had published the *Critique of Pure Reason* in 1781 and the *Critique of Practical Reason* in 1788, had passed away, Kant had contacted François Théodore de Lagarde (1756–1824). Lagarde published the *Critique of Judgment* in 1790, while a second version, corrected by Kant himself, was published in 1792 (with a print date of 1793).

In the following years, Lagarde and Kant continued to keep in touch through correspondence. In a letter dated 20 September 1793, Kant asked the publisher to send him, in place of some free copies of his *Critique of Judgement,* the book *Reisen des jüngeren Anarcharsis*[381] (Journey of the young Anacarsi) or, if not too much, the *Gedanken und Meinungen,* or the *Essays* of Michel de Montaigne, printed in German by his publishing house. In a letter of the following 24 November, Kant thanked the publisher for having sent him the *Anacarsi and Montaigne,* as well as for having given him the *Philosophie sociale:*

> den 8ten Nov. an mich abgelassenes, den 22ten ejusd. eingegangenes Schreiben, zusammt einem Theile des Anacharsis und einem des Montaigne, nebst dem beygefügten Geschenk der *Philosophie Sociale,* deren Äußerung mir viel Vergnügen gemacht hat, verdienen meinen herzlichen Danck.[382]

---

380 *Ibidem,* 569–570: [En général, on peut l'inviter à résoudre son ouvrage, à donner plus de développement à ses idées, et surtout à l'écrire avec clarté et correction, s'il veut que le public en profite].

381 Almost certainly it is the book *Les Voyages du jeune Anarcharsis en Grèce* by Jean-Jacques Barthélemy, published in 1788 by De Bure and then reprinted many times thanks to the wide success obtained also by the publishing house of Lagarde.

382 Immanuel Kant, in *Das Bonner Kant-Korpus, Briefwechsel,* Brief 643 (An François Théodore de la Garde, Koenigsberg, Nov. 24, 1794): korpora.zim.uni-duisburg-essen.de; cf. Königlich-

It's a short record, which would have been worth more to Dobruska than a long review if he had known about it. This appreciation of Kant – "I liked its observations very much" – buried in a letter published for the first time, from the manuscript legacy, only a century later, testifies, even to our eyes, that for attentive readers the book of Dobruska was, at its appearance, new and important. And what readers!

7.1.5 The Opinion of Maximilien de Robespierre

The *Philosophie sociale* was mentioned not only by scholars and sympathizers of the French Revolution but also by an illustrious lawyer and ruthless politician, none other than Maximilien de Robespierre (1758–1794). After having dominated, with his action as incorruptible guardian of the Revolution, the terrible months of Terror, Robespierre was in turn guillotined on July 28, 1794. Among the papers found in his home, there are some drafts of speeches, never made in public, and but published by the National Convention, a few months after his death.[383]

In an oration on the Chabot case, and on the supposed foreign conspiracy that saw the latter involved, Robespierre also mentions the Freys, who are branded as "monsters" and "hypocrites". The result is a surprising portrait, sarcastic and flattering at the same time, albeit in a sinister way, of Dobruska/Frey with a "red cap", always hunched over his papers and surrounded by the esteem of the other revolutionaries:

> Since the early days of the Revolution, there have been two monsters in Paris worthy of serving the cause of tyrants, because of the profound hypocrisy that characterizes them. They had lost, in Paris, their titles and the names they had at the Court of Vienna. One of the two had associated the name of the founder of Roman freedom with the one he had adopted; he was surrounded by patriotic titles, had composed eloquent works in defense of human rights and the French Revolution, had even got attestations of persecution, having been banned from Germany by Emperor Joseph II. None of the patriots he attracted to himself entered without spotting him, pen in his hand, dreaming of the rights of humanity, bent on the works of Plutarch or Jean-Jacques [Rousseau]. The austere appearance and revolutionary costume of Junius responded perfectly to the idea of a person with great character; the philosophical cut of his hair, the red cap that adorned his philosophical head, guaranteed the purity of his patriotism to the whole earth. Junius Frey had acquired the

---

Preussische Akademie der Künste, eds. *Kant's gesammelte Schriften. Kant's Briefwechsel*, Band 2. (Berlin: Georg Reimer, 1900), 511; Paul Guyer, Editor's Introduction to *Critique of the Power of Judgement*, by Immanuel Kant, transl., Eric Matthews, (Cambridge: Cambridge University Press, 2000), XLVI.

383 *Pièces trouvées dans les papiers de Robespierre et complices*, Paris 1794.

esteem of the whole section; he was linked with the patriots, who were honored by the friendship of this righteous friend of humanity.[384]

"Pen in hand, dreaming of the rights of humanity, bent on the works of Plutarch or Jean-Jacques" – a Dobruska *en philosophe*, honored and revered, at least for a few months, in Jacobin Paris. If Robespierre, the incorruptible, says so, we must believe him.

7.1.6 The Influence on Johann August Eberhard

A very particular influence, which we could define as "negative", was that exerted by Dobruska on the German philosopher Johann August Eberhard (1739–1809). Only a few months after the publication of the *Philosophie sociale*, in the third issue of the second volume of the *Philosophisches Archiv* of 1793, which was distributed in early 1794, appears the essay *Dreyerley Desorganisationen gegen das Ende unsers Jahrhunderte*.[385] Eberhard picks up Dobruska's evaluation of Kant as a great "disorganizer" of previous thought, but transforms the enthusiasm of our author into a sharp indictment. Born in Halberstadt, with Enlightenment sympathies and linked to the Berlin circle of Friedrich Nicolai and Moses Mendelssohn, Eberhard held strongly critical positions towards Kant. According to Eberhard, Kant is the protagonist of one of the three "disorganizations" running through culture and society at the end of the eighteenth century. The parallel with the words of Dobruska, who is never mentioned directly, immediately catches the eye. In Eberhard's vision, which I have already briefly mentioned in the first chapter,

---

384 Robespierre, *Pièces trouvées*, 67: [Il existe à Paris, depuis les premiers temps de la révolution, deux monstres dignes de servir la cause des tyrans, par la profonde hypocrisie qui les caractérise. Ils avoient perdu, à Paris, les titres et le nom qu'ils portoient à la cour de Vienne; l'un d'eux avoit associé à celui l'un, d'eux avoit associé à celui qu'il a adopté, le nom du fondateur de la liberté romaine; il étoit entouré de titres patriotiques; il avoit composé des ouvrages éloquens pour la défense des droits de l'homme et de la révolution française; il avoit même des brevets de persécution; il avoit été banni de l'Allemagne par l'empereur Joseph II. Aucun des patriotes qu'il attiroit chez lui, n'y entroit sans le sur prendre, la plume à la main, rêvant sur les droits de l'humanité, on courbé sur les œuvres de Plutarque ou de Jean-Jacques. L'extérieur austère et le costume révolutionnaire de Junius répondoient parfaitement à l'idée d'un si grand caractère; la coupe philosophique de sa chevelure, le bonnet rouge qui ornoit sa tête philosophique, garantissoient à toute la terre la pureté de son patriotisme. Junius Frey avoit acquis l'estime de toute sa section; il s'étoit lié avec des patriotes qui s'honoroient de l'amitié de ce' vertueux ami de l'humanité].
385 Johann August Eberhard, "Dreyerley Desorganisationen gegen das Ende unsers Jahrhunderte," *Philosophisces Archiv* 2.3 (1794), 17–31.

Kant disorganized philosophy, ruining the rational construction of Christian Wolff's thought, which had long dominated the German intellectual scene;

> [Kant] disorganized philosophy in a way of which no example had been seen before [. . .] With such a manifold disorganization of philosophy, it is no wonder that Mr. Kant [. . .] could no longer come to any systems, and that the results of his philosophy contradict his premises.[386]

It is very interesting to note how Eberhard also draws a parallel between the revolutionary scope of Kantian thought, which he assessed negatively, and the political "disorganization" brought about by the French Revolution. "France", he wrote, "is the homeland of all disorganization", or rather the land where it has found welcome and development. It is in France that the physical "disorganization", introduced by Mesmer, German by birth but so much admired in Paris,[387] has taken root to describe the manipulation of the patient".[388]

And France is naturally, for Eberhard, as for Dobruska, the place of the third, epoch-making disorganization, the political one, brought about by the Revolution of 1789.

---

386 Eberhard, "Dreyerley Desorganisationen," 22–25.

387 This is what Despina also affirms in the first act of *Così fan tutte* by Wolfgang Amadeus Mozart: "This is that piece / of magnet: / mesmeric stone, / which had its origin / in Germany, / which was then so famous / there in France".

388 Eberhard, *Dreyerley Desorganisationen*, 17–18: [Das Vaterland dieser dreyerley Desorganisationen ist eigentlich Frankreich, aus welchem sie erst zu uns gekommen sind. Denn was erstlich die körperliche Desorganisation betrifft, so hat zwar der berüchtigte Mesmer, ein Deutscher, durch einen thierischen Magnetismus dazu Anlaß gegeben; allein dieser thierische Magnetismus wurde anfangs in Deutschland wenig geachtet, und erst in Frankreich machte er sein Glück, wo er, nachdem man seiner unter dieser Benennung überdrüßig geworden war, unter dem Nahmen der Desorganisation triumphirte. In Paris, in Straßburg und andern Städten Frankreichs ließ man sich nunmehr desorganisieren, wie man sich vorher hatte magnetisieren lassen. Durch diese Operation, die in einer besondern Manipulation des Kranken mit den Fingerspitzen besteht, wird nach der Theorie der neuern Mesmerianer, das natürliche Gleichgewicht zwischen den sinnlichen Organen aufgehoben, und der auf solche Art desorganisirte Mensch in den Stand gesetzt, Wunder zu thun (The fatherland of these threefold disorganizations is actually France, from which they first came to us. For as far as physical disorganization is concerned, the infamous Mesmer, a German, gave rise to it through an animal magnetism; only this animal magnetism was little respected at first in Germany, and only in France did it make its fortune, where it triumphed under the name of disorganization, after its original designation [of magnetism] had been abandoned. In Paris, Strasbourg, and other cities in France, it was now possible to disorganize oneself as one had been magnetized before. By this operation, which consists in a special manipulation of the patient with the fingertips, according to the theory of the newer Mesmerisms, the natural balance between the organs of the senses is removed so that the disorganized person can work miracles)].

The polemical reception of disorganization, theorized in the *Philosophie sociale*, by the anti-Kantian philosopher Johann Albert Eberhard, shows us that the originality of the concept, extended by Dobruska to the philosophical, political and social world, was immediately understood, even though it was used in a negative sense.

7.2 In the Nineteenth Century: Henry de Saint-Simon and Auguste Comte

The history of the nineteenth-century fortune of the *Philosophie sociale* touches two of the greatest French thinkers of the century, Claude-Henri de Rouvroy de Saint-Simon (1760–1825), first, great exponent of French socialism, and Auguste Comte (1798–1857), universally considered the founder of sociology. But it is a story that must be indirectly reconstructed, following textual traces and theoretical paths. As far as I was able to find, neither the one nor the other author mentions the *Philosophie sociale* by name, nor expressly remembers its author.

7.2.1 The Influence on Henri de Saint-Simon

Beyond work, life. Through researching sources, which had not yet been carried out, and which I had the opportunity to accomplish for this study, it appears that the biographical path of Henri de Saint-Simon and that of Dobruska have crossed, albeit in rather unusual circumstances. The background to their meeting was not in fact the silence of a library, or the worldly atmosphere of a living room, but the most unpleasant experience of the Parisian prison of Sainte-Pélagie.

Saint-Simon and the Frey brothers were arrested and imprisoned at the same time, a few days apart from each other. In the tense atmosphere of 1793, Saint-Simon, a nobleman by birth, had chosen to prudently change his aristocratic name, and called himself Bonhomme. But it was a useless expedient: poor Bonhomme was arrested on November 19, 1793 (29 Brumaire), on the basis of an order issued by the *Comités réunis de Salut public et de Sûreté Générale* (General Public Health and Safety Committees) and executed by the *Comité de police de la Ville* (Police Committee of the City of Paris).[389] Albert Mathiez's

---

389 See Albert Mathiez, "L'arrestation de Saint-Simon," *Annales historiques de la Révolution française* 2 (1925), 571–575; 571; Idem, *Saint-Simon et Ronsin, ibidem* 3 (1926), 493–494: 494;

research shows that Saint-Simon was actually imprisoned by mistake in place of Belgian banker Henry Simon, who was in Basel, Switzerland[390] for his business at the time. From the prison, Saint-Simon wrote, dismayed:

> I think I was arrested instead of another, because the name Simon in the order of arrest of the Committees was not exactly what I had before calling me Bonhomme, and the quality of "Simon who lives on his goods", written in the order, no longer belongs to me.[391]

After his arrest, he was taken to the Sainte-Pélagie prison[392] and then, at the beginning of May 1794, transferred to the Luxembourg prison.[393] He was only released on August 28, 1794.[394]

The Frey brothers were arrested four days later, on November 23,[395] on charges of espionage on behalf of foreign powers. They were detained in several prisons: Port-Libre, De-la-Force and, finally, in the Sainte-Pélagie prison, where they certainly had a chance to meet Saint-Simon. On March 19, 1794 (29 Brumaire), wine merchant Pierre Gellibert told Judge Antoine-Mairie Maire that he had learned that Charles-Philippe Ronsin (1751–1794), general of the Revolutionary Army, had promised several prisoners, including Pereyra, Desfleux, Cazerou, Dubuisson, Bonhomme, and the Frey brothers, "relatives of Chabot on his wife's side" that he would set them free.[396] The previous day, March 18 (28 Ventôse), Emmanuel Frey, brother of Moses/Junius had reported to the police administrator François Dangé "the names of several people who could give information about Ronsin, both in favor and against him, indicating as alleged partisans Desfieux, Pereyra, and Debuisson, and as his opponents Mollin, Delonne, and Bonhomme".[397] Charles-Philippe Ronsin, accused of conspiring

---

Henri Gouhier, *La jeunesse d'Auguste Comte et la formation du positivisme*, 3 vols. Second edition (Paris; Vrin, 1964–1970) (I ed. 1933–1941), vol 2, *Saint-Simon Jusqu'à la restauration*, 84.

390 Mathiez, *L'arrestation de Saint-Simon*, 573.

391 *Loc. cit.*: [Je crois que j'ai arrêté pour un autre, car le nom de Simon porté dans l'ordre d'arrestation des Comités n'était pas exactement celui que je portais avent de m'appeler Bonhomme, et la qualité de "Simon vinant de son bien" qu'on trouve dans l'ordre de la police ne me convient davantage. On this "mistake", actually voluntary], see also Gouhier, *La jeuness d'Auguste Comte*, vol. 2, 84–85.

392 See *Ibidem*, 86 and 357, correcting Mathiez, *L'Arrestation de Saint-Simon*, 572.

393 Gouhier, *La jeunesse de Comte*, vol. 2, 85.

394 Mathiez, *L'arrestation de Saint-Simon*, 572.

395 See above, 2. 7.

396 Tuetey, *Répertoire*, vol. 10, no. 2,288, 21–522.

397 Mathiez, "Saint-Simon et Ronsin," 494. Cf. Tuetey, *Répertoire*, vol. 10, 518–519, No 2285.

with the Hérbertists, was guillotined on March 24, 1794,[398] two weeks before the Frey brothers.

The latter were evidently perfectly informed about the opinions of Saint-Simon/Bonhomme, and it is very likely that they had known him directly, from personal meetings that wouldn't have been infrequent during the common detention in Sainte-Pélagie.

Probably already in this period of imprisonment, tormented but far from intellectually inert as it was, Saint-Simon had knowledge of the political and social ideas expressed in the *Philosophie sociale*. In later years, when anxieties of Terror were no more than a memory, Saint-Simon would return to a key concept of Dobruska's thought, that of social disorganization.

In the work *De la réorganisation de la société européenne*, published by Saint-Simon, with the help of Augustin Thierry, in 1814, the process of disorganization and reorganization is placed at the center of the investigation:

> The philosophy of the last century was revolutionary: that of the nineteenth century must have an organizational character [. . .] the social order was disturbed because it no longer conformed to the dictates of the Age of Enlightenment. It's up to you to build a better one. The political body has been disintegrated: your intention must be to reconstitute it [. . .] Every institution, founded on an opinion, should not last longer than this one. Luther, shaking in people's minds that original respect that constituted the power of the clergy, disorganized Europe. Half of the Europeans freed themselves from the chains of papism, and broke the only political link that united them to the great society.[399]

The affinity with the *Philosophie sociale* concerns first of all the phase of destruction of a constituted social order (social disorganization) which must be followed by the reconstruction (social organization) and the rethinking of the major institutions. But that's not the only point of contact. The distinctive sign of Dobruska's thought is the "transversal" use of the concept of disorganization, as a meta-category that encompasses society, philosophical thought, and religion. This plurality also plays a significant role for Saint-Simon: the disorganization of society is

---

398 Auguste Philippe Herlaut, *Le général rouge Ronsin (1751–1794). La Vendée, l'armée révolutionnaire parisienne* (Paris: Clavreuil, 1956).

399 Henri de Saint-Simon and Augustin Thierry, *De la réorganisation de la société européenne, ou De la nécessité et des moyens de rassembler les peuples de l'Europe en un seul corps politique* (Paris A. Égron 1814), VIII, XII: [La philosophie du siècle dernier a été révolutionnaire celle du dix-neuvième doit être organisatrice [. . .] L'ordre social a été bouleversé parce qu'il ne convenait plus aux lumières c'est à vous d'en créer un meilleur le corps politique a été dissous, c'est à vous de le reconstituer [. . .] Toute institution fondée sur une opinion ne doit pas durer plus longtemps qu'elle. Luther, en ébranlant dans les esprits ce vieux respect qui faisait la force du clergé, désorganisa l'Europe. La moitié des Européens s'affranchit des chaînes du papisme, c'est-à-dire brisa le seul lien politique qui l'attachât à la grande société].

matched by that of philosophy and theology. The attentive reader will have noticed that Luther, mentioned here by Saint-Simon as the main disorganizer of sixteenth-century Europe, also appears in the genealogy of disorganizers identified by *Philosophie sociale*, where he is in the company of other protagonists of the Protestant Reformation ("les diverses révolutions philosophiques et sacerdotales de Luther, Zuingle, Melanchton, Calvin"[400]).

The similarities with Dobruska's work are not limited to this fundamental theoretical debt concerning disorganization/reorganization. It is the same constitutional proposal, and the method by which it is to be achieved, that recalls the words of the old fellow prisoner of Saint-Simon. In the chapter entitled *The best possible constitution*, Saint-Simon writes:

> I propose to investigate whether there is a good form of government for itself, based on certain, absolute, universal principles, independent of time and place [. . .] Until now, the method of the observational sciences has not been used in political matters. Each one has brought you his own way of seeing, reasoning, and judging. And from this follows the lack of precision in the solutions, and the uncertainty of the results achieved. The time has come for this infancy of science to come to an end.[401]

The reader of the *Philosophie sociale* here breathes a familiar air: the constitution and the government must be based on absolute principles, political issues must be addressed with the methods of the natural sciences, and it is time for the study of society and the way of governing it to come out of its infancy. If not exact sentences (Dobruska speaks of a "cradle" instead of "infancy"[402]), the concepts are the same as those that open the *Philosophie sociale*. Exactly twenty years have passed since Dobruska's death on the gallows, and his book seems to be consigned to the past. All the more reason to use it freely, without too many ceremonies.

---

400 Dobruska, *Philosophie sociale*, 48.
401 Saint-Simon, Thierry, *De la réorganisation*, 33: [Je veux chercher, s'il n'y a pas une forme de gouvernement bonne par sa seule nature, fondée sur des principes sûrs, absolus, universels, indépendans des temps et des lieux [. . .] Jusqu'ici la méthode des sciences d'observation n'a point été introduite dans les questions politique» chacun y a porté sa façon de voir, de raisonner, de juger, et de là vient qu'il n'y a eu encore ni précision dans les solutions, ni généralité dans les résultats. Le temps est venu où il doit cesser cette enfance de la science].
402 Dobruska, *Philosophie sociale*, ii: [La philosophie sociale est la science la moins avancée et la plus incertaine de toutes. Elle est encore dans son berceau].

7.2.2 The Influence on the Thought of Auguste Comte

From Dobruska to Saint-Simon, and from there to Comte. A biographical thread links the three characters in a continuous way. If the first two met, in the narrow space of the Parisian prison of Sainte-Pélagie, the personal ties between Saint-Simon and Auguste Comte are well known, and are documented since August 1817, when the young Comte becomes secretary of the older and already famous Saint-Simon. It is an intellectual bond with important consequences. Comte will write: "From this relationship I have received a great number of things that I would have searched in vain for in books".[403]

Disorganization and Social Organization

Comte had sympathized at a very young age with the ideas of the French Revolution and the construction of a Republic, thus opposing the Catholic and counter-revolutionary culture in which he had been socialized in Montpellier, a city with ancient university traditions butwhich was small and provincial.[404] Meeting Saint-Simon broadened his cultural horizons, and gave him the opportunity to showcase his talents as a writer and publicist, with a fluent pen and a philosophical vein. Already in 1817, from the collaboration between the two was born *Industrie*, a work in four parts, which outlines the idea of a culture that, after dismantling the mistakes of the past, must be able to rebuild a new method of knowledge and a society that reflects it. If this work's general conception was that of Saint-Simon, the formulations came largely out of Comte's eloquence:

> After working separately, eighteenth century writers came together in a single philosophical laboratory and created a general work, an encyclopedia that could have been called a general anti-theology. This, broadly speaking, is the way in which the first task was carried out, the task of disorganizing the theological system. Let us now consider how to proceed with the execution of the second, which will have as its purpose the organization of an earthly moral system.[405]

---

403 Gouhier, *La jeunesse de Comte*, vol. 1, 15; cf. *ibidem*, vol. 3, 167–183.
404 Mary Pickering, *Auguste Comte. An Intellectual Biography*, 3 vol. (Cambridge: Cambridge University Press 1993), vol. 1, 3.
405 "Prospectus annonçant le troisième volume de l'Industrie (1817*)*," in *Écrits de jeunesse 1816–1828. Suivis du Mémoire sur la Cosmogonie de Laplace, 1835*, by Auguste Comte (Berlin: De Gruyter, 2018) (I ed. 1970), 40: [Après avoir travaillé chacun de son côté, les écrivains du XVIIIe siècle se sont réunis en un seul atelier philosophique et ils ont fait en commun un ouvrage général, une encyclopédie à laquelle on aurait pu donner le nom d'*antithéologie* générale. Voilà, par aperçu, la manière dont la première tâche a été remplie, et cette tâche avait pour but la désorganisation du système théologique. Voyons maintenant comment on doit procéder

Note, once again, the *désorganisation du système théologique*. It is enough to leaf through the *Philosophie sociale* to understand where these anti-theological intellectuals, about to found the culture of the new age, come from:

> For you, O wise! may your first care be to overthrow (disorganize) the artificial regime, and to bring us back to the simple regime of nature, developed by a healthy culture. Let us first go back to it, examine it; and let us draw from its processes a new art, a new culture.[406]

Dobruska's approach passed to Comte, through the influence that Saint-Simon had on him. For Saint-Simon the "reorganization" of society increasingly assumed a programmatic role, became the mission of all his work and the engine of public commitment. To Comte, Saint-Simon entrusts the role of main extensor of the documents aimed at founding this reorganization and, therefore, passes to him the conceptual scheme of disorganization/reorganization, which we first found in the *Philosophie sociale*. We don't know if the two of them discussed the figure of that unusual converted Jew who died during the Revolution. It is very possible, just as it is also possible that Saint-Simon passed on some personal memories to his young secretary. But we can't be sure. Of course, Comte also seems to have had a first-hand knowledge of the *Philosophie sociale*, so evident are the similarities between his early writings and the prose, although much less elegant, of Dobruska's work.

At the beginning of 1822, Comte began to compose a text that would prove to be fundamental, not only for his personal theoretical path but for the entire development of the social sciences. The work appeared in print in April of the same year, in a few copies, in the collection *Suite des travaux ayant pour objet de fonder le système industriel. Du Contrat social*.[407] The main title page of the volume bears the name of Saint-Simon, who is actually only the author of the 14-page introduction. In this introduction there is a clear continuity with *La réorganisation de la société européenne* of 1814, which I have dealt with above, and with the *Industrie* of 1817. The basic concept is the same, aiming at the link between the disorganization of a society and its reorganization, and therefore

---

à l'exécution de la seconde, qui aura pour objet l'organisation d'un système de morale terrestre].

406 Dobruska, *Philosophie sociale*, 47: "Pour vous, ô sages! que votre premier soin soit de renverser, (désorganiser) le régime artificiel, et de nous ramener au régime simple de la nature, développé par une saine culture. Retournons d'abord à elle, examinons-la; et puisons dans ses procédés un art nouveau, une culture nouvelle".

407 Henri Saint-Simon, *Suite des travaux ayant pour objet de fonder le système industriel. Du Contrat social* (Paris: Chez les Marchands de nouveautés, 1822).

indebted – and this is what interests us most here – to the *Philosophie sociale.*
A brief quotation will be enough to understand the tone of Saint-Simon's text:

> Take the time to examine what happened in the eighteenth century, and you will recog-
> nize that the destruction of privileges was mainly determined by the *Encyclopédie*, a work
> in which the most illustrious scholars and artists of the time participated. However, it
> would be too extraordinary if their efforts had been necessary to disorganize society, and
> if society could be reorganized without them contributing to this undertaking.
>
> In a word, gentlemen, it is the scientists who must begin the work necessary for so-
> cial reorganization.
>
> In order to encourage them to use their strengths and talents in this direction, it was
> necessary for my system to be presented to them in scientific form.
>
> One of my collaborators and friends was in charge of this important operation. Here
> is his work, which corresponds to the *Preliminary Discourse to the Encyclopédie*, by
> d'Alembert.[408]

In the last sentence, Saint-Simon himself stated the link between his own approach and that of Comte, defined here as *un de mes collaborateurs et amis.* The
internal frontispiece correctly attributes everything else in the book to Comte,
under the title *Prospectus des travaux scientifiques nécessaires pour la réorgan-
iser la société.* The combination of disorganization and reorganization, which
we have seen passed from Dobruska to Saint-Simon, and already to the Comte
of 1817, is also the distinctive sign under which the treatment of the memorable
Comtian *Prospectus* of 1822 opens:

> A social system that is dying out, a new system that has reached its full maturity and
> tends to be established, this is the fundamental character assigned to the present era by
> the general path of civilization. In accordance with this state of affairs, two movements of
> a different nature are agitating society today: one of disorganization, the other of reorga-
> nization. Through the first, considered in isolation, it is pushed towards a deep moral and
> political anarchy, which seems to threaten it [i.e. society] with an imminent and inevitable
> dissolution. Through the second, it is led to the definitive social state of the human species,
> the most suited to its nature, where all means of prosperity must receive their broadest

---

408 Saint-Simon, *Suite des travaux*, 11–12: [Prenez la peine d'examiner ce qui s'est passé dans
le dix-huitième siècle, et vous reconnaîtrez que la destruction des priviléges (sic) a été princi-
palement déterminée par l'Encyclopédie, travail auquel les savants et les artistes les plus dis-
tingués de cette époque ont concouru. Or il serait par trop extraordinaire que leurs efforts
eussent été nécessaires pour désorganiser la société, et que la société pût être réorganisée sans
qu'ils devinssent auxiliaires dans cette entreprise. En un mot, Messieurs, ce sont les savants
qui doivent commencer les travaux qu'exige la réorganisation sociale. Pour les déterminer à
employer leurs forces et leurs talens dans cette direction, il était nécessaire que mon système
leur fût présenté sous la forme scientifique. Un de mes collaborateurs et amis s'est chargé de
cette importante opération Voici son travail, qui correspond au discours préliminaire de l'Encyclopédie, par d'Alembert].

development and their most direct application. It is in the coexistence of these opposing tendencies that the great crisis experienced by the most civilized nations consists. It is under these two aspects that it must be considered in order to be understood.[409]

It will be remembered that the lack of a reorganization, both political and intellectual, was the basis of the criticism made by Dobruska of Rousseau. If he had shown the need to break up the pre-revolutionary society, in which all men were in chains, and had thus become the great inspirer of the Revolution, he had not been able to indicate the path towards the construction (organization) of a new social order. We have seen how Dobruska's project was divided into two phases: 1) analysis of the "pathological causes" that had brought about the collapse of the *Ancien Régime*, and 2) formulation of a Universal Constitution, based on the most "scientific study" possible of society. The first part of the Constitution, which contains the conceptual elaborations and principles, as we know, must be the foundation on which to build a new democratic society. The program of the young Comte is very similar, oriented as it is to the renewal of the society under the impulse of Saint-Simon:

> The only way to put an end to this stormy situation, to stop the anarchy that invades society day by day, in a word, to reduce the crisis to a simple moral movement, is to push the civilized nations to leave the critical direction and to take the organic direction, to focus all their efforts on the formation of the new social system, the final object of the crisis, and for which all that has been done so far is only preparatory. This is the first necessity of the present. This is also, in summary, the general purpose of my work, and the specific purpose of this paper, which aims to bring into play the forces that must lead society on the road to the new system.[410]

---

409 Comte, "Prospectus des travaux scientifiques" *Suite des travaux*, 15 (cf. Idem, *Écrits de jeunesse*, 241): [Un système social qui s'éteint, un nouveau système parvenu à son entière maturité et qui tend à se constituer, tel est le caractère fondamental assigné à l'époque actuelle par la marche générale de la civilisation. Conformément à cet état de choses, deux mouvemens de nature différente agitent aujourd'hui la société: l'un de désorganisation, l'autre de réorganisation. Par le premier, considéré isolément, elle est entraînée vers une profonde anarchie morale et politique qui semble la menacer d'une prochaine et inévitable dissolution. Par le second, elle est conduite vers l'état social définitif de l'espèce humaine, le plus convenable à sa nature, celui où tous ses moyens de prospérité doivent recevoir leur plus entier développement et leur application la plus directe. C'est dans la co-existence de ces deux tendances opposées que consiste la grande crise éprouvée par les nations les plus civilisées. C'est sous ce double aspect qu'elle doit être envisagée pour être comprise].

410 *Ibidem*, 17 (Idem, *Écrits de jeunesse*, 242): [La seule manière de mettre un terme à cette orageuse situation, d'arrêter l'anarchie qui envahit de jour en jour la société, en un mot de réduire la crise à un simple mouvement moral, c'est de déterminer les nations civilisées à quitter la

Let us therefore see how Comte, like Dobruska, intends first and foremost to identify the causes that prevent society from progressing. After this analysis, one can think of building a new direction, which Comte calls "organic".

The Need of a Scientific Reflection on Society

How to move towards the reorganization of society? Comte is convinced that a new science must be founded, one that focuses on the analysis of "social phenomena". In the 1822 *Prospectus*, he defined this discipline as "social physics":

> In this sense, social physics, that is to say, the study of the collective development of the human species, is really a branch of physiology, that is, the study of man, conceived in all its extension. In other words, the history of civilization is nothing more than the indispensable continuation and complement of man's natural history.[411]

The objective of this new science is the collective development of the human species, which must be studied with the tools of mathematics. In short, social physics must be considered a specific branch of physiology.

In the 1825 *Considérations philosophiques sur les sciences et les savants*, we find an expanded and partly revised formulation of social physics:

> I shall limit myself here to saying, in order to prevent any confusion, that by social physics I mean the science which has as its specific object the study of social phenomena, considered with the same spirit as astronomical, physical, chemical, and physiological phenomena, that is to say subject to invariable natural laws, the discovery of which is the particular purpose of his research. In this way, it aims directly to explain, with the utmost precision, the great phenomenon of the development of the human species, considered in all its essential parts; that is to say, to discover the necessary concatenation of the successive transformations, through which the human race, starting from a state just above that of the great apes, has been gradually led to the point where it is now in civilized Europe.[412]

---

direction critique pour prendre la direction organique, à porter tous leurs efforts vers la formation du nouveau système social, objet définitif de la crise, et pour lequel tout ce qui s'est fait jusqu'à présent n'est que préparatoire. Tel est le premier besoin de l'époque actuelle. Tel est aussi en aperçu le but général de mes travaux, et le but spécial de cet écrit qui a pour objet de mettre en jeu les forces qui doivent entraîner la société dans la route du nouveau système].

411 *Ibidem*, 176 (Idem, *Écrits de jeunesse*, 311): [En ce sens, la physique sociale, c'est-à-dire, l'étude du développement collectif de l'espèce humaine, est réellement une branche de la physiologie, c'est-à-dire de l'étude de l'homme, conçue dans toute son extension. En d'autres termes, l'histoire de la civilisation n'est autre chose que la suite et le complément indispensable de l'histoire naturelle de l'homme].

412 Comte, *Écrits de jeunesse*, 335: [Je me borne ici à dire, pour prévenir toute confusion, que j'entends par physique sociale la science qui a pour objet propre l'étude des phénomènes sociaux considérés dans le même esprit que les phénomènes astronomiques, physiques, chimiques, et physiologiques, c'est-à-dire comme assujettis à des lois naturelles invariables, dont la

There is a focus on this "physics", which becomes, in a more specific way, a treatment of "social phenomena". The preoccupation with scientificity and the link with the natural sciences remains alive, so much so that social physics is taken to descend from individual physiology and is inserted in a mutual relationship with the disciplinary field of physiology.

In short, social physics must consider social phenomena in the same way as astronomical, physical, chemical, and physiological phenomena, and must go so far as to find natural laws that cannot be altered. This analogy between the treatment of social and other scientific disciplines, which today we would call "hard sciences", is exactly what Dobruska has in mind for social philosophy, which he wants to advance to the level of physics and chemistry. More precisely, social philosophy must base its thought on rationality, it must leave behind metaphysics, and find in the study of *physis* (nature) its own definitions and its own laws or principles.[413]

The development of Comte's thought is very similar, and is further specified in the *Cours de philosophie positive*, one of his mature works, published from 1830:

> Now we have a celestial physics, a terrestrial physics, both mechanical and chemical, a plant physics, and an animal physics; to complete the system of our knowledge of nature, we still need one, the last one, the social physics.[414]

In the *Cours*, social physics is no longer to be understood as a branch of physiology but as a constitutive part of positive philosophy. In the preface, Comte writes that he understands "philosophy" in the Aristotelian meaning of "general system of human conceptions".[415]

The term "positive" here indicates the set of theories, according to a certain order of ideas, which have as their object "the coordination of the observed facts". In other words, theories should not be elaborated in an *a priori* way according to a metaphysics, but should arise from the analysis of real facts that

---

découverte est le but spécial de ses recherches. Ainsi, elle se propose directement d'expliquer, avec le plus de précision possible, le grand phénomène du développement de l'espèce humaine, envisagé dans toutes ses parties essentielles; c'est-à-dire de découvrir par quel enchaînement nécessaire de transformations successives le genre humain, en partant d'un état à peine supérieur à celui des sociétés de grands singes, a été conduit graduellement au point où il se trouve aujourd'hui dans l'Europe civilisée].

413 Dobruska, *Philosophie sociale*, viii.

414 Auguste Comte, *Cours de philosophie positive*, vol. 1 (Paris: Rouen Frères, 1830), 22: [Maintenant que l'esprit humain a fondé la physique céleste, la physique terrestre, soit mécanique, soit chimique; la physique organique, soit végétale, soit animale, il lui reste à terminer le système des sciences d'observation en fondant la *physique sociale*].

415 *Ibidem*, viii.

have been observed. In particular, positive philosophy includes, in the Comtian sense, the study of any phenomenon, even if not social, provided that the positive or scientific method of the natural sciences is used.[416]

Connection between Forms of Thought and Social Organization

The 1822 *Prospectus* has gone down in history above all because in it, for the first time, Comte formulated his famous *Law of Human Progress* or *Law of the Three Stages*:

> By the very nature of the human mind, each branch of our knowledge is necessarily subject in its course to three different consecutive theoretical states: the theological or fictitious state; the metaphysical or abstract state; and, finally, the scientific or positive state.[417]

Schematic, simple to the point of appearing simplistic, and precisely for this reason so fortunate, the law of the three stages of Comte has the ambition to embrace in a single formulation cultural models and social organization:

> If we consider politics as a science, and apply the previous observations to it, we find that it has already passed through the first two stages, and that it is now ready to reach the third stage. The doctrine of kings represents the theological stage of politics [. . .] The doctrine of peoples expresses the metaphysical stage of politics. It is entirely based on the abstract and metaphysical assumption of a primitive social contract, before any development of human faculties by civilization [. . .] Finally, the scientific doctrine of politics considers the social stage under which the human species has always been found by observers as the necessary consequence of its organization.[418]

Where does this scanning of the history of thought come from in three distinct, successive, necessary degrees? The most attentive readers have noticed the

---

416 Compare *Philosophie sociale,* iv.

417 Comte, *Prospectus des travaux scientifiques,* in Suite *des travaux,* 71 (Idem, *Écrits de jeunesse,* 268): [Par la nature même de l'esprit humain, chaque branche de nos connaissances est nécessairement assujettie dans sa marche à passer successivement par trois états théoriques différents: l'état théologique ou fictif; l'état métaphysique ou abstrait; enfin l'état scientifique ou positif].

418 *Ibidem,* 74–75 (Idem, *Écrits de jeunesse,* 269): [En considérant la politique comme une science, et lui appliquant les observations précédentes, on trouve qu'elle a déjà passé par les deux premiers états, et qu'elle est prête aujourd'hui à atteindre au troisième. La doctrine des rois représente l'état théologique de la politique [. . .] La doctrine des peuples exprime l'état métaphysique de la politique. Elle est fondée en totalité sur la supposition abstraite et métaphysique d'un contrat social primitif, antérieur à tout développement des facultés humaines par la civilisation [. . .] Enfin, la doctrine scientifique de la politique considère l'état social sous lequel l'espèce humaine a toujours été trouvée par les observateurs comme la conséquence nécessaire de son organisation].

similarities with the theories of the three ages of man, formulated by Giambattista Vico in his *Scienza nuova* of 1725, a work that aimed to read, in a new way, the history of mankind. According to Vico, all nations would pass through three ages: gods, heroes and men. The first is characterized by the senses and imagination and dominated by religion. The second sees the attribution of divine attributes to heroes, and the establishment of the law of the strongest, while the last age, that of men, is marked by reason. For Vico, however, it is not a matter of a substantially linear progress, as in Comte, but of a cyclical alternation, through which each people pass, and then fall back, from the third, to the first age. It is likely that Dobruska, who knew Italian well, had read Vico and had made the most of it. It is certain that in the *Philosophie sociale* we find a very similar scheme, although less concise than that offered by Comte. And it is a scheme that, unlike the Vichian "corsi" and "ricorsi", of circular trend, is pervaded by undeniable enlightenment optimism. The three phases of thought and society on which Dobruska is based are the same as those immortalized by the law of the three stages of Comte:

> In ancient times, the entire earth was subject to the sovereignty of the gods. The kings were their representatives. All forms of government were theocratic [. . .]

> Where legislation has found a solid foundation in nature and applies physics perfectly, metaphysics will no longer be needed. That is to say, when we know nature, we will no longer have anything to look for beyond it.[419]

Dobruska states even more clearly, a little further on, that the time has come to overcome the metaphysics that is no longer needed. Dobruska writes:

> It is true that when the legislation will have found the solid foundations of nature, and will apply in a perfect way the physics, we will no longer need the metaphysics, in this sense we can say with Bacon *post veram inventam phisicam nulla metaphysica erit*. That is to say, once we have known nature, we must no longer look beyond it.[420]

Readers will forgive me if I have put together passages that, in the *Philosophie sociale*, are further apart. What is important is to show that even the starting point for this succession of stages of civilization and thought – theology, metaphysics, nature – may well have come to Comte from a reading of Dobruska, perhaps through the usual mediation of Saint-Simon, who already in the *Réorganisation* of

---

419 *Philosophie sociale*, 40 (see above, 3. 9) and 55 (see above, 3. 10).
420 *Loc. cit.*: [Il est vrai que lorsque la législation aura trouvé les bases solides de la nature, en fait l'application parfaite de la physique, nous n'aurons plus besoin de la métaphysique, dans ce sens, nous pourrions dire avec Bacon, *post veram inventam phisicam nulla métaphysica erit*. C'est-à-dire, quand nous connoîtrons une fois la nature, nous n'aurons plus à chercher au-delà d'elle].

1814 distinguished between theological and metaphysical ages. With one caveat. Among the many gifts of our social philosopher from Brno was not the gift of conciseness. If not complete originality, Comte's Law of the three states has the merit of having used a prose of Cartesian compactness.

Division of Labor for the Reorganization of Society between Theory and Practice

Another surprising analogy between the thinking of Moses Dobruska and that of Auguste Comte concerns the division of labor necessary to reorganize society.

As already mentioned above, the *Philosophie sociale* provides that the Constitution is divided into two parts.

The first part, which is binding, contains the principles governing the life of individuals in society, while the second part, which is subordinate to the first, represents the application of the principles set out in the first part. If the theoretical part requires, in order to be formulated, abstract competence and rational rigor, the realization of the second part of the Constitution is instead the task of the general assemblies.[421] It is no coincidence that the *Philosophie sociale* only deepens the first part of its Constitution and does not deal with the second. For Dobruska, in short, a strict division of labor is necessary in order to be able to rebuild the social order in France, after the fall of the absolute monarchy: on the one hand a work of theoretical reflection, on the other hand legislative practice and the activity of government.

We find such a division of labor, between theory and practice, almost replicated in Comte's thought. The 1822 *Prospectus* reads:

> It follows from the above that the major mistakes made by peoples in their conception of the reorganization of society are mainly due to the fallacious procedure on the basis of which they carried out this very reorganization; the flaw of this procedure consists in the fact that the social reorganization has been considered as a purely practical operation, whereas it is essentially theoretical; that the nature of things and the most convincing historical experiences demonstrate the absolute necessity of dividing the overall work of reorganization into two series, one theoretical and the other practical, the first of which must be carried out in advance, and must serve as a basis for the second; that the preliminary execution of the theoretical work requires the activation of a new social force, distinct from those who have occupied the scene so far and who are absolutely incompetent; finally, that, for several very stringent reasons, this new force must be that of the scientists [*savants*], who devote themselves to the study of observational sciences.[422]

---

421 *Ibidem*, 53.
422 Comte, *Prospectus des travaux scientifiques*, in *Suite des travaux*, 69–70 (Idem, *Écrits de jeunesse*, 267): [Il résulte, de tout ce qui précède, que les erreurs capitales commises par les

And again, a few pages later:

> The very nature of the work to be carried out indicates, as clearly as possible, the class to which it is to be assigned. Since these works are theoretical, it is clear that the men who by profession elaborate theoretical combinations followed methodically, that is, the scientists [*savants*] who deal with the study of the sciences of observation, are the only ones whose type of intellectual capacity and culture meets the necessary conditions.[423]

The theoretical part of the reorganization of society will have to be elaborated by the *savants*. Moreover, the idea of attributing the reconstruction of society to intellectuals, artists, and artisans is one of the cornerstones of Saint-Simon's program, also reaffirmed in the introduction to the Comtian *Prospectus*. Dobruska could not have agreed more, he who had called the wise to celebrate their new cult: "Religion of the truth of the princes! I already see the nameless wise prepare all their hearts to receive your worship".[424]

7.3 In the Twentieth Century: The Study of Gershom Scholem

The rediscovery of Moses Dobruska, and of the fascinating tangle of his biography, is due to Gershom Scholem. Scholem, father of the modern study of the kabbalah, is interested above all in the intellectual parable of Dobruska, from the heretical Jewish environment of his birth, to his conversion to Catholicism and

---

peuples dans leur manière de concevoir la réorganisation de la société, ont, pour cause première, la marche vicieuse d'après laquelle ils ont procédé à cette réorganisation de la société; que le vice de cette marche consiste en ce que la réorganisation sociale a été regardée comme une opération purement pratique, tandis qu'elle est essentiellement théorique; que la nature des choses et les expériences historiques les plus convaincantes prouvent la nécessité absolue de diviser le travail total de la réorganisation en deux séries, l'une théorique, l'autre pratique, dont la première doit être préalablement exécutée, et est destinée à servir de base à la seconde; que l'exécution préliminaire des travaux théoriques exige la mise en activité d'une nouvelle force sociale, distincte de celles qui ont jusqu'ici occupé la scène, et qui sont absolument incompétentes; enfin, que, par plusieurs raisons très-décisives, cette nouvelle force doit être celle des savants adonnés à l'étude des sciences d'observation].

423 *Ibidem*, 59 (Idem, *Écrits de jeunesse*, 262): [La nature des travaux à exécuter indique d'elle-même, le plus clairement possible, à quelle classe il appartient de les entreprendre. Ces travaux étant théoriques, il est clair que les hommes qui font profession de former des combinaisons théoriques suivies méthodiquement, c'est-à-dire les savans occupés de l'étude des sciences d'observation, sont les seuls dont le genre de capacité et de culture intellectuelle remplisse les conditions nécessaires].

424 *Philosophie sociale*, 50: [Religion de la vérité des principes ! je vois déjà des savans sans nombre préparer tous les cœurs à recevoir ton culte. Viens, ô viens, et qu'après tant d'idolâtries et d'idoles, qui t'ont occupée, l'humanité jouisse une fois de ta divinité!].

adhesion to Freemasonry, up to his political commitments between the Jacobins of Strasbourg and Paris, and at his end at the gallows. Scholem's essay, published in 1981, shortly before his death in 1982,[425] has its strength in its evaluation of the esoteric Dobruska, the adventurer who knows how to play cunning with the courts and governments, and who subjugates at will the noble and powerful. Given this orientation, it is not surprising that Scholem dedicates only a few pages to the *Philosophie sociale*. It is a sketchy outline, offered more for duty of completeness than for real interest. However, it is still a description from the pen of a great scholar, and it is worth remembering its salient elements. Scholem believes in the sincerity of Dobruska/Frey's commitment to the ideals of the French Revolution and breaks a lance in favor of the good faith of the multifaceted man of letters and action, who, he thinks, was truly convinced "of the moral, political, and social principles that he sets out"[426] in his work. For those who know the caustic vein of the master of Jewish studies, who over time had maintained much of his polemical Berlin attitude, already this admission of sincerity, in a biographically ambiguous charactersuch as Dobruska, is surprising. The *Philosphie sociale* is presented by Scholem as a philosophical reflection, "a synthesis of the ideas of Locke, Rousseau and Kant",[427] which arose from the discussion of a new constitution for the French people. Although he is convinced that "the work deserves a detailed analysis",[428] Scholem sees it above all in the framework that is closest to his heart, that is, as a document of the links between the Jewish sectarian movements – in particular Sabbatianism and its later variant, Frankism – that criticized the religious orthodoxy of the Rabbis of the time, and the philosophy of the Enlightenment. Among the many topics dealt with in Dobruska's book, the passages dedicated to religion are thus highlighted, which, according to Scholem, are "animated by an enlightened radicalism that, in the eyes of the Frankists, does not contradict the esoteric mysticism, on the contrary, completes it".[429]

---

425 Gershom Scholem, *Du Frankisme au jacobinisme. La vie de Moses Dobruska, alias Thomas von Schönfeld alias Junius Frey,* which was presented at the conference of May 23, 1979, as part of a cycle dedicated to Marc Bloch, at the École des Hautes Études en Sciences Sociales. This essay was translated into French by Naftali Deutsch and published two years after the conference. It contains the most important results of Gershom Scholem's studies on Moses Dobruska. Some of these results had already been published first in German and in Hebrew. Scholem's essay was translated into Italian by Elisabetta Zevi and published in Gershom Scholem, *Le tre vite di Mosess Dobrushka*, (Milano: Adelphi, 2014), edited by Saverio Campanini.
426 Scholem, *Du Frankisme au jacobinisme,* 73.
427 *Loc. cit.*
428 *Loc. cit.*
429 *Loc. cit.*

According to Scholem, Dobruska's thesis is that "every political regime is like a religion, endowed with its own theology" and therefore it is also possible to search for the theological foundations of the democratic regime. For this reason, Dobruska "initiates a critical analysis of the systems and constitutions of Moses, Solon, and Jesus. And here – writes Scholem – is revealed the last Jewish avatar" of Dobruska. Scholem correctly emphasizes the harsh criticism that the *Philosophie sociale* addresses to the "Constitution" of Moses, "as a system [. . .] founded on superstition, the work of a man who knew the truth, but concealed it". Moses thus becomes "the most reprehensible of all the legislators, since he was the one who had the greatest chance: that of giving form to an entire people entrusted to his authority during forty years in the desert, in total isolation; he could have guided this formless body to the Enlightenment, but he preferred to direct it in the name of a imposture presented as of divine origin".[430] Scholem sees in this criticism by Dobruska of Moses a certain closeness to Frankist thinking. Jakob Frank, shortly before his death, had stated in his book *Words of the Lord* that the laws of Moses "weigh on the people [of Israel] and harm them, but the law of the Lord is whole (*temimah*) because it has never been spoken".[431] Despite these Frankist assonances, Scholem believes that Dobruska's reflections owe more to Voltaire than to Frank. The Scholemian analysis of the *Philosophie sociale* concludes in laudatory terms. In Scholem's assessment, the principles of a Universal Constitution (the third part of the work) are "permeated by the thought of Rousseau and Locke". They defend a radical democracy, which identifies in the "equality of rights [. . .] the authentic freedom of each individual". In short, the Constitution proposed by Dobruska reflects "the liberal and patriotic spirit of Jacobinism that precedes Terror".[432]

Although brilliant, this brief profile of the *Philosophie sociale* shows some forcing. First of all, it does not seem correct to say, as Scholem does, that Dobruska wanted to seek theological foundations for the nascent democratic regime and for its Universal Constitution. On the contrary, the first part of the work, the most revolutionary, makes it clear that a condition for the birth of a democracy is good legislation and the contribution of good lawmakers. And good legislation, based on the principles of truth, must be completely separated from a system of religious beliefs.[433]

---

430 *Ibidem*, 74.
431 *Loc. cit.*
432 *Ibidem*, 75.
433 Dobruska, *Philosophie sociale*, 30–31: [L'éclat emprunté de la religion, ajouté à la vérité d'un système de législation, sous couleur de le rendre ainsi plus intelligible et plus sacré pour

If Dobruska praises the message of Christ, which for him has nothing to do with the institutionalization of Christian doctrine (the "Church", as he calls it) – he does so only in consideration of moral precepts (love your neighbor as yourself), certainly not for the search for a divine foundation of the new Constitution. The foundation of Dobruska's constitutional project is secular, based on truth, reason, and nature.

Likewise, the Scholemian definition of the *Philosophie sociale* as a "synthesis of the ideas of Rousseau, Locke and Kant" does not seem to be acceptable. Although Dobruska dialogues with the works of these authors and quotes some of their theories and concepts, he often criticizes them and distances himself from them. According to Dobruska, the influence of "the immortal Kant", as he is praised in the *Philosophie sociale*, is hindered by the philosophical language he has chosen to use: a metaphysical lexicon, incomprehensible to ordinary readers. Moreover, Dobruska has elaborated his own theoretical vision above all in reference to the social, something that Scholem either does not grasp or ignores.

Thanks to Scholem's studies, other authors in the twentieth century have dealt with the biography of Moses Dobruska and his involvement in the French Revolution.[434] Rare, on the other hand, are the mentions of the *Philosophie sociale*. Diego Scarca has pointed out how Dobruska in his work theorizes a great distance between primitive man in the state of nature compared to the man of culture.[435] Carol Blum in her book on Rousseau recalls how Junius Frey recognized the decisive role of Rousseau in "provoking and determining the French Revolution".[436]

7.4 In the Twenty-First Century: Little Attention, and Not Very Flattering

In the last decade, Dobruska/Frey has received some attention, not only from scholars of Jewish culture[437] but also from philosophers and, in particular, from

---

le peuple, ne fut que nuisible dans tous les tems [sic], pernicieux et destructif pour la bonne cause].

434 See for instance Arthur Mandel, *The Militant Messiah or, The Flight from the Ghetto. The Story of Jacob Frank and the Frankist Movement*, Atlantic Highlands, NJ: Humanities Press, 1979.

435 Diego Scarca, *L'albero della civiltà. Primitivismo e utopia in Francia tra Sette e Ottocento* (Genève: Slatkine, 1990), 32.

436 Carol Blum, *Rousseau and the Republic of Virtue. The Language of Politics in the French Revolution* (Ithaca: Cornell University Press, 1989), 149.

437 Laurence Sigal-Klagsbald, *Juifs et Citoyens.* (Paris: A.I.U., 1989), 69–71.

social philosophers. Among others, a brief entry about our author appeared in the *Bloomsbury Dictionary of the Eighteen century German philosophers.*[438]

In the *Manifeste pour une philosophie sociale,* published in 2009, the French-Swiss philosopher Franck Fischbach reflects on the role of social philosophy, and highlights the marginalization of the discipline in the French academic world. Fischbach focuses on the main characteristics that social philosophy must have in order to be able to be called such. Among the five characteristics elaborated by Fischbach, the most important one, as already for Axel Honneth, is the ability to be critical of the existing social reality. In the first chapter, entitled *La philosophie sociale: une inconnue française, ou presque,* he erroneously states that for the first time the term *philosophie sociale* was coined in the anonymous *Philosophie sociale,* attributed, in the note, to Junius Frey.

As mentioned above, and already anticipated in an essay of mine in 2016,[439] the expression *philosophie sociale* was first used by Jean-Baptiste Durosoy in 1783.

Thomas Bedorf and Kurt Röttgers propose a somehow sketchy evaluation of the *Philosophie sociale* in their edition of the German translation of the *Manifeste* by Fischbach:[440]

> The text is nothing more than a draft Constitution inspired by Kant and the Sabbatian sect for an ideal Constitution for France, in keeping with freedom, i.e. a political philosophy and not a social philosophy as a separate discipline.[441]

Kurt Röttgers had already dealt very briefly with the *Philosophie sociale* on two previous occasions. In *Die Entstehung der Sozialphilosophie im Spannungsfeld*

---

438 See Christian Buder, s.v. *Frey, Junius,* in *The Bloomsbury Dictionary of the Eighteenth-century German philosophers,* eds. Heiner F. Klemme and Manfred Kuehn (London-New York: 2016), 236–237. At the end of the bibliographic profile, Buder mentions the publications of Dobruska / Frey, including the *Philosophie sociale* of 1793, but without giving even a brief description of it.

439 Greco, "Heresy, Apostasy and the Beginnings of Social Philosophy. Moses Dobruska reconsidered," 442.

440 See Thomas Bedorf and Kurt Röttgers, "Einleitung", in Franck Fischbach, *Einführung in die Sozialphilosophie,* transl. from French by Lilian Peter (Hagen: FernUniversität in Hagen, 2017), 3; Thomas Bedorf and Kurt Röttgers, "Nachwort", in Franck Fischbach, *Manifest für eine Sozialphilosophie,* transl. from French by Lilian Peter (Bielefeld: 2016), 141.

441 Bedorf, Röttgers, "Einleitung," in Franck Fischbach, *Einführung in die Sozialphilosophie,* 4: [Die Schrift ist nichts anderes als ein von Kant und der Sekte der Sabbatianer inspirierter Verfassungsentwurf zu einer der Freiheit angemessenen idealen Verfassung für Frankreich, d.h. eine politische Philosophie und nicht eine Sozialphilosophie als davon unterschiedene Disziplin].

von Neukantianismus, Soziologie und Kulturphilosophie, published in 1995, he denied that Dobruska's text could be considered true "social philosophy". Rather, it should be seen as "Jacobin philosophy of happy life in society, written for the people and against a philosophy of the State, designed by the rulers to deceive the people".[442] Röttgers also criticizes the enthusiasm of Dobruska/Frey for Kant, saying that it does not correspond to a positive knowledge of Kantian philosophy: according to Röttgers, Jacobinism would stand in contrast to the foundations of Kantian practical philosophy.

In 2009, in *Kritik der kulinarischen Vernunft. Ein Menü der Sinne nach Kant*, Röttgers seems to have changed his mind about this. He mentions some authors who have distanced themselves from Kant because of the latter's lack of reflection on social issues. One of the first who undertook such a path would have been Rudolf Stammler with the work *Wirtschaft und Recht nach der materialistischen Geschichtsauffassung* of 1896, where one finds:

> The scientific task of Kant's life was to re-establish philosophy as a systematic science, but without extending it to the social sphere. He has not created [. . .] a comprehensive social philosophy [. . .].[443]

According to Röttgers, Rudolf Stammler has a precursor: Moses Dobruska, alias "Franz Thomas Edler von Schönefeldt (*sic*), alias Lucius-Junius Frey". This mention is followed, a few pages later, by exactly the same criticism of the *Philosophie sociale* already offered in 1995.[444]

---

442 Kurt Röttgers, "Die Entstehung der Sozialphilosophie im Spannungsfeld von Neukantianismus, Soziologie und Kulturphilosophie," in *20. Jahre Fernuniversität. Daten, Fakten, Hintergründe. Festschrift zur 20-Jahr-Feier der Fernuniversität*, ed. Volker Hagen-Schmidtchen (Hagen: FernUniversität in Hagen, 1995), 159–185: [*Philosophie sociale* als einer jakobinischen Philosophie des glücklichen Lebens in der Gesellschaft, geschrieben für das Volk und gegen die Staatsphilosophie, die die Herrschenden entwerfen, um das Volk zu täuschen].
443 Kurt Röttgers, *Kritik der kulinarischen Vernunft. Ein Menü der Sinne nach Kant* (Bielefeld: Transcript, 2009), 18: "Kant hat seine wissenschaftliche Lebensaufgabe, die Neubegründung der Philosophie als systematischer Wissenschaft, auf das soziale Gebiet nicht ausgedehnt. Er hat [. . .] keine zusammenhängende Sozialphilosophie geschaffen".
444 *Ibidem*, 20.

8 Concluding Remarks

Moses Dobruska's *Philosophie sociale* must be seen within the troubled context of the French Revolution. It is an age of intense transformations, of febrile activism, in which social theories born out of the Enlightenment fight their way into real life. During such a period of upheaval, intellectuals were compelled to work at full steam in order to keep pace with the political arena.

Today we know that from this period of transformation also comes the first formulation of the term "sociology". I have already mentioned above the intuition of Sieyès, who lists "sociologie" within a synoptic table devoted to society and social organization.[445] His manuscript having remained unpublished for two-centuries, Sieyès' coinage of the word didn't have any direct impact on later studies. Such an early emergence of the idea of sociology, however, is quite interesting, especially considering the fact that Sieyès is the author of one the most influential texts of the French Revolution. His *Qu'est-ce que est le tiers état?*, published in 1789, had an enormous impact in voicing the vision of a new social order.[446]

In some respects, the case of the forgotten *sociologie* of Sieyès and of the conceptual innovations of Dobruska that were submerged by his tragic end, share some affinities.

In both circumstances, the intense power of innovation in social theories that characterizes the late eighteenth century has remained buried under the more vociferous and less troubled nineteenth century scholarship. When asked what he did during the Terror, Sieyès laconically answered "J'ai vécu",[447] a healthy albeit modest goal Dobruska was unable to attain.

At first reading, the intellectual pedigree of the *Philosophie Sociale* seems easily ascertained. Hobbes, Montesquieu, Locke, Rousseau, Kant – Dobruska repeatedly quotes some of the most influential thinkers of the great age of Enlightenment. Instead of mentioning a vast array of men of learning, he prefers to focus on big names, and spares no effort in showing that he can match the most revered protagonists of seventeenth- and eighteenth-century social philosophy.

In some crucial points, Dobruska's social theories are modeled on his predecessors. From Hobbes and Rousseau, he adopts the idea of a social contract;

---

445 See above, 1. 2.
446 Emmanuel Joseph Sieyès, *Qu'est-ce que est le tiers état?* [s.l. 1789].
447 Kurt Röttgers, *Kritik der kulinarischen Vernunft. Ein Menü der Sinne nach Kant* (Bielefeld: Transcript, 2009), William H. Sewell, *A Rhetoric of Bourgeois Revolution the Abbé Sieyès and What is the Third Estate?* (Durham: Duke University Press, 1994), 19.

his emphasis on education owes much to Montesquieu; the methodological foundations of his *Philosophie sociale* draw on Kant, and his idea of freedom is influenced by Locke, although Dobruska's approach is in some ways very different from that of his great English predecessor.

A more in-depth reading of the *Philosophie sociale*, however, leads one to rethink the hasty reading described above. It is neither a hodgepodge of the opinions of others, nor, as has recently been said, a simple draft of a Constitution, lacking originality.

In the present study, I have tried to give this "second chance" to the *Philosophie sociale*. The reader will judge whether it was worth it and whether, as I believe, this review casts a new light on a phase still little studied, but fundamental, for the history of social thought in the modern age.

In order to understand the *Philosophie sociale*, and to insert it correctly in its historical context, it is first necessary to go through the life of Moses Dobruska, so troubled and full of transformations.

After a general introduction on my work and its aims, in the second chapter I have thus sketched the biography of our author, which extends across various countries, during the second half of the eighteenth century. We first went to Brno in Moravia under the Habsburg dynasty, where Moses was born into a Jewish family that had risen to considerable wealth. As Gershom Scholem's research has shown, his mother, Schöndl, and probably also his father, Solomon, were followers of the Sabbatian sect, and therefore had a position in contrast to rabbinical orthodoxy. We followed Moses to Prague, where he converted to Catholicism in, and then to Vienna. It is here that his considerable economic and social rise takes place. Made noble by Maria Theresa as a reward for conversion, Moses entered the imperial court under the new name of Franz Thomas von Schönfeld, until he became a valued entrepreneur and supplier to the Habsburg army. In 1792 we saw a turning point in his life. Perhaps due to problems with the court of Leopold II, who became emperor after the death of his brother Joseph II, Moses left Vienna for Strasbourg, where he began engaging in political activity within the ranks of the Jacobins, under the name of Sigismond-Gottlob (later Junius) Frey. From Strasbourg he arrived in Paris, and at the end of June 1793 he published the *Philosophie sociale*. His revolutionary season, however, only lasted a few months. Charged with treason, he was arrested and executed on April 5, 1794.

The third chapter brought us into contact with the main topic of my work, namely an in-depth examination of the *Philosophie sociale*. Starting from the title, the book makes us immediately enter into the reflection on social reality, and proposes many research questions and reflections, to which Dobruska intends to respond with the elaboration of articulate theories.

As we have seen, these research questions are those that sociologists and social philosophers still ask themselves today: what are the needs of men, how and why do men live in society, what do they get out of it? And again, what impact do laws have on the behavior and customs of individuals, how social bonds are defined; what is the morality of the individual and what is the morality of the State, what is selfishness, and what is reciprocity? What may not work in society, and what prevents proper social organization? A question crowns all previous ones. How does man achieve happiness? Which social system is best suited to achieving universal happiness?

The answers Dobruska gives to these questions occupy the central part of my work. The fourth chapter deals with man and society, while the fifth and the sixth chapters deal, respectively, with political systems and structures – democracy, aristocracy and monarchy – and the ultimate goal of future democracy, namely the happiness of citizens.

In the course of the analysis, I have focused on two dimensions of the *Philosophie sociale*, which are linked to each other. I have defined the first component of Dobruska's thought as a sociological approach, which observes human behavior and social interaction from an objective, purposely scientific perspective. By choosing such a scientific approach, Moses Dobruska anticipated some important issues, concepts, and theories that were later developed by the founding fathers of sociology and even by the sociologists of the 20th century.

Dobruska's new founded discipline has three core aims.

The first aim of the *Philosophie sociale* is to assess the old social order, pulling out all of its "negative outcomes" for the majority of the population. Dobruska describes the "disorganizing" political and social phenomena such as tyranny, privileges, and the power abuses of aristocracy and clergy, that caused the *Ancien Régime* to collapse.

The second aim of Dobruska's work is to understand the society of the late eighteenth century, and to explain the motivations of individuals and their behaviors. He wants to analyze both society as a collective structure and through lone individuals – their motivation, desires, ambitions, morality, and behaviors.

The third aim is to delineate social rules and principles, based on the observation of human nature and human experience, and not on some "metaphysical or religious principles". The principles, rules and social institutions we encounter in the *Philosophie sociale* are related to seventeen different topics: human beings; social contracts; principles, duties and selfishness; individual morality; morality and immorality of society; the right of the strongest and the right of trickery; laws, power, legislative bodies; the sovereign; public contributions; government; liberty; equality; education; pains and offense; unity of interests; democracy, aristocracy, monarchy, and representative democracy. Already this sketchy list shows Dobruska's ambitious idea of an all-encompassing categorization of society, and his painstaking effort to base constitutional theory on social dynamic.

In other words, Moses Dobruska aims at developing an analytical and descriptive science of society, which later on became known as "sociology".

Given such a theoretical frame, we can appreciate how Moses Dobruska is the first to formulate concepts that have had a very important role in the following sociological thinking.

The first of these concepts is social disorganization (*désorganisation sociale* in Dobruska's French text).

The second concept, which derives from the first and completes it in a positive sense, is that of social organization and social cohesion. In his *Philosophie sociale* Moses Dobruska aims at defining principles, social rules, and norms for the construction of a new democratic society. According to his social-philosophical thought and to his empirical, sociological understanding of individuals living in a society, he asserts the importance of morality, of reciprocity in social interaction, and of the overcoming of selfishness. As a result, he tackles one of the most important issues of sociological debate since its early stage: the topic of social cohesion. His treatment of this topic intends to answer a question that has played a major role in sociology from its conception until today: how is society possible and how can it perpetuate itself? While the founding fathers of sociology[448] and later sociologists have answered this question very differently, according to their different theoretical perspectives,[449] Moses Dobruska must be considered one of first inquirers of social cohesion as a prerequisite to social organization.

The third innovative concept is that of social treasure (*trésor social, soziales Tresor* in the German draft). According to Dobruska, the social treasure consists in "all the means of culture and its instruments, i.e. the material and intellectual appetitive faculty".[450] This social treasure can only be developed within the society, and it belongs to the community, i.e. to the social self. After Dobruska, and most probably on the basis of his work, we find mention of the social treasure in a patriotic poem by Paul-Èmile Raboteau, published in 1830,

---

448 See, for example, Emile Durkheim, *De la division du travail social. Étude sur l'organisation des sociétés supérieures*, Paris: Félix Alcan, 1893.
449 Noah F. Friedkin, "Social Cohesion," *Annual Review of Sociology* 30 (2004), 409–425; Caroline Guibet Lafaye, "Modèles de la cohésion sociale", *European Journal of Sociology / Archives Européennes de Sociologie / Europäisches Archiv für Soziologie* 50 (2009) 3, 389–427; Paul Spicker, "Cohesion, Exclusion and Social Quality," *The International Journal of Social Quality* 4 (2014): 95–107.
450 Dobruska, *Philosophie sociale*, 150.

and in the *Harmonies économiques* by Fréderic Bastiat.[451] Later on, it was used by Ferdinand de Saussure in linguistics, and by no less writer than Marcel Proust.[452] As is well known, Pierre Bourdieu has stressed how culture, in its different forms, constitutes a "treasure", which he termed "cultural capital". Bourdieu speaks of a threefold capital: i) "embodied state" – i.e. inherited and acquired properties in one's self; i) "objectified cultural goods"; iii) "institutionalized cultural entitlement".[453] While Dobruska's theory of a social treasure is less articulated than Bourdieu's cultural capital, it nevertheless posits the core idea of a cultural asset, socially determined, that can be deployed individually.

The fourth concept is that of a social ego or social self (*moi social*). Moses Dobruska distinguishes between an "individual self" and a "social self". According to him, the individual self that exists in the state of nature is transformed into a social self in the state of culture, that is, within the fabric of society.[454] In his *Du contrat social*, Jean-Jacques Rousseau had already spoken of a *moi commun* as a kind of collective personality, expressing a rational consensus (*volonté générale*) of all individuals within a community.[455] Dobruska transforms the Rousseauian "moi commun" into a sociological category by eliminating its voluntarist overtones, while stressing the social interaction and solidarity implicit in the distinction between the individual self and the social one.

---

451 Paul-Émile Raboteau, *Poème* (Paris: Chez l'Auteur, 1830), 77: [au trésor social chacun doit ses tributs]; Fréderic Bastiat, *Harmonies économiques*, (Bruxelles: Meline, Cans et Compagnie, 1850): [Et remarquez que Robinson [Crusoe] portait avec lui dans la solitude un autre trésor social mille fois plus précieux et que les flots ne pouvaient engloutir: je veux parler de ses idées, de ses souvenirs, de son expérience, de son langage même, sans lequel, il n'aurait pus s'entretenir avec lui-même, c'est-à-dire penser]. Cf. Silvana Greco, "Heresy, Apostasy, and the Beginnings of Social Philosophy. Moses Dobruska reconsidered," *Materia giudaica* 20–21 (2015–2016), 454.

452 Ferdinand de Saussure, *Cours de linguistique Générale* (Paris 1972 (I ed. 1913), 30; Marcel Proust, *A la recherche du temps perdu*, vol. 7, *Le côté de Guermantes* (Paris: Gallimard, 1919), 221–222: [La nubilité plus accentuée s'était marquée quand Albertine, parlant d'une jeune fille qui avait mauvaise façon, avait dit: 'On ne peut même pas distinguer si elle est jolie, elle a un pied de rouge sur la figure.' Enfin, quoique jeune fille encore, elle prenait déjà des façons de femme de son milieu et de son rang en disant, si quelqu'un faisait des grimaces: 'Je ne peux pas le voir parce que j'ai envie d'en faire aussi', ou si on s'amusait à des imitations: 'Le plus drôle, quand vous le contrefaites, c'est que vous lui ressemblez.' Tout cela est tiré du trésor social].

453 Pierre Bourdieu, *The Forms of Capital*, in *Handbook for Theory and Research for the Sociology of Education*, ed. John G. Richardson (Westport: Greenwood, 1986), 241–258. Seoyong Kim, Hyesun Kim, "Does Cultural Capital Matter? Cultural Divide and Quality of Life," *Social Indicators Research* 93 (2009), 296–297.

454 *Philosophie sociale*, 214.

455 See above, 4. 3.

The second component of Moses Dobruska's thought is its social-philosophical side. Thisdiffers from the avowedly scientific approach, which I have termed socio-logical, in its evaluative and normative-ethical dimension. It is a goal- and target-oriented philosophy. Indeed, Moses Dobruska evaluates and criticizes the social order of the *Ancien Régime* and diagnoses all of the social and political dysfunc-tions that were responsible for the collapse of feudalistic society. Moreover, with his Universal Constitution he gives clear indications about the ethical principles, social institutions, and norms that must permeate a new democratic society. Fi-nally, Moses Dobruska addresses his work to specific social actors: to all the men of thought (*hommes qui pensent et, qui jugent par eux-mêmes*), who are seeking the truth, and to the French people. Led by his *Philosophie sociale* they will engage in transformative action towards the existing social reality.

After completing this long journey into the social thought of Dobruska, in the seventh chapter I demonstrated the depth of the reception and influence of the *Philosophie sociale*. I believe that the results of this investigation are new and important. Step by step, I have recorded the texts which, without mentioning it, most likely take up ideas expressed for the first time by Dobruska. The cata-logue is amazing. They range from the provisional Constitution of December 4, 1793, whose extender, Jacques-Nicolas Billaud-Varenne, treasures the *Philosophie sociale*,[456] to the works of two great masters of French social thought, Henri de Saint-Simon and Auguste Comte.[457] Textual and philological comparison allows us to follow the echoes of cultural and social disorganization/reorganization, so characteristically theorized by Dobruska, first in Saint-Simon and then in Comte. But the loans from the *Philosophie sociale* don't stop there. The famous Comtian law of the three stages also has its direct precedent in Dobruska, as I think I have demonstrated in a philologically clear manner.

In this way, a hitherto underestimated bond is reconstructed, linking the sociology-in-progress of Montesquieu – which Raymond Aron rightly consid-ered the first exponent of the discipline, if not in name, in its cognitive inten-tions – to that of Auguste Comte, already formed and self-aware. Between the former and the latter, both rightly considered leading exponents of European thought, our Moses Dobruska, an outsider by origin and by tormented bio-graphical fate, has carved out a distinguished intellectual role.

---

456 See above, 7. 1. 2.
457 See above, 7. 2. and 7. 3.

Appendix 1: Glossary of the Universal Constitution

The glossary contains in alphabetical order the principal definitions of the concepts elaborated by Moses Dobruska for the Universal Constitution.

Definitions	English translation	Original French text in Dobruska's *Philosophie sociale*
Legislative Body	The legislative body is the delegate of the people, with the aim of representing moral faculties, sentiment and reason, and to seek and express determination through the principle and for the principle.	*Le corps législatif est le délégué du peuple, pour représenter les facultés morales, le sentiment et la raison, pour chercher et pour exprimer la détermination par le principe et pour le principe, (120).*
Civil and Political Law	What is civil and political law? The duty of the relationship according to the principle.	*Qu'est-ce que le droit civil et politique? Le devoir de la relation pour le principe, (9).*
The Right of the Strongest and of Deception	The right of the strongest and of deception are sacred rights indefence of the principle; the right of the strongest is a tyranny; the right of deception is a murder, as an offence against the principle.	*Le droit du plus fort et le droit de ruse sont des droits sacrés, comme défense pour le principe, (113); Le droit du plus fort est une tyrannie; le droit de la ruse est un assassinat, comme offense contre le principe, (114)*
The Right of the Strongest	The right of the strongest is that measure of strength which was given solely by nature to defend the principle, and which then degenerated, in the action of tyrants, into a power which offends the principle.	*Le droit du plus fort est cette mesure de force qui fut donnée uniquement par la nature pour la défense du principe, et qui a dégénéré depuis par le fait des tyrans en pouvoir offensif contre le principe, (110).*
Right in the State of Nature	What is natural law? Duty to principle.	*Qu'est-ce que le droit naturel? Le devoir pour le principe (90).*
Duty	is the duty of the relationship according to the principle, so the principle is individual preservation. Duty: it's only obedience to the principle.	*est devoir de la relation pour le principe, donc le principe est la conservation individuelle, (177).* *Devoir: n'est que l'obéissance au principe, (91).*

(continued)

Definitions	English translation	Original French text in Dobruska's *Philosophie sociale*
Selfishness	The selfish person makes himself the center of the relationships of all external and extraneous activities [. . .] In a few words, in order to achieve his goal, [the selfish person] tries to be relative to others, and is not relative to them, that is to say, he rejects the reciprocity of the relationship. Selfishness is also individual preservation, but by rejecting the reciprocity of the relationship, it refuses its duty. Selfishness is the opposite of morality: the former accepts without wanting to give, the latter gives without wanting to be given back.	*L'égoïsme fait de son moi le centre des relations de toutes les activités extérieures et étrangères [. . .]. En un mot, qui pour arriver à son but, cherche a être relatif pour les autres, et à ne pas l'être envers eux, c'est-à-dire, qu'il refuse la réciprocité de relation, (97).* *L'égoïsme est aussi la conservation individuelle, mais qui refusant la réciprocité de la relation, refuse son devoir, (98). L'égoïsme est l'opposé de la morale, celui ci accepte sans vouloir rendre, celle-là donne sans vouloir qu'on lui rende, p. 107.*
Appetising, Material and Intellectual Faculty	What do we mean by appetitive faculty, both material and intellectual, perfected and developed? The mature instinct formed by society.	*Que doit-on entendre par la faculté appétitive, matérielle et intellectuelle perfectionnée et développée? L'instinct mûri et formé par la société, (85), (135).*
Moral Faculties of Man	Man has two moral faculties, reason and feeling. Sometimes feeling desires what reason doesn't want at all; and sometimes reason desires what repels feeling. The heart is often in opposition to the head.	*L'homme a deux facultés morales, la raison et le sentiment. Le sentiment désire quelquefois ce que la raison ne veut point; et la raison veut quelquefois ce qui répugne au sentiment. Le cœur se trouve souvent en opposition avec la tête, (115).*
Immorality of the State	The immorality of the State is the non-consequence of individual morality.	*L'immoralité de l'état est la non conséquence de la moralité individuelle, (108).*
Inequalities in Talent and Skills	The natural inequality of human talents and abilities.	*L'inégalité naturelle des talens et de la capacité des hommes (207).*

(continued)

Definitions	English translation	Original French text in Dobruska's *Philosophie sociale*
Law	Law is the expression of the determination of moral faculties through principle, and for the principle. Laws are not, and must not be, but the guarantee of freedom and equality, or of the right of all his efforts [i.e. of the individual], to achieve supreme happiness in society.	*La loi est l'expression de la détermination des facultés morales par le principe, et pour le principe (117).* *Les loix ne sont donc et ne doivent être que la garantie de la liberté et de l'égalité, ou du droit de l'exercice de tous ses efforts, pour atteindre le suprême bonheur dans la société, (89).*
Freedom	Freedom is the equality of rights. The freedom of each individual is the most perfect equality of rights.	*Liberté est l'égalité des droits, (175), (181).* *Liberté de chaque individu est l'égalité des droits la plus parfaite, (88).*
Morality of the State	The morality of the State is the consequence of individual morality.	*La moralité d'état est la conséquence de la moralité individuelle, (108).*
Morality	Morality is the voluntary partial relationship to the principle of another. Morality is the opposite of selfishness, because the principle draws from it profit and is damaged by selfishness. Morality, which is a license, a crime for man in the state of nature, becomes his greatest virtue in the social order, and the most majestic, the most irrefutable testimony that he was born for society.	*La moralité est la relation volontaire partielle pour le principe d'un autre, (100).* *La moralité est l'opposé de l'égoïsme, en ce que le principe gagne par elle, et perd par l'égoïsme, (12).* *La moralité qui est une licence, un crime pour l'homme dans l'état de nature, devient sa plus haute vertu dans l'ordre social, et le témoignage le plus auguste, le plus irrécusable, qu'il est né pour la société, (107).*
Ultimate Principle of Law	The principle of law is individual preservation. Individual preservation is therefore the eternal principle, the fundamental basis of any justice and injustice.	*Le principe de tout droit est la conservation individuelle, p. 90.* *La conservation individuelle est donc le principe éternel, la bâse fondamentale de toute justice et injustice, (98).*

(continued)

Definitions	English translation	Original French text in Dobruska's *Philosophie sociale*
General Prosperity	General prosperity is but the sum of the happiness of each of the members who make up [society].	*La prospérité générale, n'est que la somme réunie du bonheur de chacun des membres qui le composent, (227).*
Rebellion of the citizen	Rebellion is then nothing more than holy resistance to oppression.	*Rébellion qui n'est alors que la sainte résistance à l'oppression, (89).*
Company	What is society? A new set or rather a sovereign and independent whole, spontaneously composed of isolated primitive sets, equally independent, sovereign and with equal rights, multiplied in the same and homogeneous way, and not increased differently.	*Qu'est-ce que c'est que la société? Un nouvel ensemble ou un tout souverain et indépendant, spontanément composé d'ensembles primitifs isolés, aussi indépendans souverains et égaux en droits, multipliés d'une manière égale et homogène, mais non pas augmentés différemment (134–135).*
Social Treasure	The means of culture, with their vehicle, the appetitive faculty, material and intellectual, extended and perfected, constitute the social treasure.	*Les moyens de culture avec leur véhicule, la faculté appétitive matérielle et intellectuelle, étendue et perfectionnée, constituent le trésor social, p. 148.*
Equality	Equality of rights is the true freedom of everyone.	*L'égalité des droits, est la véritable liberté d'un chacun, (211).*
Man in Society or State of Culture (Mensch im Sozialzustand)	In the state of culture, the individual man, who has become dependent on others, ceases to be a perfect whole. His sovereignty has passed to society as a whole. In the state of culture, the individual self is transformed into the social self.	*Dans l'état de culture, l'homme individuel étant devenu dépendans des autres, cesse d'être un tout parfait. Sa souveraineté est passée à la société entière, (143). Le moi individuel étant dans l'état de culture changé dans le moi social, (219).*

(continued)

Definitions	English translation	Original French text in Dobruska's Philosophie sociale
Man in the State of Nature (Naturmensch)	In the state of nature, the individual man, independent outside himself, is a perfect being. What is a man in the state of nature? A sovereign whole, a perfect and isolated whole, whodepends on himself and is independent outside himself. What is the property of being-man in the state of nature? All the natural forces and means that can lead him to the goal required by the principle; that is to say, to the most perfect satisfaction of the animal and undeveloped appetitive faculties, which is nothing more than the instinct through which, in that state, the principle directs all the natural forces and means that, combined together, constitute the property of the primitive sovereign.	Dans l'état de nature, l'homme individuel étant indépendant hors de soi, est un tout parfait, un être souverain, (142). Qu'est-ce que l'être-homme dans l'état de nature? Un ensemble souverain, un tout parfait et isolé dépendant de soi-même et indépendant hors de soi, (134). Quelle est la propriété de l'être-homme dans l'état de nature ? toutes les forces et moyens naturels qui peuvent le conduire au but exigé par le principe; c'est-à-dire, au plus parfait contentement de sa faculté appétitive animale et non développée, qui n'est autre chose que l'instinct, par lequel dans cet état, le principe dirige toutes ces forces et moyens naturels qui combinés ensemble, constituent la propriété du souverain primitif, (135).
Man (Being a Man)	Man is a living being whose instinct is susceptible to the widest development and the greatest perfection.	L'être-homme est un être vivant dont l'instinct est susceptible du développement le plus étendu et de la plus grande perfection, (81).

Appendix 2: The Seventy Principles of the Universal Constitution

L'homme et le contrat social

I.

L'homme reçoit de la société le seul développement de sa faculté appétitive, matérielle et intellectuelle qui est: L'instinct mûri et formé par la société.

II.

Pour que cette recette de la société soit une recette réelle et obligatoire, il faut qu'elle ait la liberté d'employer tous ses efforts pour satisfaire ses desirs de la manière. la plus complette, ou pour atteindre son suprême bonheur, conformément au développement de sa faculté appétitive.

III.

Cette liberté de chaque individu est l'égalité des droits la plus parfaite.

IV.

Personne ne peut aliéner cette égalité libre ou liberté égale, sans se déclarer prodigue ou foible, trompé ou forcé, cas dans lesquels tout contrat d'aliénation est nul de fait, parce que la faculté appétitive cessant par cette aliénation d'être un avantage réel, cesseroit aussi d'être obligatoire.

V.

Il est clair que le développement de la faculté appétitive intellectuelle doit suivre les mêmes principes. Toute formule coercitive de penser ou de croire est donc une infraction à la liberté égale et à l'égalité libre.

VI.

Dans le seul cas où les efforts d'un individu empêcheroient les efforts de l'autre, l'usurpation de la liberté égale doit être réprimée par la loi, afin de mettre en sûreté les droits que tous les individus de la société ont au bonheur.

VII.

Les loix ne sont donc et ne doivent être que la garantie de la liberté et de l'égalité, ou du droit de l'exercice de tous ses efforts, pour atteindre le suprême bonheur dans la société.

VIII.

Sans ce droit, le développement de la faculté appétitive cesse d'être un bénéfice réel: et dans ce cas-là l'individu ne doit plus rien à la société ; et la loi devenue trop foible pour garantir ses droits, met hors de responsabilité sa *rébellion* qui n'est alors que la sainte résistance à l'oppression. Oui, elle sanctifie son insurrection, et lui en fait un devoir. Ses facultées développées et puis réprimées par la force ou la ruse justifient sa vengeance, et demandent la punition des tyrans par ces mêmes principes qui sanctifient les loix et les peines.

Principe, Droits & Égoïsme
I.
La conservation individuelle, est le principe de tout droit, et de tout ce qui est contre droit.

II.
Dans l'état de nature le devoir de la relation, n'a lieu qu'en vers les membres *du moi* individuel. Dans l'état de société, au contraire, il se porte sur les mêmes membres du moi *social* avec la même latitude que dans l'état de nature, où il agit sur tous les membres du moi individuel. Et comme, dans l'état de société, l'homme a besoin de la relation de ses semblables pour la conservation individuelle, et la satisfaction de la faculté appétitive développée, le besoin établit le devoir de la relation de son côte, et fait un droit de cette réciprocité nécessaire.

III.
Le droit naturel, est le devoir pour le principe.

IV.
Le droit civil et politique, est le devoir de la relation pour la conservation individuelle, qui est, et qui reste aussi son principe éternel.

V.
Toute contribution nécessaire à la conservation individuelle, que la majorité exige de la minorité en vertu du principe, est fondée en droit; étant le devoir de la relation pour le principe.

VI.
L'égoïsme est aussi la conservation individuelle, mais qui refusant la réciprocité de la relation, refuse son devoir, n'est pas en droit. La conservation individuelle est donc le principe éternel, la bâse fondamentale de toute justice et injustice (i).

VII.
Toute société, dont la majorité commande à la minorité un devoir, un sacrifice du moi individuel, sans que le moi social en exige la nécessité, s'éloigne du droit en s'éloignant du devoir de la relation pour le principe. Elle tombe dans le refus de la réciprocité de la relation ; dans l'égoïsme, principe infâme, étant aussi la conservation individuelle; mais dont la ligne de démarcation trop déliée, n'est distinguible qu'aux connoisseurs, se glisse bientôt dans la société comme véritable principe, dont il détruit la divinité d'un intérêt commun; et en introduisant l'enfer d'un intérêt partiel, engloutit le droit véritable; et en vomissant l'exécrable droit du plus fort dans la société, rend l'un coupable, et l'autre misérable, confond l'erreur avec la vérité, obscurcit le sentier simple de la nature et de la raison, en compliquant la philosophie sociale, et en trompant sur-tout l'humanité dans la science de vivre.

Moralité de l'individu
I.
La moralité est la relation volontaire partielle pour le principe (I) d'un autre.
(I) Toutes les fois que nous parlerons dans la suite du principe en général, nous entendrons la conservation individuelle, définition du principe général de tout être créé, comme nous l'avons posé dans le troisième chapitre.

II.

Aucune moralité n'est possible envers la société; chaque sacrifice n'agit qu'en droit, parce qu'il se porte toujours réciproquement sur le moi individuel.

III.

Dans l'état de nature, la moralité n'est autre chose qu'une liberté poussée trop loin, une licence, un crime. L'étincelle morale court en lui, pour ainsi parler, mais l'exercice de la relation volontaire (la moralité) dans l'état de nature ne peut le conduire qu'à sa perte. L'heureux lien de la société ne l'a pas encore attaché à son prochain, ne le connoissant pas encore, il ne peut avoir aucune relation volontaire avec lui, et l'exercice de son impulsion morale est encore contre le droit.

IV.

La moralité qui est une licence, un crime pour l'homme dans l'état de nature, devient sa plus haute vertu dans l'ordre social, et le témoignage le plus auguste, le plus irrécusable, qu'il est né pour la société.

V.

L'égoïsme est l'opposé de la morale, celui-ci accepte sans vouloir rendre, celle-là donne sans vouloir qu'on lui rende.

Moralité et immoralité de la société
I.

La moralité d'état est une chose partielle qui n'a qu'une existence isolée, bornée dans le partiel. Elle est la plus haute vertu de l'humanité qu'elle honore; mais liée aux principes conservateurs du grand tout, empiétant sur le grand moi de la société, elle affoiblit, elle énerve, elle tue le droit, elle est un crime que les loix doivent réprimer et punir (I).
(I) La loi contre les émigrés n'est pas un acte immoral, mais au contraire bien fondé en droit.

Du droit du plus fort et du droit de la ruse
I.

Le droit du plus fort et le droit de ruse sont des droits sacrés, *comme défense pour le principe*.

II.

Le droit du plus fort est une tyrannie; le droit de la ruse est un assassinat, *comme offense contre le principe*.

III.

Cette différence constitue les deux sortes de majorité: l'une comme défense pour le principe, agit en véritable droit, et peut même sacrifier la minorité, étant un moyen conservateur pour la partie plus grande du corps du *moi social*; et l'autre comme offense contre le principe, agit en droit du plus fort, qui n'est qu'une tyrannie, et qui transmet le véritable droit à la minorité, qui peut se servir alors de tous les mêmes moyens, pour abattre la majorité rébelle, agissant toujours en véritable droit.

Loi, Pouvoir, Corps législatif
I.

La loi est l'expression de la détermination des facultés morales, dirigées par le principe, et pour le principe.

II.

Le pouvoir n'est qu'un seul. Il est législatif et exécutif en même-temps, car il est la mesure déterminative et le régulateur du corps législatif, des facultés morales.

III.

Le corps législatif est le délégué du peuple, pour représenter les facultés morales, *le sentiment* et *la raison*, pour chercher et pour exprimer la détermination par le principe et pour le principe.

IV.

Le corps législatif étant obligé de déterminer par le principe et pour le principe, il est donc aussi chargé de l'exercice du seul pouvoir, il est donc en même-temps comme le pouvoir lui-même, législatif et exécutif.

V.

Si-tôt que le corps législatif cesse de représenter ces facultés morales en s'écartent de leur marche naturelle, il cesse d'être corps législatif entièrement comme particulièrement. Sa mission est finie, puisque son but est manqué. Il est rappellés par le pouvoir (I). (I) Au peuple seul appartient la sanction des loix; mais comme chaque loi doit être précédée d'un considérant explicatif des principes du droit, sur lequel cette loi se fonde ; que le peuple n'en peut rejetter ni recevoir aucune, qu'en faisant précéder également sa décision d'un semblable considérant; pour mettre un frein aux entreprises du corps législatif, il suffira de poser en principe, i°, que chaque loi, comme chez les Romains, aura force jusques au rassemblement des Sections populaires, qui aura. lieu de trois mois en trois mois. 2°. Que chaque loi sera rendue par appel nominal, lequel sera envoyé avec la loi aux sections populaires, où il sera proclamé. 3°. Que lorsqu'un délégué aura voté pour trois loix, que le peuple conduit par le considérant explicatif des principes du droit, posé dans la première partie de la Constitution aura rejetées, le Secrétaire de la Section populaire fera passer au corps législatif le procès-verbal, qui établit que tel délégué a voté trois fois contrairement au principe, et sans autre formalité, le membre sera exclu de l'assemblée législative. Ce moyen aussi simple que juste, ne sera sujet â aucun inconvénient, puisque le membre exclu, sera exclu par le principe, seul pouvoir légitime.

VI.

Si-tôt que le corps législatif cesse de se faire déterminer, par cette autorité médiatice, par le principe, ses résultats cessent d'être *loi*.

Du souverain
I.

Dans l'état de nature, l'homme individuel étant indépendant hors de soi, est un tout parfait, un être souverain.

II.

Dans l'état de culture, l'homme individuel étant devenu dépendans des autres, cesse d'être un tout parfait. Sa souveraineté est passée à la société entière.

III.

La propriété du souverain primitif de l'homme, dans l'état de nature, consiste dans toutes les forces et moyens naturels qui peuvent conduire l'homme à son but, exigé par le principe.

IV.

La propriété du nouveau souverain de la société, consiste dans toutes les forces et moyens de culture, qui se réunissent aux forces et moyens naturels antérieurs de chacun de ses membres.

V.

La contribution, est l'emploi de toutes les forces et moyens naturels (de toute sa propriété dans cet état) pour atteindre le but exigé par le principe, lesquels constituent les devoirs et les fonctions du souverain primitif, dans l'état primitif.

VI.

Ces devoirs et obligations du souverain primitif, peuvent être requis tant qu'ils restent moyens pour le but, et qu'ils ne sont pas contre le but, car ils agiraient alors contre le principe; et comme le principe est le seul pouvoir, seul, il peut exiger une contribution, un devoir. C'est donc hors du pouvoir en droit du souverain légitime, de commettre une action quelconque contre le principe et par conséquent, il n'est nullement du droit du souverain de se faire mal à lui-même, quoiqu'il puisse le faire.

VII.

Dans l'état de culture, les droits du nouveau souverain s'étendent sur ses membres dans la même mesure. Toutes les contributions et devoirs qu'il exige, ne doivent être que pour le but, et non lui être contraires, pour le principe, qui demeure le seul pouvoir, et par conséquent le pouvoir de faire mal à lui-même est hors du droit du souverain quoiqu'il le pût faire. Cette distinction entre pouvoir faire en droit ou contre droit, pouvoir agir contre le principe ou pour le principe, constitue seule la différence absolue entre la liberté et la licence.

VIII.

La conduite du souverain primitif dans cette contribution de ses forces et moyens naturels pour le principe, est une offre entière sans nulle économie ou restriction, il suit constamment la loi inviolable qui dit: *Que cela soit: la victoire ou la mort.*

IX.

La conduite du souverain primitif, dans l'état de nature, est la sainte et inviolable formule du nouveau souverain de la société. Dans l'état de culture, quand il s'agit d'une contribution de tous les moyens de culture (des propriétés sociales) pour défendre son but, exigé par le principe, nulle économie, nulle restriction, il faut employer le tout pour défendre le tout.

X.

Le nouveau souverain occupant la place du souverain primitif, et entrant dans tous ses droits, aucuns de ses membres individuellement, nulle corporation, quelle qu'elle soit, ne peut avoir aucun prétexte pour s'approprier un intérêt inégal ou plus important, quand même on voudroit ou pourrait faire davantage pour cet intérêt plus important, puisqu'on raison de l'acquisition de sa faculté appétitive, tant matérielle qu'intellectuelle, perfectionnée et développée, chaque membre, dans cet état est redevable au nouveau souverain de tout ce dont il peut concourir par ces nouveaux moyens de culture, ainsi que guidé par son instinct animal, il l'aurait fait autrefois pour son souverain primitif, l'être-homme dans l'état de nature.

XI.

Quoiqu'il soit bien avéré qu'aucun individu isolé en son particulier, ni toute autre corporation sous quelque unité nouvelle adoptée qu'elle subsiste, ne puisse pas acquérir dans la société un intérêt inégal et plus important. Il n'est pas moins constant que ce nouveau souverain lui-même, n'a pas le droit de céder ou transporter à un individu isolé ce nouvel intérêt inégal et plus important, quelque soit cet individu, ni même à une corporation quelconque, sous quelque dénomination qu'elle existe, c'est-à-dire que le nouveau souverain ne peut abuser du trésor social.

XII.

L'établissement ou l'admission d'un second intérêt; privilège différent pour un individu où corporation, étant le renversement de la bâse naturelle de l'unité d'intérêt, tant de l'ancien que du nouveau souverain, puisque ce nouvel intérêt ne peut se nourrir qu'au détriment de l'autre, il en résulte que cette introduction d'un second intérêt; sort du cercle du juste pouvoir de l'ancien et du nouveau souverain, et qu'elle dégénère en usurpation et tyrannie, ainsi seroit le suicide, auquel l'ancien et le nouveau souverain pourroit également se livrer mais dont aucun n'osera faire usage en droit.

XIII.

L'établissement en introduction d'un intérêt second et différent, privilège pour un individu isolé ou une corporation quelconque un roi ou sénat héréditaire, étant une aliénation et abus du trésor social, est nécessairement par sa propre nature, une lésion du droit de propriété des autres membres du grand tout, et ensemble parfait du nouveau souverain, parce que cette aliénation et abus du trésor social, ne sont pas plus autorisés par l'existence du nouveau souverain, que le souverain primitif poussé par son instinct animal, n'auroit été autorisé à l'entreprendre contre un, ou plusieurs de ses membres.

Contributions publiques
I.

Dans le souverain primitif, aucun de ses membres ne sollicite ni n'usurpe la délégation ou les fonctions des autres, puisqu'au lieu d'y gagner, il se chargeroit uniquement d'une peine plus grande. Ainsi c'est l'instinct, la nécessité qui règle le régime dans le souverain primitif, et qui oblige alternativement l'un de commander, et l'autre d'obéir.

II.

Il n'en est pas ainsi pour le nouveau souverain (la société); car ici l'intérêt qu'ils y pourraient trouver fait craindre à chaque instant l'usurpation d'un ou de plusieurs membres réunis, ou du moins la rend très possible. Il faut que la justice, les connoissances de l'instinct mûri et perfectionné exercent par rapport au grand tout, la surveillance que nous voyons l'instinct animal observer dans l'état de pure nature, c'est-à-dire, que par la fixation du *maximum* contributionnel des moyens de chaque membre représentant la nécessité générale du *Corps* entier, ils mettent un obstacle, ou déjouent toutes les entreprises de ces agens représentatifs, contre la sûreté, ou l'existence du grand tout.

III.

Quand l'être homme, ce tout singulier et particulier, s'est réuni à plusieurs êtres de sa nature pour former son instinct et le leur, et par là multiplier mutuellement leur jouissances, il a voulu *gagner*; mais il n'a prétendu rien perdre, ni renoncer à rien par cette réunion. Cela seroit contre le principe.

IV.

Le nouveau souverain (la société) ne peut donc jamais exiger de lui comme une contribution nécessaire soit morale ou physique, et palpable même, la moindre obéissance, action, sacrifice, fût-il de son abondance ou luxe moral ou physique, si le sacrifice n'est pas évidemment et indispensablement nécessaire dans le moment, pour la défense du principe du moi social, du nouveau souverain, auquel la souveraineté primitive a été transmise et dont il est devenu un membre dépendant. L'obéissance envers chaque fonctionnaire représentant au moment de sa fonction pour le souverain et pour le principe; chaque sacrifice exigé de sa propriété pour la nécessité évidente et indispensable du soutien et de la défense du souverain pour le principe est fondé en droit, et doit être rendu sans restriction; mais dans le cas contraire, ou dans toute autre occasion, la moindre obéissance ou préférence qu'un membre exigera involontairement d'un autre, ou même le moindre sacrifice contributionnel du besoin ou du luxe, que le gouverne' ment exigera d'un individu, seroit une tyrannie, une licence, un attentat à la propriété individuelle. En outre, comme il n'a jamais renoncé à sa souveraineté primitive, que la nature ne s'est rien moins qu'engagée à payer aux dépens de sa propriété et de ses propres fonds les dettes contractées par l'art, qu'il est bien plus juste, au contraire, que la nature surveille toujours cet être nouveau l'art, afin d'empêcher la dilapidation de ses facultés; il en résulte qu'on ne peut jamais ordonner à un des membres de l'association, la déposition des armes qui servent à sa défense personnelle, ni l'en priver. Ainsi dans le cas d'usurpation des biens individuels du souverain primitif, on ne peut sous aucun prétexte exiger d'un individu le sacrifice de ses moyens de défense, ni le faire renoncer à la faculté d'en user. A moins que la défense du nouveau souverain (la société) ne soit tellement confondue dans la défense du souverain primitif *l'être-homme*, c'est-à-dire, qu'il s'agisse pour le principe de la conservation de la base naturelle, la liberté et l'unité d'intérêt. Parce qu'alors la querelle intéresse à la fois le corps entier, que tous combattent pour le tout, et que *le tout* doit intéresser tous; ou le moi individuel est changé et remplacé par le moi social.

V.

Dans cette hypotèse, le souverain primitif, (l'être-homme) sert encore de modèle au nouveau souverain *la société*, parce que touchant la faculté d'éloigner le mal et les efforts pour parvenir au souverain bien, le triomphe de l'un est aussi le triomphe de l'autre, et que la perte du premier, entraîne après elle la chute du second. Alors l'abandon de la faculté de se défendre soi-même, l'enlèvement des armes, et le sacrifice de tous moyens de défense personnelle, qui ne peuvent en aucuns cas être exigés d'un membre de l'association comme contribution, peuvent lui être imposés comme peines, et ce cas arrive lorsque la liberté d'un individu ayant dégénéré en coupable licence, elle entrave l'exercice de la juste liberté d'autrui, ce qui peut se rencontrer surtout dans l'état social, ou un membre pouvant usurper l'intérêt égal des autres, il finiroit par rendre dépendant le souverain primitif (l'être-homme), lequel n'a jamais pré, tendu résigner sa souveraineté individuelle,

VI.

Quand aux membres fonctionnaires représentans, il nous faudra bien exactement suivre A leur égard le procédé du souverain primitif, et notamment dans le cas où ils tiennent toutes les autres forces et ressources comme enchaînées, et ce, dans l'attente de la fin de l'opération, que la nécessité de sauver le corps entier peut leur prescrire quelquefois dans des circonstances délicates. Il faut que malgré cette résignation apparente, tous les autres membres tiennent préparés tous les moyens de défense dont ils ne doivent jamais se dépouiller, et qu'ils soient dans un tel état d'application et d'examen intérieur sur le membre qui agit, qu'ils ayent plutôt l'air d'attendre la fin de l'opération avec calme et dignité, que de la servir; et l'on doit en agir avec d'autant plus de rigueur sur ce chapitre dans l'état social, qu'on a à redouter ici tous les accidens qui sont à craindre pour le souverain primitif, dans une situation pareille.

Gouvernement
I.

Dans l'état primitif de pure nature, tons les membres concourent au besoin et au contentement de tout le corps, aucun ne s'en dispense par privilège, aucun ne s'y porte par préférence, et nul ne peut demeurer dans une coupable neutralité, quand il s'agit de leur égal intérêt relativement au but, au principe.

II.

Tous les membres de la société doivent concourir de tous leurs moyens au besoin et au contentement du tout. Aucun ne peut avoir le privilège de s'en dispenser: aucun ne doit s'y immiscer par préférence, et nul ne peut rester dans une inertie ou neutralité coupable, quand il s'agit de l'intérêt égal relativement au but (le principe).

III.

Le gouvernement de la société doit être d'après le régime de la nature, qui est l'unique forme de gouvernement juste et exacte.

IV.

Chaque fonctionnaire public est un véritable représentant du peuple, dont l'élection se fait par le peuple même, ou par un corps électoral, élu par le consentement général, et muni de pouvoirs pour l'élection des fonctionnaires.

V.

L'élection de chaque membre du corps législatif inclusivement, tous les fonctionnaires, si petit que soit leur emploi, se doit faire par appel nominal nominal à haute voix, et aucun fonctionnaire ne pourra parvenir à aucune place sans cette formalité.

VI.

Le terme des représentations principales et en chef, doit être le plus court possible, et une prolongation occasionnée par une réélection illimitée n'y a pas lieu.

VII.

La séparation, et le morcellement des pouvoirs, et des forces nécessaires dans les agens représentatifs principaux et en chef est inévitable, et de toute nécessité dans le corps social.

VIII.

Tous les représentans du peuple en chef, doivent être non-seulement de la durée la plus courte possible, mais il faut aussi que la surveillance générale du peuple porte toute son attention sur ses fonctionnaires en chefs, qui durant le court espace de leurs fonctions, semblent réunir tous les moyens de la société. Il faut que le peuple entier soit dans un tel état de réunion et de vigilance, et garde un calme tel et majestueux, qu'il semble plutôt les surveiller, que les servir en esclave. C'est ainsi que le peuple reste toujours en même tems le monarque et le sujet.

IX.

Les représentans subalternes de la force M se suppléent dans la nature l'un à l'autre. En cas de besoin, le membre le plus proche agit pour l'autre. Lorsqu'il se passe dans un endroit du territoire de la société un événement décisif pour le corps entier, où il est besoin d'une représentation rapide et instantanée de la force d'un membre absent, ou que par impossibilité, le peuple entier ne peut pas être présent lui-même, alors le district et département, commune, section, individu, enfin le membre le plus à portée doit, sans contredit, suppléer les autres en droit strict et véritable, parce qu'il est en devoir pour le principe.

X.

Les seules fonctions que le peuple entier, le souverain est en état d'exercer lui-même, sont la défense pour son moi social, les élections de ses représentans, la confiance et la tranquillité générale, l'insurrection et la surveillance générale.

Liberté
I.

Liberté est, *l'égalité des droits.*

II.

Chaque liberté, par préférence d'un membre ou corporation quelconque, est une puissance partielle aux dépens d'autrui, au détriment du principe, est licence.

III.

Tout ce qui est contraire au principe est une liberté liberticide; une licence, et licence que le souverain n'a pas le pouvoir de souffrir, soit qu'une telle licence se cache sous le masque de la liberté d'opinions, de la presse, de la politique, de la religion, qu'elle se nomme tolérance, ou sous quelque forme qu'elle se présente; elle est attentatoire au corps social dans son intégrité, et doit être punie de mort.

Egalité
I.

L'égalité des droits, est la véritable liberté l'un chacun.

II.

Chaque législateur, voulant forger une égalité, de manière à satisfaire l'inégalité des nuances de la faculté appétitive, découlant de la différence naturelle des diverses organisations, surpasse les bornes de son pouvoir, agir contre droit, et improuvé par la nature, repoussé par le principe, même sous le prétexte d'améliorer par des loix les mœurs, la moralité des individus; parce que chaque action forcée cesse d'être moralité, en cessant d'être un acte volontaire: et devient de la part du législateur, tyrannie, n'ayant pas le droit d'enchaîner le droit égal de la plus parfaite liberté d'un chacun de satisfaire sa faculté appétitive d'une manière différente, selon son organisation et son plaisir licite.

III.

Chaque loi qui exige des sacrifices involontaires, concernant le luxe, l'abondance, (excepté dans les momens impérieux, où ils sont exigés par la nécessité pour le salut public), est attentatoire à la propriété individuelle, est oppressive, vexatoire, criminelle, est repoussée par le principe.

IV.

Le partage des terres ne pouvant jamais se trouver dans le cas d'être exigé pour le soutien et la défense du principe, il reste toujours hors du pouvoir du souverain, et ne peut avoir lieu de nulle manière dans une législation.

Éducation
I.

Le principe d'une république démocratique, est, *la vraie connoissance des charmes et avantages réels qu'elle nous donne.*

II.

Pour élever la jeunesse en républicains démocrates, il n'y a d'autre méthode, que d'avoir une constitution instructive et convaincante, qui conduise la jeunesse républicaine au but nécessaire, d'après la mesure de la nature, par les attraits du plaisir.

Peines et délits
I.

Les peines sont fondées dans la nature, et doivent être en proportion avec les délits; elles doivent être fixées par degrés.

II.

La Société ne peut punir aucun de ses membres de la peine de mort, s'il n'a commis un délit contre le corps entier. Le moi individuel étant dans l'état de culture changé dans le moi social; et le principe, la conservation, individuelle, étant devenu la conservation individuelle de la société entière, il en résulte, que l'on ne peut commettre un crime contre le principe, si l'on ne le commet point contre le corps de la société entière.

Appendix 3: The German Draft of the *Philosophie Sociale*

The transcription is based on the autograph preserved in Paris, *Archives Natio-nales, T 1524* (for a brief description of the entire set of papers, confiscated from Dobruska upon arrest, see Susanne Wölfle-Fischer, *Junius Frey (1753–1794). Jude, Aristokrat und Revolutionär*, (Frankfurt a. M.: Peter Lanf, 1997), 20–26.

CHAPITRE VIII.	Abtheilung VIII
Du souverain.	Der Souverain
I.	I.
Qu'est-ce que l'être-homme dans l'état de nature? *Un ensemble souverain, un tout parfait et isolé dépendant de soi-même et indépendant hors de soi.*	Was ist d[er] [.] Naturmensch? – ein einzelnes von sic[h selbst] abhängendes, von außen independentes Souveraines Ganze (C. §)
II.	2.
Qu'est-ce que c'est que la société ? *Un nouvel ensemble ou un tout souverain et indépendant, spontanément composé d'ensembles primitifs isolés, aussi indépendans souverains et égaux en droits, multipliés d'une manière égale et homogène, mais non pas augmentés différemment.*	Was ist die Sozietät? – ein vo[n] einzelnen, independenten, in Rechten gleichen Souverainen ältern Ganzen, freiwillig zusammengestelltes neues Ganze, gleichartig vervielfältigt aber nicht verschiedentlich vermehrt.
III.	3.
Que reçoit le souverain primitif (l'être homme) dans l'état de nature du nouveau souverain, (la société) il en reçoit *la faculté appétitive tant matérielle qu'intellectuelle perfectionnée et développée.*	Was erhält der alte Souverain (: der individuelle Naturmensch) von dem neuen Souverain (: die Sozietät)? – das erhöhte und entwickelte materielle und intellektuelle Begehrungsvermögen (C. I.§4. C.II.§.4).
IV.	4.
Que doit-on entendre par la faculté appétitive, matérielle et intellectuelle perfectionnée et développée? *L'instinct mûri et formé par la société.*	Was ist der erhöhte und entwickelte materielle und intellektuelle Begehrungsvermögen? – es ist der großgewachsene von der Gesellschaft erzogene, ausgebildete Instinkt.

(continued)

CHAPITRE VIII.	Abtheilung VIII
V.	5
Quelle est la propriété de l'être-homme dans l'état de nature ? *toutes les forces et moyens naturels qui peuvent le conduire au but exigé par le principe*; c'est-à-dire, au plus parfait contentement de sa faculté appétitive animale et non développée, qui n'est autre chose que l'instinct, par lequel dans cet état, le principe dirige toutes ces forces et moyens naturels qui combinés ensemble, constituent la propriété du souverain primitif.	Was ist das Eigenthum des alten Souverains? (des individuellen Naturmenschen)? – alle seine Kräfte und Naturmittel zu Erreichung seines eingeschränkten Zwecks – die höchsten Befriedigung seiner unentwickelten animalischen Begehrungsvermögen welches der Instinkt ist, <so> der Leiter dieser Kräfte und Naturmittel ist, und mit ihren zusammen das Eigenthum des alten Souverains ausmacht.
VI.	6.
En quoi consiste la propriété du nouveau souverain? (la société) dans toutes les forces et moyens de culture, qui se réunissent aux forces et moyens naturels antérieurs de chacun de ses membres, pour étendre la sphère de ses jouissances par le plus parfait contentement de sa faculté appétitive tant matérielle qu'intellectuelle perfectionnée et développée; et c'est la réunion de ces forces et moyens de culture qui constitue la propriété du nouveau souverain. La société	Was ist das Eigenthum des neuen Souverains (die Sozietät)? – alle <zu seinen alten Kräften und Naturmitteln hinzugekommen> neue Kräfte und Kulturmittel zu Erreichung des ausgedehnteren Zweckes – das höchsten Befriedigung ihres höchsten und entwickelten materiellen und intellektuellen Begehrungsvermögen (84) welches der Leiter dieser neuen entwickelten Kräfte und Kulturmittel ist, und mit ihren zusammen das Eigenthum des neuen Souverains (die lieson soziale {liaison sociale}) ausmachen.
VII.	7.
Quels sont les devoirs et fonctions du souverain primitif (l'être-homme dans l'état de nature) en vers lui-même ? La contribution et l'emploi de toutes ses forces et moyen naturels pour atteindre le but qu'exige le principe, c'est-à-dire le plus parfait contentement de la faculté appétitive non développée, et de l'instinct, qui réunis, constituent la propriété du souverain primitif, et qui doivent s'accorder une protection réciproque et s'entre-aider mutuellement.	Was sind die Pflichten des alten Souveraines (das individuelle Naturmenschen) gegen sich selbst? – sie sind die Beisteuer aller seiner Kräfte und Naturmittel zu Errichtung ihres eingeschränkten Zweckes – der höchsten Befriedigung ihres animalischen Leiters, des Instinktes, welcher mit ihren zusammen das Eigenthum des alten Souverains (95.) ausmacht, die sich untereinander Hülfe und reziproken Schutz leisten müßen.
VIII.	8.
Jusqu'où s'étendent les devoirs et obligations du souverain primitif; (c'est-à-dire l'être-homme dans l'état de nature) en vers	Wie weit gehen die Pflichten des alten Souverains (des individuellen Naturmenschen) gegen sich selbst? – So weit,

(continued)

CHAPITRE VIII.	Abtheilung VIII
soi-même? Ils s'étendent autant que ses moyens, c'est-à-dire autant que restant moyens ils ne touchent point au but. D'où il résulte que toutes ses prétentions qui touchent au but sortent du cercle de son juste pouvoir et dégénèrent en usurpation tyranniqe, parce que c'est alors contre le principe; tels que le suicide qu'il ne doit point commettre, quoiqu'il soit en son pouvoir de de le faire,	als sie <u>Mittel</u> bleiben, und nicht mit dem Zweck vertauscht werden; daher alle Forderungen sobald sie den Zweck berühren, außer der Souverains Gerechtigkeit liegen, und werden zur Usurpazion und Tirannie, zum Selbstmord, welchen – ob er ihn gleich ausüben kann – doch sicher nicht ausüben darf.
IX.	9.
Quelle est la conduite du souverain primitif dans cette contribution de ses forces et moyens naturels? je veux dire les employe-t-il avec une économie scrupuleuse ou avec profusion? Économise-t-il cette contribution, quand il s'agit de défendre sa propriété pour ne pas manquer à son but exigé par le principe? Non. Il suit constamment la loi invariable qui dit, que cela soit. La victoire ou la mort; et il s'acquitte involontairement de sa contribution, tant qu'il lui reste un moyen de défendre cette propriété relativement au but exigé par le principe, car tous ses moyens tendans vers ce but, n'ont qu'une existence relative à lui et finissent aussitôt qu'il cesse d'exister; d'ailleurs, l'instinct ou élan tendant à obtenir ce but, est tellement lié à l'instinct conservateur de leur propre existence, au principe, qu'ils sont obligés de déployer toutes leurs ressources pour ne pas périr eux-mêmes en perdant leur but: je veux dire pour ne pas se perdre absolument, ayant encore l'espoir de parvenir à conserver leur existence, par la possibilité de triompher et d'atteindre le but.	Wie benimmt sich der alte Souverain (der individuelle Naturmensch) in dieser Beisteuer seiner Kräfte und Naturmittel, d.i. giebt er sie kärglich, oder genugsam, geitzt und [.] in Ansehung dieser Neuer, wenn es daraus ankommt {ankommt} sein Eigenthum zu stützen, um seines Zweckes nicht verlustig zu werden? – nein! Er weichet nicht in geringsten ab, von seinen unerschütterlichen Gesetzen, das da heißt: so und nicht anders! Ding, ohne Vermischung! – er leistet seinen Steuer (die Mittel) unwillkürlich, und zwar in so lange, was ihm nur noch ein einziges Mittel übrig bleibt, dieses Eigenthum, um des Zweckes willen zu beschützen; denn da alle seine Mittel zu Erreichung dieses Zwecks nur eine für diesen Zweck relative Existenz haben, und sogleich aufhören würden, wenn dieses Zweck aufhört; so ist der Trieb zu Erreichung ihres Zweckes so genau mit dem Erhaltungstriebe ihrer eignen Existenz verbunden, daß sie alles ausbietet müßen, um nicht mit dem Verluste ihres Zweckes selbst verlohren (!) zu seyn <um nicht in diesen Falle <u>gewiß</u> verlohren zu seyn>, da sie durch höchstmöglichen Beisteuer (§) dennoch ihre Existenz durch den möglichen Sinn der Erreichung des Zweckes vi[e]lleicht retten können.

(continued)

CHAPITRE VIII.	Abtheilung VIII
X.	10.
En quoi consistent les devoirs du nouveau souverain, la société, envers lui-même? Ils consistent dans la contribution de tous les moyens de culture réunis aux moyens naturels de chacun de ses membres, afin d'arriver par elle à la satisfaction la plus entière de la faculté appétitive perfectionnée et développée, l'instinct formé pour le principe, moyens dont la réunion présente la propriété du nouveau souverain, c'est-à-dire le trésor social, et qui sont obligés de se prêter un secours mutuel relativement au but exigé par le principe, c'est-à-dire, pour pouvoir se conserver dans l'état de culture.	Was sind die Pflichten des neuen Souverains (die Sozietät) gegen sich selbst? Sie sind die Beisteuer aller zu ihren Naturmittels hinzu gekommen Kulturmitteln zur Erreichung ihres nun ausgedehnten Zweckes – der höchsten Befriedigung ihres neuen Leiters, des erhöhten und entwickelten Begehrungsvermögens, des ausgebildeten Instinktes (§ 4) – welche zusammengesetzten des Eigenthum (§ 6) des neuen Souverains (der Tresor Sozial) ausmachen, und sich untereinander reziprok beyhülfen müßen, um des Zweckes willen, von welchen ihre Erhaltung abzwingt.

Bibliography

Acte constitutionnel du Peuple Français avec le Rapport, la Déclaration des Droits et le Procès-verbal d'inauguration. Paris: Imprimerie nationale, 1793.

Archives parlementaires de 1787 à 1860, Première série, vol. 69, *Du 19 février 1793 au 8 mars 1793*. Paris: Imprimerie nationale, 1901.

Aron, Raymond. *Les étapes de la pensée sociologique. Montesquieu, Comte, Marx, Tocqueville, Durkheim, Pareto, Weber.* Paris: Gallimard, 1967.

Aron, Raymond. *Main Currents in Sociologcal Thought: Volume One. Montesquieu, Comte, Marx, De Toqueville: The Sociologistis and the Revolution of 1848.* London and New York: Routledge, 2019.

Artaize, Henri de Feucher. *Réflexions d'un jeune homme.* London [but Paris]: Chez Royez, 1786.

Aubert, "Madame". *Les charmes de la société du chrétien.* Paris: Jacques Estienne, 1730.

Aulard, François A. *La Société des Jacobins. Recueil de documents pour l'histoire du club des Jacobins de Paris*, vol. 3, *Juillet 1791 à juin 1792.* Paris: Joaust – Noblet – Quantin, 1892.

Baden, Karl Friedrich von. *Abrégé des principes de l'économie politique.* Paris: Chez Lacombe, 1772.

Baecque, Antoine de. *Le corps de l'histoire. Métaphores et politique, 1770–1800.* Paris: Calmann-Lévy, 1993.

Bagnasco, Arnaldo, Maurizio Barbagli, and Alessandro Cavalli. *Corso di sociologia.* Bologna: Il Mulino, 1997.

Bailey, Gauvin A. *The Spiritual Rococo. Decor and Divinity from the Salons of Paris to the Missions of Patagonia.* Farnham: Ashgate, 2014.

Barberini, Antonella "La proprietà della Costituzione." *Proprietà e diritti reali*, 1. (2011): 43–87.

Bastiat, Fréderic. *Harmonies économiques.* Bruxelles: Meline, Cans et Compagnie, 1850.

Bedorf, Thomas, and Kurt Röttgers. "Einleitung." In *Einführung in die Sozialphilosophie*, by Franck Fischbach, 1–12. Hagen: FernUniversität in Hagen, 2017.

Bedorf, Thomas, and Kurt Röttgers. "Nachwort." In *Manifest für eine Sozialphilosophie*, by Franck Fischbach, 137–153. Bielefeld: Transcript, 2016.

Beccaria, Cesare. *Dei delitti e delle pene.* Livorno: Coltellini, 1764.

Beccaria, Cesare. *Traité des Délits et des Peines, traduit de l'italien d'après la troisième édition, revue et corrigée et augmentée par l'auteur, avec des additions de l'auteur qui n'ont pas encore paru en italien.* Lausanne [but Paris]: without publisher, 1766.

Bellebaum, Alfred and Robert Hettlage, eds. *Glück hat viele Gesichter. Annäherungen an eine gekonnte Lebensführung.* Wiesbaden: VS Verlag, 2010.

Benoît, Michel. *1793 La République de la tentation. Une affaire de corruption sous la Ière République.* Précy-sous-Thil: Éd. de l'Armançon, 2008.

Biester, Erich J. "Magnetische Desorganisation und Sonnambulism." *Berlinische Monatschrift* 9 (1785): 126–160.

Blum, Carol. *Rousseau and the Republic of Virtue. The Language of Politics in the French Revolution.* Ithaca: Cornell University Press, 1989.

Bobbio, Norberto. "Hobbes e il Giusnaturalismo." *Rivista critica di storia della filosofia* 17 (1962): 470–485.

Bonald, Louis Gabriel A. de. *François Chabot, membre de la Convention (1756–1794).* Paris: Émile-Paul Éditeur, 1908.

Bord, Gustave. *La fin de deux légendes: l'affaire Léonard, le Baron de Batz.* Paris: Daragon, 1909.

Bourdieu, Pierre. "The Forms of Capital. " In *Handbook for Theory and Research for the Sociology of Education*, edited by John G. Richardson, 241–258. Westport: Greenwood, 1986.

Breiger, Ronald L. "Baruch Spinoza. Monism and Complementarity." In *Sociological Insights of Great Thinkers: Sociology through Literature, Philosophy, and Science*, edited by Christofer Edling and Jens Rydgren, 255–262. Santa Barbara, CA: Praeger, 2011.

Buder, Christian s.v. "Frey, Junius." In *The Bloomsbury Dictionary of the Eighteenth-century German philosophers*, edited by Heiner F. Klemme, and Manfred Kuehn, 236–237. London-New York: Bloomsbury Publishing Plc, 2016.

Burgio, Alberto. "Tra diritto e politica. Note sul rapporto Beccaria-Montesquieu." *Rivista di Storia della Filosofia* 51 (1996): 659–676.

Busino, Giovanni. "Pavane pour l'histoire de la sociologie." *Revue européenne des sciences sociales* 31 (1993): 95–123.

Campanini, Saverio. "Da Giacobbe ai Giacobini." In *Le tre vite di Moses Dobrushka*, by Gershom Scholem, edited by and with an essay by Saverio Campanini, translated by Elisabetta Zevi. 159–231. Milano: Adelphi, 2014.

Cassirer, Ernst, Paul Oskar Kristeller, and John Herman Randall Jr., eds., *The Renaissance Philosophy of Man*. Chicago: University of Chicago Press, 1948.

Cerulo, Massimo. *Sociologia delle emozioni*. Bologna: Il Mulino, 2018.

Chabot, François. "François Chabot, représentant du peuple, à ses concitoyens qui sont les juges de sa vie politique. Mémoire apologétique publié pour la première fois." *Annales révolutionnaires* 6 (1913) 533–550, 681–706; 7 (1914), 224–247, edited by Albert Mathiez.

Chabot, François. "Histoire véritable du mariage de François Chabot avec Léopoldine Frey en réponse à toutes les calomnies que l'on a répandues à ce sujet." *Annales révolutionnaires* 7 (1914): 248–254, edited by Albert Mathiez.

Clapiers de Vauvenargues, Luc de. *Oeuvres complètes*, Paris: Hachette, 1968.

Clark, Andrew E., Sarah Flèche, Richard Layard, Nattavudh Powdthavee, and George Ward. "The Key Determinants of Happiness and Misery." *World Happiness Report 2017*, edited by John Helliwell, Richard Layard and Jeffrey Sachs, 122–143. New York: Sustainable Development Solutions Network, 2017.

Clément, Denis-Xavier. *Exercices de l'âme pour se disposer aux sacrements de pénitence et d'eucharistie*, Paris: Guerin, 1758.

Comte, Auguste. *Cours de philosophie positive*, vol. 1. Paris: Rouen Frères, 1830.

Comte, Auguste. *Écrits de jeunesse 1816–1828. Suivis du Mémoire sur la 'Cosmogonie' de Laplace, 1835*. Berlin: De Gruyter, 2018 (I ed. 1970).

Comte, Auguste. *Physique sociale. Cours de philosophie positive (leçons 46–60) [1840–1842]*. Paris: Hermann, 1975.

Comte, Auguste. "Prospectus annonçant le troisième volume de l'Industrie (1817*)."* In *Écrits de jeunesse 1816–1828. Suivis du Mémoire sur la 'Cosmogonie' de Laplace, 1835*, by Auguste Comte, 39–42. Berlin: De Gruyter, 2018 (I ed. 1970)

Conlon, Pierre M. *Prélude au siècle des lumières en France, répertoire chronologique de 1680 a 1715*, 5 vols. Genève: Droz, 1970–1974.

Corbetta, Piergiorgio. *Metodologia e tecnica della ricerca sociale*. Bologna: Il Mulino, 1999.

Coser, Lewis A. *Masters of Sociological Thought. Ideas in Historical and Social Context*, 2nd ed. San Diego: Harcourt Publishers, 1977 (I ed. 1971).

Costa, Emanuele. "Uno Spinoza sistemico. Strumenti per un'interpretazione sistemica del pensiero di Spinoza." *Rivista di Filosofia Neo-Scolastica* 106 (2014): 525–535.

Dangers, Yves. "*Ephraim Josef Hirschfeld et les 'Frères de l'Asie'.*" *Le Symbolisme* 375–376 (1966): 41–359.

Dayé, Christian, and Stephan Moebius. "Einleitung." In *Soziologiegeschichte. Wege und Ziele*, edited by Christian Dayé and Stephan Moebius, 7–13. Frankfurt: Suhrkamp 2015.

De Rossi, Giovanni B. *Dizionario storico degli autori ebrei e delle loro opere*, 3 vols. Parma: Stamperia Reale, 1802.

Déclaration des droits de l'homme, et articles de Constitution présentés au Roi, avec sa réponse. Paris: chez Baudoiun, imprimeur de l'Assemblé nationale, 1789.

Déclaration des droits de la femme et de la citoyenne. [Paris: 1791].

Décret du 14 frimaire, précédé du rapport fait au nom du Comité de salut public sur un mode gouvernement provisoire et révolutionnaire par Billaud-Varenne, à la séance du 28 brumaire, l'an second de la République française, une et indivisible. Paris: Imprimerie nationale, 1793.

Descharrères, Jean J. C. "Vie de Monseigneur Casimir-Fréderic des Barons de Rathsamhausen." *Revue d'Alsace* 10 (1859): 347–348.

Descharrères, Jean J. C. *Essai sur l'histoire littéraire de Belfort et du voisinage.* Belfort: J. P. Clerc, 1808.

Die Brüder St. Johannis des Evangelisten aus Asien in Europa oder die einzige wahre und ächte Freimaurerei nebst einem Anhange, die Fesslersche Kritische Geschichte der Freimaurerbrüderschaft und ihre Nichtigkeit betreffend. Berlin: Schmidt, 1803.

Dioni, Gianluca. "Perfectibilité e perfectio. Rousseau e Wolff, armonie e dissonanze." In *La filosofia politica di Rousseau*, edited by, Giulio Maria Chiodi and Roberto Gatti, 151–160. Milano: Franco Angeli, 2012.

Dobruska, Moses *alias* Junius Frey. *Les aventures politiques du père Nicaise, ou l'Anti-fédéraliste.* Paris: De l'imp. De J. Grand, 1793.

Dobruska, Moses *alias* Junius Frey. *Philosophie sociale, dédiée au peuple françois par un Citoyen de la Section de la République Françoise, ci-devant du Roule.* Paris: Froullé, 1793.

Dobruska, Moses. *Die zwo Amaryllen, ein Schäferspiel in einem Auszuge.* Prag: Wolfgang Gerle, 1774.

Durkheim, Emile. *De la division du travail social. Étude sur l'organisation des sociétés supérieures.* Paris: Félix Alcan, 1893.

Durkheim, Emile. *Les règles de la méthode sociologique.* Paris: Félix Alcan, 1895.

Durosoy, Jean Baptiste. *Der christliche Weltbürger oder Grundsätze des socialen Lebens ein Versuch über unsere Pflichten als Menschen und Staatsbürger.* Münster: Theissing, 1852.

Durosoy, Jean-Baptiste. *Philosophie sociale ou essai sur les devoirs de l'homme et du citoyen.* Paris: C.P. Berton, 1783.

Eberhard, Johann A. "Dreyerley Desorganisationen gegen das Ende unsers Jahrhunderte." *Philosophisces Archiv* 2.3 (1794): 17–31.

Eibeschütz, Jonathan. *And I Came this Day unto the Fountain*, critically edited and introduced by Pawel Maciejko. Los Angeles: Cherub Press, 2014.

Fassò, Guido. *Storia della filosofia del diritto. II. L'età moderna.* Bari-Roma: Laterza, 2001 (I ed. 1968).

Felice, Domenico. "Nota al testo." In *Tutte le opere (1721–1754)* by Montesquieu facing French text, ed, Idem, (Milano: Bompiani 2014), 885–893.

Ferrara, Alessandro. "Autenticità, normatività dell'identità e ruolo del legislatore in Rousseau." In *La filosofia politica di Rousseau*, edited by Giulio Maria Chiodi and Roberto Gatti, 9–34. Milano: Franco Angeli, 2012.

Ferrara, Alessandro. "The Idea of a Social Philosophy." *Constellations* 9 (2002): 419–435.

Ferrarotti, Franco. *Lineamenti di storia del pensiero sociologico*. Roma: Donzelli, 2002.

Fischbach, Franck. *Manifest für eine Sozialphilosophie*, transl. Lilian Peter, with an afterword by Thomas Bedorf and Kurt Röttgers. Bielefeld: Transcript, 2016.

Fischbach, Franck. *Manifeste pour une philosophie sociale*. Paris: La Decouverte, 2009.

Flam, Helena. *Soziologie der Emotionen. Eine Einführung*, Konstanz: UVK, 2002.

Formentin, [?] *Traité du bonheur*. Paris: J. Guilletat,1706 [but 1705].

Friedkin, Noah F. "Social Cohesion." *Annual Review of Sociology* 30 (2004): 409–425.

Geck, Adolph L. H. "Die Aufgaben einer Christlichen Gesellschaftslehre als einer Wissenschaftlichen Disziplin." *Jahrbuch für christlichen Sozialwissenschaften* 11 (1970): 259–289.

Gough, Hugh. "Jean-Charles Laveaux (1749–1827). A Political Biography." PhD. diss., University of Oxford, 1974.

Gouhier, Henri. *La jeunesse d'Auguste Comte et la formation du positivisme*, 3 vols. Second edition. Paris: Vrin, 1964–1970 (I ed. 1933–1941).

Graham, Ruth. "Les mariages des ecclésiastiques députés à la Convention." *Annales historiques de la Révolution française* 262 (1985): 480–499.

Greco, Silvana, Mary Holmes, and Jordan McKenzie. "Friendship and Happiness from a Sociological Perspective." In *Friendship and Happiness. Across the Life-Span and Culture*, edited by Melikşah Demir, 19–35. New York: Springer, 2015.

Greco, Silvana. "Heresy, Apostasy, and the Beginnings of Social Philosophy. Moses Dobruska reconsidered." *Materia giudaica* 20–21 (2015–2016): 439–464.

Greco, Silvana. "Soziologie des Judentums in Deutschland. Markante Felder, Perspektiven und Methoden." In *Ein halbes Jahrhundert deutscher Forschung und Lehre über das Judentum in Deutschland*, edited by Andreas Lenhardt, 131–148. Berlin: De Gruyter, 2017.

Guastini, Riccardo. "Sulla validità della costituzione dal punto di vista del positivismo giuridico." *Rivista internazionale di filosofia del diritto* 66 (1989): 424–436.

Guerci, Luciano. "Per una riflessione sul dibattito politico nell'Italia del Triennio repubblicano." In *Universalismo e nazionalità nell'esperienza del giacobinismo italiano, (1796–1799)*, edited by Luigi Lotti and Rosario Villari, 305–321. Roma-Bari: Laterza, 2003.

Guibet Lafaye, Caroline. "Modèles de la cohésion sociale." *European Journal of Sociology / Archives Européennes de Sociologie / Europäisches Archiv für Soziologie* 50 (2009) 3: 389–427.

Guilhaumou, Jacques. "Sieyès et le non-dit de la sociologie. Du mot à la chose." *Revue d'histoire des sciences humaines* (2006): 117–134.

Gutkas, Karl. *Kaiser Joseph II. Eine Biographie*. Wien – Darmstadt: Zsolnay, 1989.

Guyer, Paul. "Editor's Introduction." In *Critique of the Power of Judgement*, by Immanuel Kant, translated by Eric Matthews, xiii-lii. Cambridge: Cambridge University Press, 2000.

Hascher, Tina. "Learning and Emotions. Perspectives for Theory and Research." *European Educational Research Journal* 9 (2010): 13–27.

Heitz, Friedrich Carl. *Les sociétés politiques de Strasbourg pendant les années 1790 à 1795: Extraits de leurs procès-verbaux publiés par F.C.H.* Strasboug Fréderic-Charles Heitz, 1863.

Herlaut, Auguste P. *Le général rouge Ronsin (1751–1794). La Vendée, l'armée révolutionnaire parisienne*. Paris: Clavreuil, 1956.

Herriger, Norbert. *Empowerment in der Sozialen* Arbeit. *Eine Einführung*, 6., extended and upsated edition. Stuttgart: Verlag W. Kohlkammer, 2019 (I ed. 2002).

Higonnet, Patrice. "Sociability, Social Structure, and the French Revolution." *Social Research* 56 (1989): 99–125.

Hobbes, Thomas. *Leviathan*, London: Crooke, 1651.

Honegger, Claudia and Theresa Wobbe, eds. *Frauen in der Soziologie. Neun Porträts*. München: Beck, 1998.

Honneth, Axel, ed. *Pathologien des Sozialen. Die Aufgaben der Sozialphilosophie*. Frankfurt am Main: Fischer, 1994.

Izzo, Alberto. *Storia del pensiero sociologico*. Bologna: Il Mulino, 2005.

Jaeggi, Rahel, and Robin Celikates. *Sozialphilosophie. Eine Einführung*. München: Beck, 2017.

Kahn, Léon. *Les Juifs de Paris pendant la révolution*. Paris: Paul Ollendorff, 1899.

Karniel, Josef. "Jüdischer Pseudomessianismus und deutsche Kultur. Der Weg der frankistichen Familie Dobruschka-Schönfeld im Zeitalter der Aufklärung." In *Gegenseitige Einflüsse deutscher und jüdischer Kultur von der Epoche der Aufklärung bis zu Weimarer Republik*, edited by Walter Grab, 31–54. Tel Aviv: Nateev-Printing and Publ. Enterprises, 1982.

Katz, Jakob. *Jews and Freemasons in Europe. 1723–1939*. Cambridge: Harward University Press (Mass.), 1970.

Katz, Jakob. "Moses Mendelssohn und Ephraim Josef Hirschfeld." *Bulletin des Leo Baeck Institutes* 28 (1964): 295–311.

Kim, Seoyong, and Hyesun Kim. "Does Cultural Capital Matter? Cultural Divide and Quality of Life." *Social Indicators Research* 93 (2009): 295–313.

Klausnitzer, Ralf. *Poesie und Konspiration. Beziehungssinn und Zeichenökonomie von Verschwörungsszenarien in Publizistik, Literatur und Wissenschaft 1750–1850*. Berlin, New York: De Gruyter, 2007.

Kley, Andreas and Richard Amstutz. *Gironde-Verfassungsentwurf aus der französischen Revolution vom 15./16. Februar 1793 deutschsprachige Übersetzung mit einer Einleitung und kommentierenden Anmerkungen*. Zürich: Nomos, 2011.

Koch, Patrick. B. "Ein verschollener jüdischer Mystiker? Gershom Scholems Nachforschungen zu Ephraim Joseph Hirschfeld." In *Gershom Scholem in Deutschland*, edited by Gerold Necker, Elke Morlok and Matthias Morgenstern, 219–242. Tübingen: Mohr Siebeck, 2014.

Königlich-Preussische Akademie der Künste, eds. *Kant's gesammelte Schriften. Kant's Briefwechsel*, Band 2. Berlin: Georg Reimer, 1900.

Kraus, Samuel. *Joachim Edler von Popper. Ein Zeit- und Lebensbild aus der Geschichte der Juden in Böhmen*. Wien: Selbstverlag, 1926.

La Constitution du 24 juin 1793. L'utopie dans le droit public français?, texts collected by Jean Bart, Jean-Jacques Clère, Claude Courvoisier, and Michel Verpeaux, coordination Françoise Naudin Patriat. Dijon: Editions universitaires de Dijon, 1997.

Leser, Norbert. *Sozialphilosophie. Grundlagen des Studiums*. Wien: Böhlau, 1997.

Lestapis, Arnaud de. *La "Conspiration de Batz" (1793–1794)*. Paris: Société des études robespierristes.

Locke, John. *An Essay Concerning Human Understanding*, edited by Peter H. Nidditch. Oxford: Oxford University Press, 1975.

Locke, John. *An Essay Concerning Humane Understanding*. London: The Basset, 1690 [but 1689].

Locke, John. *Essai philosophique concernant l'entendement humain*, trans. by Pierre Coste. Amsterdam: Pierre Mortier, 1770.

Locke, John. *Saggio sull'intelletto umano*, edited by Marian and Nicola Abbagnano. Torino: Utet, 1971.

Loty, Laurent. *Que signifie l'entrée du bonheur dans la Constitution*, in *Le bonheur au XVIIIe siècle*, texts gathered and presented by Guilhem Farrugia, and Michel Delon. Rennes: Presses Universitaires de Rennes, 2015.

Maciejko, Pawel. *The Mixed Multitude. Jacob Frank and the Frankist Movement, 1755–1816*. Philadelphia: University of Pennsylvania Press, 2011.

Mandel, Arthur. *The Militant Messiah or, The Flight from the Ghetto. The Story of Jacob Frank and the Frankist Movement*. Atlantic Highlands, NJ: Humanities Press, 1979.

Mannucci, Erica J. *Baionette nel focolare. La Rivoluzione francese e la ragione delle donne*. Milano: Franco Angeli, 2016.

Maslow, Abraham H. "A Theory of Hominoid Motivation." *Psychological Review* 50 (1943): 370–396.

Maslow, Abraham H. *Motivation and Personality*. New York: Harper & Row Verlag, 1970.

Mathiez, Albert. "Histoire véritable du mariage de François Chabot avec Léopoldine Frey en réponse à toutes les calomnies que l'on a répandues à ce sujet." *Annales révolutionnaires* 7 (1914): 248–254.

Mathiez, Albert. *La révolution et les étrangers. Cosmopolitisme et défense nationale*. Paris: Renaissance du Livre, 1918.

Mathiez, Albert. "L'arrestation de Saint-Simon." *Annales historiques de la Révolution française* 2 (1925): 571–575.

Mathiez, Albert. "Saint-Simon et Ronsin." *Annales historiques de la Révolution française* 3 (1926): 493–494.

Mauzi, Robert. *L'idée du bonheur dans la littérature et la pensée françaises au XVIIIe siècle*. Paris: Colin, 1965.

McPhee, Peter. *A Social History of France 1780–1914*. New York: Palgrave, 2004.

Merçon, Juliana. "La filosofía de Spinoza y el pensamiento sistémico contemporáneo." *Revista de Filosofía (Universidad Iberoamericana)* 133 (2012): 83–101.

Mirabeau, Honoré Gabriel de Riqueti. *Discours de monsieur Mirabeau l'ainé sur l'éducation nationale*. Paris: Lejay, 1791.

Moebius, Stephan, Andrea Ploder, Nicole Holzhauser, and Oliver Römer, eds. *Handbuch Geschichte der deutschsprachigen Soziologie*, [herausgegeben von], 3 vols. Wiesbaden: Springer, 2017–2019.

Moebius, Stephan, and Gerhard Schäfer, eds. *Soziologie als Gesellschaftskritik. Wider den Verlust einer aktuellen Tradition*. Hamburg: VSA, 2006.

Moebius, Stephan. "Die Geschichte der Soziologie im Spiegel der Kölner Zeitschrift für Soziologie und Sozialpsychologie (KZfSS)." *Kölner Zeitschrift für Soziologie und Sozialpsychologie*, Sonderheft 56 (2017): 3–44.

Moebius, Stephan. *René König und die "Kölner Schule". Eine soziologiegeschichtliche Annäherung*. Wiesbaden: Springer, 2015.

Molm, Linda D., David R. Schaefer, and Jessica L. Collett. "The Value of Reciprocity." *Social Psychology Quarterly* 70 (2007): 199–217.

Montesquieu, Charles-Louis de. *The complete Works of M. de Montesquieu*. Volume the First. Dublin: W. Watson, 1777.

Montesquieu, Charles-Louis de. *Tutte le opere (1721–1754)*, Frontal French text, ed., Domenico Felice. Milano: Bompiani, 2014.

Montesquieu, Charles-Louis de. *Pensées – Le Spicilège*, edition established by Louis Desgraves. Paris: Laffont, 1991.

Mousset, Sophie. *Women's Rights and the French Revolution. A Biography of Olympe de Gouges*. New Brunswick: Transaction, 2007.

Önnerfors, Andreas. "Freemasonry and Civil Society: Reform of Manners and the Journal für Freymaurer (1784–1786)." In *The Enlightenment in Bohemia: Religion, Morality and Multiculturalism*, edited by Ivo Cerman, Rita Kruger, and Susan Reynolds, 111–128. Oxford: Voltaire Foundation, 2011.

Parry, Richard D. "Morality and Happiness. Book IV of Plato's 'Republic'." *The Journal of Education* 178 (1996): 31–47.

Pfest, Ladislaus L. *Die Jahreszeiten. Eine Liederlese für Freunde der Natur*. Salzburg: Mayr'schen Buchhandlung, 1812.

Pickering, Mary. *Auguste Comte. An Intellectual Biography*, 3 vol. Cambridge: Cambridge University Press, 1993.

Pico della Mirandola, Giovanni. *Discorso sulla dignità dell'uomo*, edited by Francesco Bausi. Parma: Guanda, 2003.

Pope, Alexander. *An Essay on Man. Epistle I-IV*. London: J. Wilford, 1733–1734.

Proust, Marcel. *A la recherche du temps perdu*, vol. 7, *Le côté de Guermantes*. Paris: Gallimard, 1919.

Raboteau, Paul-Émile. *Le patrotisme français. Poème*. Paris: Chez L'Auteur, 1830.

Rehberg, Karl-Siegbert, and Hans Vorländer, eds. *Symbolische Ordnungen. Beiträge zu einer soziologischen Theorie der Institutionen*. Baden-Baden: Nomos, 2014.

Rehberg, Karl-Siegbert. "Die Unverzichtbarkeit historischer Selbstreflexion der Soziologie." In *Soziologiegeschichte. Wege und Ziele*, edited by Christian Dayé and Stephan Moebius, 431–464. Frankfurt: Suhrkamp, 2015.

Rehberg, Karl-Siegbert. "The Fear of Happiness. Anthropological motives." *Journal of Happiness Studies* 1 (2000): 479–500.

Rehberg, Karl-Siegbert. "Institutionelle Analyse und historische Komparatistik." In *Dimensionen institutioneller Macht. Fallstudien von der Antike bis zur Gegenwart*, edited by Gert Melville and Karl-Siegbert Rehberg, 417–443. Köln, Weimar, Wien: Böhlau, 2012.

Rehberg, Karl-Siegbert. "Institutionelle Machtprozesse im historischen Vergleich. Einleitende Bemerkungen." In *Dimensionen institutioneller Macht. Fallstudien von der Antike zur Gegenwart*, edited by Gert Melville and Karl-Siegbert Rehberg, 1–16. Köln, Weimar, Wien: Böhlau, 2012, pp. 1–16

Reinhalter, Helmut. *Joseph II. und die Freimaurerei im Lichte zeitgenössischer Broschüren*. Wien, Köln, Graz: Böhlaus, 1987.

Robespierre, Maximilien de. *Œuvres de Robespierre*, collected and annotated by Auguste-Jean-Marie Vermorel. Paris: F. Courmol, 1866.

Robespierre, Maximilien de. *Pour le bonheur et pour la liberté. Discours*, selected and presented by Yannick Bosc, Florence Gauthier, and Sophie Wahnich. Paris: La Fabrique, 2000.

Robin, Audrey. *Une sociologie du beau sexe. L'homme et les soins de beauté de hier à aujourd'hui*. Paris: L'Harmattan, 2005.

Röttgers, Kurt. "Die Entstehung der Sozialphilosophie im Spannungsfeld von Neukantianismus, Soziologie und Kulturphilosophie, in *20. Jahre Fernuniversität. Daten, Fakten, Hintergründe. Festschrift zur 20-Jahr-Feier der Fernuniversität*, edited by Volker Hagen-Schmidtchen, 159–185. Hagen: FernUniversität in Hagen, 1995.

Röttgers, Kurt. *Kritik der kulinarischen Vernunft. Ein Menü der Sinne nach Kant*. Bielefeld: Transcript, 2009.

Rouillé d'Orfeuil, Auguste. *L'alambic moral, ou, Analyse raisonnée de tout ce qui a rapport à l'homme*. [but Paris?]: Maroc, 1773.

Rousseau, Jean-Jacques. *Discours sur l'origine et les fondements de l'inégalité parmi les hommes*. Amsterdam: Chez Marc-Michel Rey, 1755.

Rousseau, Jean-Jacques. *Du contrat social. Ou, Principes du droit politique*. Amsterdam: Chez Marc-Michel Rey, 1762.

Rousseau, Jean-Jacques. *The Social Contract, and Discourses*, introduction by George D. H. Cole. London: J.M. Dent & Sons, Ltd, 1910.

Sabine, George H. *A History of Political Theory*, revised by T. Landon Thorson, Fourth edition. Hinsdale: Dryden Press, 1973 (I. ed. 1937).

Saint-Just, Louis A. de. *Rapport sur la nécessité de déclarer le gouvernement révolutionnaire jusqu'à la paix*. In *Œuvres choisies. Discours, rapports, institutions républicaines, proclamations, lettres*, by idem. Paris: Gallimard 1968.

Saint-Simon, Henri de [Comte, Auguste]. *Suite des travaux ayant pour objet de fonder le système industriel. Du Contrat social*. Paris: Chez les Marchands de nouveautés, 1822.

Saint-Simon, Henri de, and Augustin Thierry. *De la réorganisation de la société européenne, ou De la nécessité et des moyens de rassembler les peuples de l'Europe en un seul corps politique*. Paris: A. Égron, 1814.

Saussure, Ferdinand de. *Cours de linguistique générale*. Paris: Payot, 1972 (I ed. 1913).

Scarca, Diego. *L'albero della civiltà. Primitivismo e utopia in Francia tra Sette e Ottocento*. Genève: Slatkine, 1990.

Scherke, Katharina. *Emotionen als Forschungsgegenstand der deutschsprachigen Soziologie*. Wiesbaden: Spriger, 2009.

Scholem, Gershom. "Ein verschollener jüdischer Mystiker der Aufklärungszeit. Ephraim Josef Hirschfeld." *Leo Baeck Institute Yearbook 7* (1962): 247–279.

Scholem, Gershom. *Du Frankisme au jacobinisme. La vie de Moses Dobruska, alias Franz Thomas von Schönfeld alias Junius Frey*. Paris: Gallimard, 1981.

Scholem, Gershom. *Le tre vite di Moses Dobrushka*, ed. and with an essay by Saverio Campanini, trans. by Elisabetta Zevi. Milano: Adelphi, 2014.

Scholem, Gershom. *Sabbatai Sevi. The Mystical Messiah*. London: Routledge, 1973 (Heb. ed. 1957).

Schönpflug, Daniel. *Der Weg in die Terreur. Radikalisierung und Konflikte im Straßburger Jakobinerklub (1790–1795)*. München: Oldenbourg, 2002.

Sigal-Klagsbald, Laurence. *Exposition Juifs et Citoyens*. Paris: A.I.U. 1989.

Sewell, William H. *A Rhetoric of Bourgeois Revolution the Abbé Sieyès and What is the Third Estate?*. Durham: Duke University Press, 1994.

Simmel, Georg. *Soziologie. Untersuchungen über die Formen der Vergesellschaftung*. Leipzig: Duncker & Humblot, 1908.

Spicker, Paul. "Cohesion, Exclusion and Social Quality." *The International Journal of Social Quality* 4 (2014): 95–107.

Steckner, Carl H. "Karl August Wilhelm Weissenbruch (1744–1826)." In *Saarländische Lebensbilder*, edited by Peter Neumann, 39–58. Saarbrücken: Saarbrücker Dr. u. Verl.

Steuckardt-Moreau, Agnès. "Endormeur chez Marat (1790–1792)." In *Dictionnaire des usages socio-politiques (1770–1815)*, by INALF: 87–110. Paris: Klincksieck, 1989.

Strauss, Leo. "On classical political Philosophy." *Social Research* 12 (1945): 98–117.

Strong, Tracy B. *Jean-Jacques Rousseau. The Politics of the Ordinary*. Lanham: Rowman & Littlefield, 2002 (I ed. 1994).

The Political State of Europe for the Year 1793, vol. 3. London: J.S. Jordan, 1793.

Theodorson, George A., and Achilles Theodorson, eds. *A Modern Dictionary of Sociology*. New York: Crowell, 1969.

Trapp, Bruno M. "Dobruschka – Schönfeld – Frey." *[Brünner] Tagesbote* (January 16 1928): 5.

Trénard, Louis. "Pour une histoire sociale de l'idée de 'bonheur' au XVIIIe siècle." *Annales historiques de la Révolution française* 35, n. 173 (1963): 309–330.

Trigg, Andrew B. "Deriving the Engel Curve. Pierre Bourdieu and the Social Critique of Maslow's Hierarchy of Needs." *Review of Social Economy* 62 (2004): 393–406.

Tuetey, Alexandre. *Répertoire général des sources manuscrites de l'histoire de Paris pendant la Révolution française*, 12 vols. Paris: Imprimerie Nouvelle (Association ouvrière), 1890–1914.

Uhlíř, Dušan. "Juden in Mähren und das Mährische Zentrum des Frankismus im ausgehenden 18. Jahrhundert." *Aufklärung, Vormärz, Revolution* 4 (1999): 45–54.

Veltri, Giuseppe, Gerold Necker, and Patrick Koch. "Die versuchte Wiederaufnahme des jüdischen Freimaurers geheimer Rapport." *Judaica* 68 (2012): 129–155.

Weber, Max. "Der Sinn der 'Wertfreiheit' der soziologischen und ökonomischen Wissenschaften." *Logos* 7 (1917): 40–88.

Wölfle-Fischer, Susanne. *Junius Frey (1753–1794). Jude, Aristokrat und Revolutionär*. Frankfurt a. M.: Peter Lang, 1997.

Index of Names

Index of Concepts

∂ Open Access. © 2022 Silvana Greco, published by De Gruyter. [(cc) BY] This work is licensed under the Creative Commons Attribution 4.0 International License.
https://doi.org/10.1515/9783110758825-014